Cruising Guide to British Columbia Vol. III

Sunshine Coast

Fraser Estuary and Vancouver to Jervis Inlet

by Bill Wolferstan

with Fraser Estuary chapters by Peggy Ward
and aerial photos by George McNutt

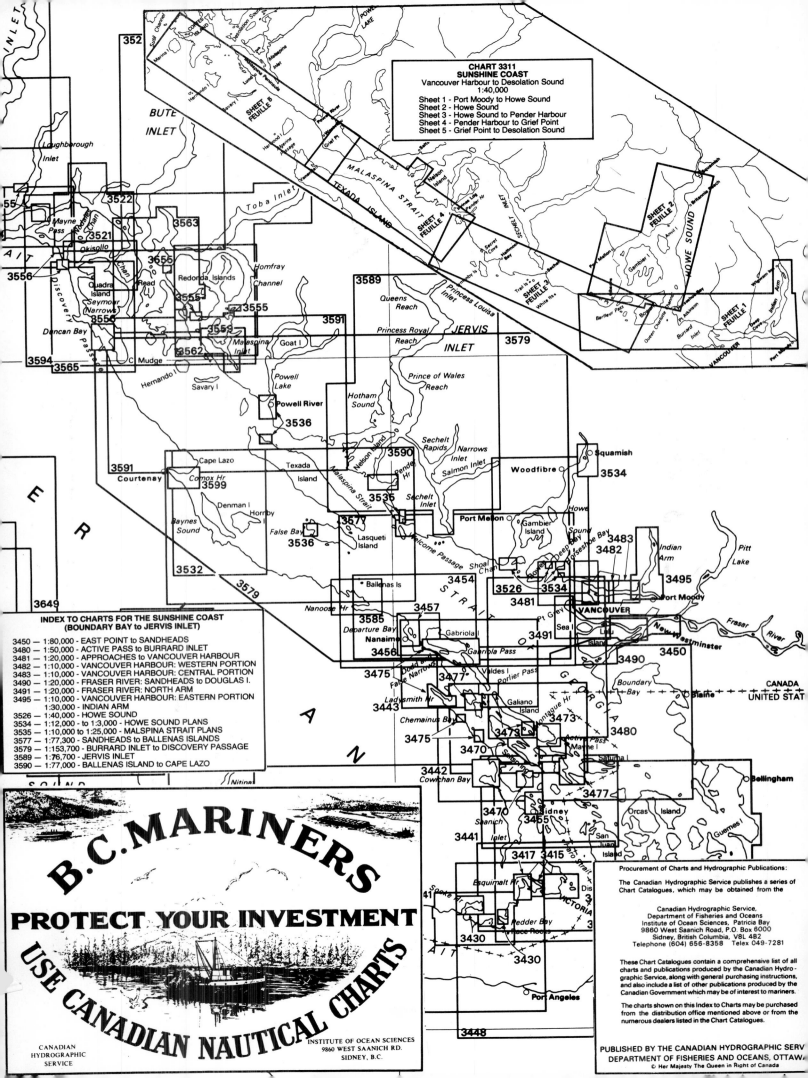

CHART 3311
SUNSHINE COAST
Vancouver Harbour to Desolation Sound
1:40,000
Sheet 1 - Port Moody to Howe Sound
Sheet 2 - Howe Sound
Sheet 3 - Howe Sound to Pender Harbour
Sheet 4 - Pender Harbour to Grief Point
Sheet 5 - Grief Point to Desolation Sound

INDEX TO CHARTS FOR THE SUNSHINE COAST
(BOUNDARY BAY to JERVIS INLET)

3450 — 1:80,000 - EAST POINT to SANDHEADS
3480 — 1:50,000 - ACTIVE PASS to BURRARD INLET
3481 — 1:20,000 - APPROACHES to VANCOUVER HARBOUR
3482 — 1:10,000 - VANCOUVER HARBOUR: WESTERN PORTION
3483 — 1:10,000 - VANCOUVER HARBOUR: CENTRAL PORTION
3490 — 1:20,000 - FRASER RIVER: SANDHEADS to DOUGLAS I.
3491 — 1:20,000 - FRASER RIVER: NORTH ARM
3495 — 1:10,000 - VANCOUVER HARBOUR: EASTERN PORTION
       1:30,000 - INDIAN ARM
3526 — 1:40,000 - HOWE SOUND
3534 — 1:12,000 - to 1:3,000 - HOWE SOUND PLANS
3535 — 1:10,000 to 1:25,000 - MALSPINA STRAIT PLANS
3577 — 1:77,300 - SANDHEADS to BALLENAS ISLANDS
3579 — 1:153,700 - BURRARD INLET to DISCOVERY PASSAGE
3589 — 1:76,700 - JERVIS INLET
3590 — 1:77,000 - BALLENAS ISLAND to CAPE LAZO

B.C. MARINERS
PROTECT YOUR INVESTMENT
USE CANADIAN NAUTICAL CHARTS

INSTITUTE OF OCEAN SCIENCES
9860 WEST SAANICH RD.
SIDNEY, B.C.

CANADIAN
HYDROGRAPHIC
SERVICE

Procurement of Charts and Hydrographic Publications:

The Canadian Hydrographic Service publishes a series of
Chart Catalogues, which may be obtained from the

Canadian Hydrographic Service,
Department of Fisheries and Oceans
Institute of Ocean Sciences, Patricia Bay
9860 West Saanich Road, P.O. Box 6000
Sidney, British Columbia, V8L 4B2
Telephone (604) 656-8358   Telex 049-7281

These Chart Catalogues contain a comprehensive list of all
charts and publications produced by the Canadian Hydrographic Service, along with general purchasing instructions,
and also include a list of other publications produced by the
Canadian Government which may be of interest to mariners.

The charts shown on this Index to Charts may be purchased
from the distribution office mentioned above or from the
numerous dealers listed in the Chart Catalogues.

PUBLISHED BY THE CANADIAN HYDROGRAPHIC SERV
DEPARTMENT OF FISHERIES AND OCEANS, OTTAWA
© Her Majesty The Queen in Right of Canada

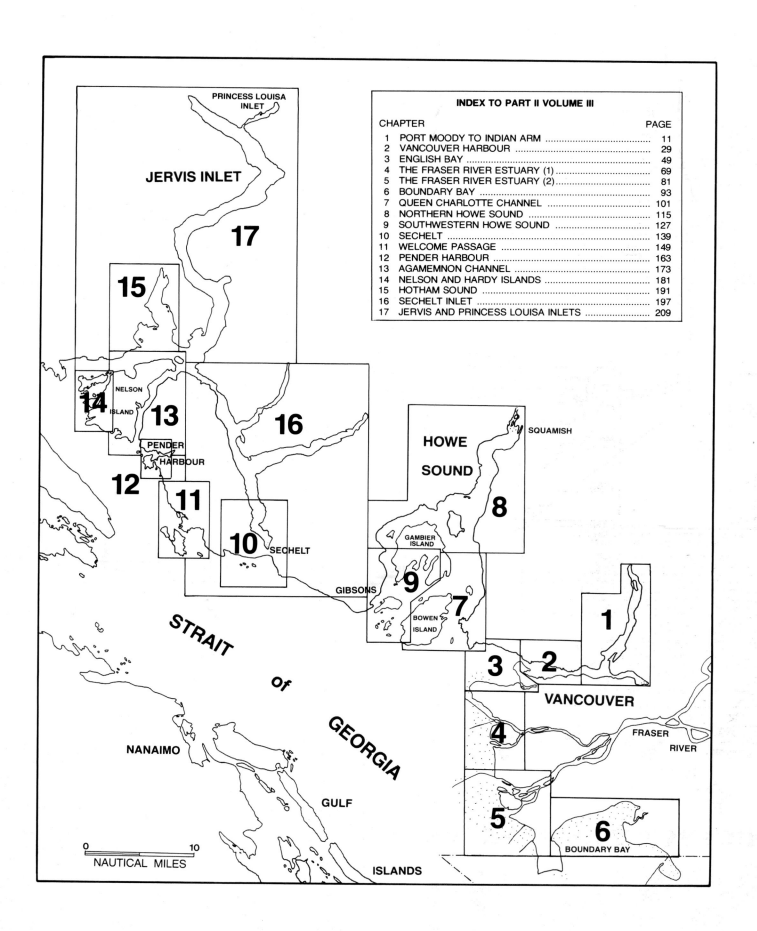

INTRODUCTION

The term "Sunshine Coast" was coined in the early part of this century when the principal means of travel north of Vancouver was by steamship. Today, ferries and thousands of small craft provide even greater opportunities to explore this coast, and to experience the same feelings evoked by a visitor to Vancouver in 1894:

I took passage on a radiant summer morning and the first breeze of Burrard Inlet soon inspired a feeling of buoyancy and vigour after spending several days in the railway cars.

Our first stopping place is Gibsons Landing, at the west entrance of Howe Sound. On the shore is descried Bowen Island teeming with deer . . . Outside lie Paisley and Ragged Islands, sometime the camps of whalers who harpooned these waters profitably.

We observe the gay sea dog or seal, who loves to lie a-basking in the sun. . . . We too on deck bask on . . . past occasional shanties and clearances that skirt the shores of Georgia's Gulf . . . As we sail through Welcome Pass the sun is setting in a wealth of colour over the north end of Texada Island.

(W.F.G. in *Whistle Up the Inlet*)

This Guide is similar in format to Volume 1, *Gulf Islands* and Volume II, *Desolation Sound* in this series. Part One presents an introduction to the Sunshine Coast area, including Vancouver and the Fraser Estuary, with maps depicting weather and sea conditions, geology, fishing areas, government floats, anchorages, marinas, settlements, roads, major parks and charts drawn by the early explorers. Part Two describes in detail seventeen separate areas from the viewpoint of a cruising yachtsman. Three of these areas, incorporating the mouths of the north, middle and main (south) arms of the Fraser River and Boundary Bay, have been contributed by Peggy and Bill Ward. Peggy is the author of *Explore the Fraser Estuary!*, a detailed guide to the attractions of the estuary. Each area is introduced by a chart showing the exact location of parks, marinas, anchorages and government (public) floats. Temporary anchorages which can be used subject to prevailing wind and tide conditions are also suggested. Log booms stored along the shore may also be used occasionally as a temporary tie-up moorage (see bottom of page 132). Most of the aerial photographs were taken as close to spring low water as possible to reveal rocks and shoals which are normally hidden at mean or high tide.

Every cove and harbour described in this book have been visited by the authors. While every effort has been made to ensure that the information in this guide is accurate, readers should be cautioned that the information, maps and illustrations are not to be solely relied on for navigation. Prior to exploration of these waters, yachtsmen should also study and have on board the *Small Craft Guide*, Vol. 2 and the pertinent Canadian Hydrographic Charts (see end-papers for index).

ACKNOWLEDGEMENTS

The author wishes to thank all the cruising yachtsmen, coastal people and others who have assisted in my research or helped in putting this volume together. In particular: Jamie Alley, Wayne Campbell, Lynn Cobb, Chuck Davis, Helen Dawe, Alan Ferguson, Brock Friesen, Norman Hacking, Rick Hankin, Chris Hatfield, Gerry Kidd, Clio Matheson, Sharon McLellan, George McNutt, Jill Newby, David Oliver, Yvonne Olsen, Elizabeth Owen, Lester Peterson, John Rich, Joan Robertson, Gary Robinson, Jack Stathers, Mel Turner, Bill and Peggy Ward, Howard White, Graeme Matheson, Paul Burkhart, Rex Armstead, Alan Crockford, and the staff of *Pacific Yachting*, Vancouver Typesetting, the B.C. Maritime Museum, the Vancouver City Archives, B.C. Provincial Archives and the Canadian Hydrographic Service.

Peggy Ward wishes to acknowledge the assistance of Al Brown, Bev Evers, Larry Giovando, Tom Grozier, Bob Richardson, Marielle St. Germain and the staff of the Canadian Coast Guard Hovercraft Base, Sea Island, Richmond.

For Clementien,
Jonathan, Matthew, Thomas, and Elizabeth

And there's another country
I've heard of long ago—
Most dear to them that love her
most great to them that know:

—Sir Cecil Spring Rice

CONTENTS

ADDENDA to JANUARY 1992

Major corrections to the **Cruising Guide to British Columbia: Volume III, SUNSHINE COAST** are listed below. Readers should also refer to the annual Boating Services Directory published every May by *Pacific Yachting* for an up-to-date listing of marine facilities, services, and amenities.

Page 26: Wigwam Inn is now a private RVYC outstation with limited reciprocal privileges.

Page 30: Vancouver Harbour (from Point Atkinson and Point Grey into and including Burrard Inlet, Indian Arm, False Creek and English Bay) is under the control of the Port of Vancouver Corporation.

Page 58: Beach Avenue Marina (685-9874) located at Boaters Village.

Page 60: Maritime Market includes Cooper Boating Centre (687-4110), Pacific Quest Charters (682-2205), and the Granville Island Hotel and Marina (Pelican Bay, 683-7373) at the east end.

Page 61: False Creek Marina demolished; old Granville Slopes Marina under bridge now the False Creek Yacht Club (682-3292) with limited transient moorage.

Page 78: new **Marina at Bridgeport** (273-8560) is located immediately southwest of the Oak Street bridge and offers moorage, market, and access to all facilities in vicinity.

Page 97: Crescent Beach Marina (538-9666); bridge will be opened on 3 horn blasts between 0630 and 2230 hours.

Page 111: new **Union Steamship Company Marina** in Snug Cove (947-0707) provides access to pub and new and restored resort facilities.

Page 113: new **Halkett Bay Marine Park** on Gambier Island has walk-in campsites.

Page 137: new **Gibsons Marina** (886-8686) has transient moorage, showers, laundry, charts, tackle, chandlery, fuel, restaurants, and provisions.

Page 146: new **Blue Heron Inn** (885-3847) in Porpoise Bay provides accommodation and free moorage to diners.

Page 152: new **Simson Marine Park** is located on east shore of South Thormanby Island from Dennis Head to northeast corner of island; no facilities to date.

Page 154: new **Buccaneer Bay Marine Park** at the southern tip of North Thormanby Island.

New Charts

3463 - for Fraser Estuary, Boundary Bay (replaces 3450)

3499 - for Roberts Bank, Tsawwassen

3493 - Vancouver Harbour (replaces 3482)

3512 - for Howe Sound, Sechelt Inlet, mouth of Jervis Inlet (replaces 3577, 3589, 3590)

3514 - for Jervis Inlet (replaces 3589)

3212 - new Atlas of charts includes Jervis and Sechelt inlets

PART ONE

Introduction to the
SUNSHINE COAST
from the Fraser Estuary to Jervis Inlet

WEATHER AND SEA

The map opposite summarizes the average summer wind and water conditions which can be expected by anyone cruising the central Strait of Georgia-Sunshine Coast region. Up-to-date weather reports, collected from the stations indicated on the map, are broadcast regularly on local radio stations. See Appendices VII and VIII in the *Small Craft Guide*, Vol. 2, for more details.

Wind. Summer winds in this region are strongly influenced by the local topography. In good weather, daytime winds tend to blow onshore: up the Strait of Georgia and mainland inlets (from the south and southeast), and through Burrard Inlet (from the west). At night, winds are generally lighter and offshore: down the Strait and mainland inlets (from the north and northwest) and out of the Lower Mainland (from the east). In winter, and at times of bad weather in the summer months, southeasterlies prevail in the Strait of Georgia, bringing strong winds, cloudy skies and rainfall. Outbreaks of cold, arctic air from the interior periodically blow out of some mainland inlets with considerable force. The "Squamish" wind of Howe Sound is a notable example. Wind roses, depicting percentage frequency wind direction for the month of July, are shown on the map.

Seas. The most dangerous seas which can be experienced in the central Strait of Georgia occur off Sand Heads when northwesterly winds blow against outflowing currents from the main arm of the Fraser River. Other areas which can experience occasionally high waves, swells, tide rips or turbulent seas occur on open coastlines with long fetches, in tidal passes, rivers, off headlands or areas of frequent large vessel movements.

Because of the protection afforded by Vancouver Island, local waters are remarkable for their relative calmness. Wave heights will seldom exceed 4 feet in the most exposed parts of the Strait even under extreme wind conditions. Off Sturgeon Bank, the most exposed shore in the central Strait of Georgia, wave heights exceed 3 feet less than 10% of the time (Thomson, 1981).

The waters of the Sunshine Coast which are most likely to be placid most of the time are indicated on the map. These areas are generally the safest for canoe, kayak or other small boat exploration.

Sunshine. In the summer months, the Sunshine Coast, including the Fraser estuary and English Bay, receives large quantities of sunshine. In July, there are more than 300 hours of bright sunshine as a mean average. The Sunshine Coast itself (from Gibsons to Powell River) has one of the highest totals of sunshine in Canada (up to 2400 hours of annual sunshine). Throughout the year, Vancouver and the mainland inlets are *occasionally* overcast and . . . damp, especially in December, when the mean monthly sunshine drops to 44 hours (annual total for Vancouver is over 1900 hours).

Rainfall. In July, the Sunshine Coast (including Vancouver) averages less than 5 days with measurable precipitation (totalling 1.2 inches or 30mm.). In the winter months (October to March) this area can more appropriately be called a "raincoast", with more than 15 days in every month bringing the bulk of the lower coast's total of 40 inches (1000 mm) of mean annual precipitation.

Fog. Fog may occur during any month but is most common during the fall and winter months. Vancouver averages 6 to 11 days of fog per month from September to March and less than 2 days of fog in the each of the months of April to July.

Temperatures. Mean daily temperatures along the Sunshine Coast average more than 15°C (60°F) with mean daily maximums of over 20°C (70°F) in the summer months. Near the heads of the mainland inlets, away from the moderating effect of the Strait of Georgia, extreme maximum temperatures can approach 40°C (100°F). In the winter months, mean daily temperatures average 5°C (40°F).

Tides. The maximum rise and fall of the tide varies from 10 feet inside Sechelt Inlet to 14 feet at White Rock and 18 feet at Egmont.

GEOLOGY
(adapted from Gerhard H. Eisbacher, Vancouver Geology)

The mountainous backdrop of the Sunshine Coast owes its beauty to the geologic evolution of the Pacific seaboard over the last 150 million years. The oldest rocks are those that stand out as crags and sea cliffs. This terrain was once an ocean basin with chains of volcanic islands: the volcanoes grew by the eruption of dark lavas (green on map), flowing over a pedestal of chrystalline quartz-diorite or grandiorite rock (blue on map). Rock outcroppings give the observer some idea of how the volcanic strata were arranged in these rugged islands.

From about 30 to 80 million years ago low hills framing the Vancouver area were gradually worn down and rivers deposited sediments (also shown as green on the map) over a gently undulating surface of chrystalline rocks. Parts of this ancient land surface can be recognized along the southern slope of the Sunshine Coast mountains. The gravel, sand and mud was eventually cemented into conglomerate, sandstone and mudstone. Thin layers of plant debris, which had accumulated between the strata of sand, were converted to small seams of lignite coal, such as those found at Coal Harbour. Today the sandstone strata form cliffs and other erosional remnants stretching from Kitsilano to Burnaby Mountain. They are particularly visible along the sea wall of Stanley Park.

Siwash Rock, off Stanley Park, is a remnant of a volcanic vent. This hard rock has resisted the beating action of the sea better than the friable sandstone enveloping it. Black volcanic rock also supports the spectacular ledge of Prospect Point. Volcanic activity may not yet be finished in southwestern B.C. — near Mt. Garibaldi, visible from Howe Sound, volcanic

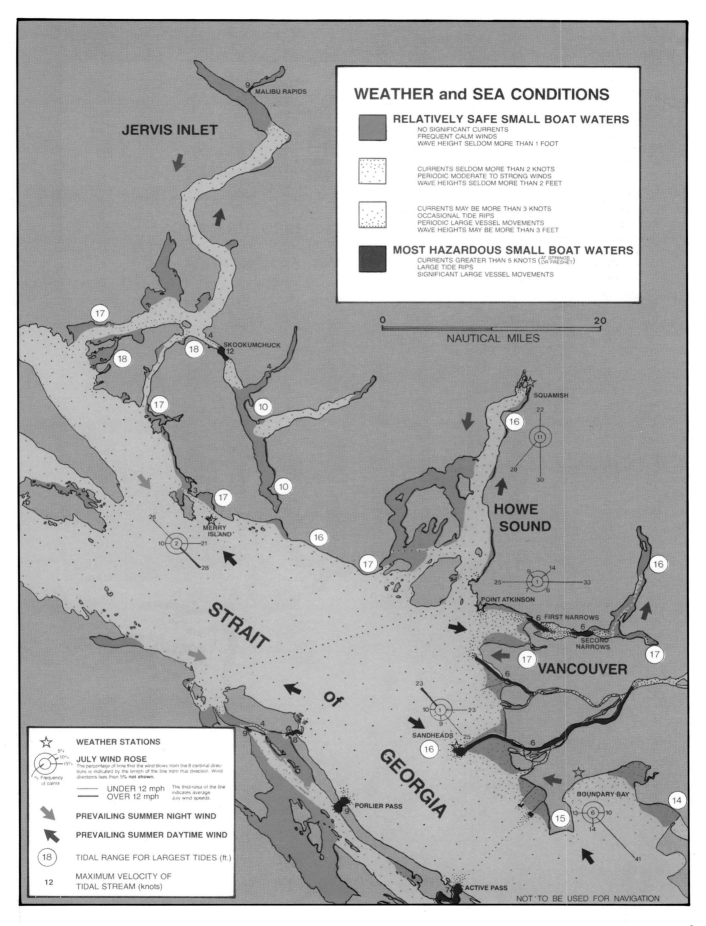

WEATHER and SEA CONDITIONS

RELATIVELY SAFE SMALL BOAT WATERS
NO SIGNIFICANT CURRENTS
FREQUENT CALM WINDS
WAVE HEIGHT SELDOM MORE THAN 1 FOOT

CURRENTS SELDOM MORE THAN 2 KNOTS
PERIODIC MODERATE TO STRONG WINDS
WAVE HEIGHTS SELDOM MORE THAN 2 FEET

CURRENTS MAY BE MORE THAN 3 KNOTS
OCCASIONAL TIDE RIPS
PERIODIC LARGE VESSEL MOVEMENTS
WAVE HEIGHTS MAY BE MORE THAN 3 FEET

MOST HAZARDOUS SMALL BOAT WATERS
CURRENTS GREATER THAN 5 KNOTS (AT SPRINGS OR FRESHET)
LARGE TIDE RIPS
SIGNIFICANT LARGE VESSEL MOVEMENTS

JERVIS INLET

MALIBU RAPIDS

SKOOKUMCHUCK
12

SQUAMISH

HOWE
SOUND

MERRY
ISL'AND

POINT ATKINSON

FIRST NARROWS

SECOND
NARROWS

VANCOUVER

STRAIT

of

GEORGIA

SANDHEADS

PORLIER PASS

BOUNDARY BAY

ACTIVE PASS

0   20
NAUTICAL MILES

WEATHER STATIONS

JULY WIND ROSE
The percentage of time that the wind blows from the 8 cardinal directions is indicated by the length of the line from that direction. Wind directions less than 5% not shown.

UNDER 12 mph
OVER 12 mph

The thickness of the line indicates average July wind speeds.

PREVAILING SUMMER NIGHT WIND

PREVAILING SUMMER DAYTIME WIND

TIDAL RANGE FOR LARGEST TIDES (ft.)

MAXIMUM VELOCITY OF
TIDAL STREAM (knots)

NOT TO BE USED FOR NAVIGATION

1

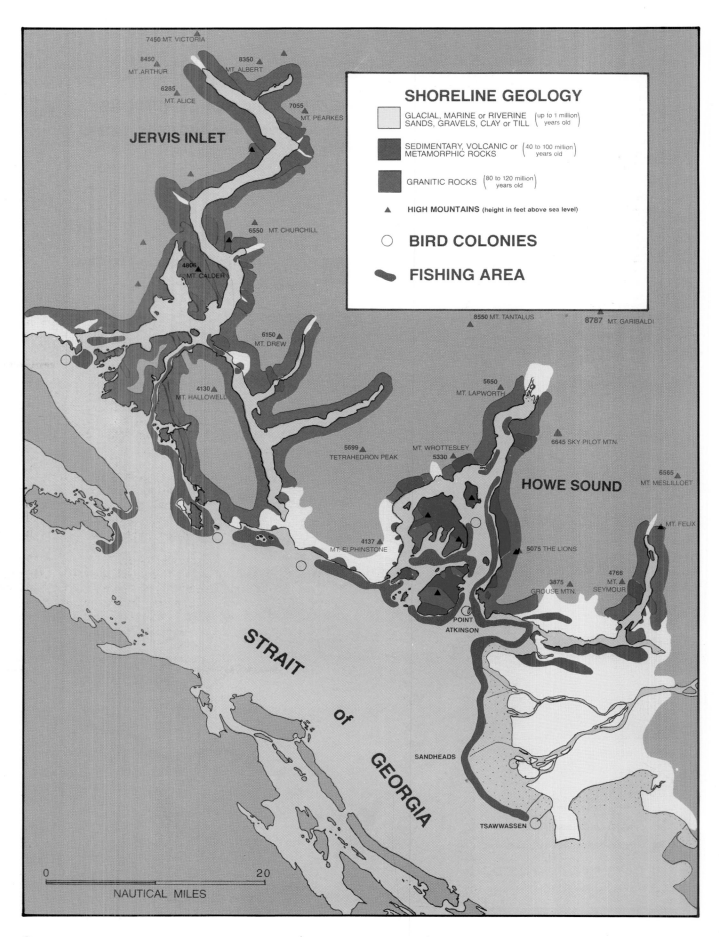

SHORELINE GEOLOGY

GLACIAL, MARINE or RIVERINE SANDS, GRAVELS, CLAY or TILL (up to 1 million years old)

SEDIMENTARY, VOLCANIC or METAMORPHIC ROCKS (40 to 100 million years old)

GRANITIC ROCKS (80 to 120 million years old)

▲ HIGH MOUNTAINS (height in feet above sea level)

○ BIRD COLONIES

FISHING AREA

7450 MT. VICTORIA

8450 MT. ARTHUR

8350 MT. ALBERT

6285 MT. ALICE

7055 MT. PEARKES

JERVIS INLET

6550 MT. CHURCHILL

4806 MT. CALDER

6150 MT. DREW

8550 MT. TANTALUS

8787 MT. GARIBALDI

4130 MT. HALLOWELL

5650 MT. LAPWORTH

6645 SKY PILOT MTN.

5699 TETRAHEDRON PEAK

MT. WROTTESLEY
5330

HOWE SOUND

6565 MT. MESLILLOET

MT. FELIX

4137 MT. ELPHINSTONE

5075 THE LIONS

3875 GROUSE MTN.

4766 MT. SEYMOUR

POINT ATKINSON

STRAIT of GEORGIA

SANDHEADS

TSAWWASSEN

0   20
NAUTICAL MILES

2

eruptions were common only a few thousand years ago.

From about one million years ago up to only 10,000 years ago glaciers advanced and retreated over this area several times. These glaciers left hard packed stones and clay ("till") and unconsolidated sands and gravels as "drift" deposits (yellow on map). These deposits were first quarried commercially in the 1860's by "Navvy" Jack from his West Vancouver beach. The history of the different layers of clay, sands and till can be seen in the cliffs of Point Grey and Thormanby Island.

Also at that time the Fraser River began to build its delta of sand, silt, clay and peat. It is still advancing at a rate of about 10 feet a year, and should connect with the Gulf Islands in five or six thousand years. Parts of the Fraser delta are, however, being steadily eroded by wave action. The Point Grey cliffs are retreating at an average rate of 1 foot a year, supplying a fairly reliable "feed" of sand to the beaches of Spanish Banks, Kitsilano and English Bay.

SPORT FISHING
(adapted from BC Outdoors magazines' Fishing Guide)

Tsawwassen Jetty:

Good salmon fishing much of the year for coho and chinook. Trolling, mooching for salmon, bait-fishing for sole and flounder on the shelf; troll or mooch for salmon on the dropoff. This area is very close to the U.S. border; care must be taken not to drift across the line, as a Washington State marine licence is required.

Steveston Jetty:

Most fishing is done near the seaward end of the seawall, and in the vicinity of the Sand Heads Light Station. Fishing conditions vary greatly with Fraser River freshets but most of the huge salmon runs bound for the immense spawning area upriver must pass through here. Mooching and stripcasting are popular; both coho and chinook are often taken close to the surface. Good sockeye, pink and chum salmon in their "big run" seasons. Bottom fish are also plentiful on the sandy, silty bottom in shallower water. This is a heavily used shipping lane; a constant stream of tugs, freighters, and fishing boats keep waters rough. In addition, with a moderate west wind and outrunning tide, a dangerous, nearly vertical chop develops on the tideline.

Fraser North Arm to Burrard Inlet:

Coho, chinook, pink and sockeye salmon are found here at the same times as they move into the Steveston Jetty area. Good fishing also continues around the Point Grey bell buoy into Burrard Inlet. Mooching, trolling, stripcasting for salmon, and bait-fishing for bottom fish all year.

Horseshoe Bay:

One of the most popular salmon fishing spots on coast. Mooching best near the Hole in the Wall, three hundred yards north of the ferry slips. Chinook all year, peaking November-December, coho summer and fall.

Howe Sound:

Famous for its "Howe Sound Chinooks", hot spots are Britannia, Furry Creek, Porteau, Bowyer Island; south of Horseshoe Bay in Queen Charlotte passage, Grebe Islets. On west side, Defense Islands and McNabb Creek are best spots. The waters around Gambier, Bowen and Keats Islands are good for salmon. Mostly chinooks, year around. Troll, mooch, stripcast. Some coho, summer and fall.

Gibsons Landing to Roberts Creek:

Home Island, off the south end of Keats Island, gathers chinook, coho and salmon fishermen in large numbers, along its south edge. Fishing the dropoff along the shelf between Keats and Steep Bluff is also productive, as is the dropoff along Gower Point. There is good fishing along this dropoff right to Roberts Creek, with a hot spot at Camp Byng.

Rock Point to McNaughton Point:

The shallow shelf continues along here, with good fishing on the dropoff. Some chinook spring and fall, and excellent coho fishing July-August, peaking in September. Trolling, strip-casting and mooching are all effective at times. Shore-fishing, for both chinook and coho, are becoming very popular along here, with Buzzbomb and Stingsilda being cast from piers, and points of land. Trail Islands and Sargeant Bay are hotspots near Sechelt. The waters all around Thormanby Island provides excellent trolling and mooching, hotspots in Halfmoon Bay, Wilbraham Point, Pirate Rock and Merry Island.

Bjerre Shoal:

This shoal comes to within 2½ fathoms of the surface, in line with Francis Peninsula and North Thormanby Island. Good mooching or casting water on the shoal; troll around the dropoff for bluebacks April-May; coho June-September. A few chinook present much of the year.

Francis Peninsula, Pender Harbour:

Good trolling, mooching along outside (west) edge of Francis Peninsula for blueback and coho, summer. Pender Harbour has been a very popular year-round mooching area for chinook for many years. Bargain Bay, a niche between Francis Peninsula and the mainland, is also a good coho mooching or casting area. Fish just off the two small islands, on the 8 to 29 fathom line. Good mooching for winter chinook.

Egmont:

Excellent chinook waters in Agamemnon Channel, Jervis Inlet and Sechelt Inlet are reached from Egmont, near the Earl's Cove ferry landing. Winter chinook show here early in September, continue through the winter. Good summer mooching for chinook, some coho. The awesome Skookumchuck lies 2 miles east of Egmont on Sechelt Inlet. This is a good fishing area but no place to be during tide runs, when the narrows becomes a roaring torrent.

Hotham Sound, Saltery Bay, Scotch Fir Point:

This is good water for chinook mooching, with hot spots along the east shore and in St Vincent Bay. Some coho fishing in summer. Good fishing from Saltery Bay south; Scotch Fir Point, with many underwater reefs, is good coho water, mooching or surface trolling.

3

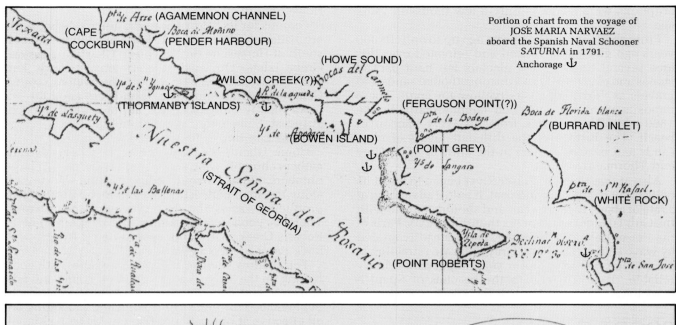

Portion of chart from the voyage of
JOSÉ MARIA NARVAEZ
aboard the Spanish Naval Schooner
SATURNA in 1791.
Anchorage ⚓

(CAPE COCKBURN)
pta de Arze (AGAMEMNON CHANNEL)
Boca de Moñino (PENDER HARBOUR)
(HOWE SOUND)
Bocas del Carmelo
WILSON CREEK(?)
R de la aguada
(THORMANBY ISLANDS)
Yta de Sn Ygnacio
Ya de Lasquety
(FERGUSON POINT(?))
Boca de Florida blanca (BURRARD INLET)
Ys de Anada
(BOWEN ISLAND)
pta de la Bodega
(POINT GREY)
Nuestra Señora del Rosario
pta de Sn Rafael (WHITE ROCK)
Ys de Langara
Ys de las Ballenas
(STRAIT OF GEORGIA)
Ysla de Zepeda
Declinac observa
(POINT ROBERTS)
pta de San Jose

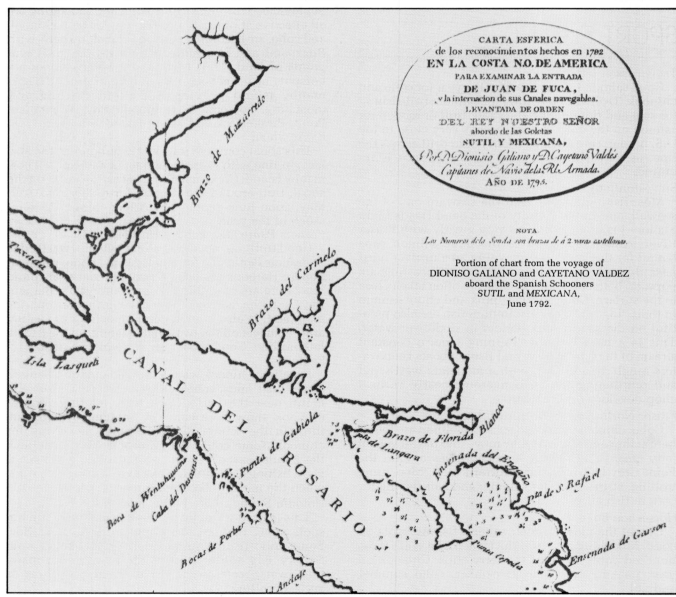

CARTA ESFERICA
de los reconocimientos hechos en 1792
EN LA COSTA N.O. DE AMERICA
PARA EXAMINAR LA ENTRADA
DE JUAN DE FUCA,
y la internacion de sus Canales navegables.
LEVANTADA DE ORDEN
DEL REY NUESTRO SEÑOR
abordo de las Goletas
SUTIL Y MEXICANA,
Por D. Dionisio Galiano y D. Cayetano Valdés
Capitanes de Navio de la Rl. Armada.
AÑO DE 1795.

NOTA
Los Numeros de la Sonda son brazas de á 2 varas castellanas.

Portion of chart from the voyage of
DIONISO GALIANO and CAYETANO VALDEZ
aboard the Spanish Schooners
SUTIL and MEXICANA,
June 1792.

Brazo de Mazarredo
Tavada
Brazo del Carmelo
Isla Lasqueti
CANAL DEL ROSARIO
Brazo de Florida Blanca
Boca de Wentuhuysen
Cala del Descanso
Punta de Gabiola
pta de Langara
Ensenada del Engaño
pta de S. Rafael
Bocas de Porlier
Punta Cepeda
Ensenada de Garzon
I Andase

4

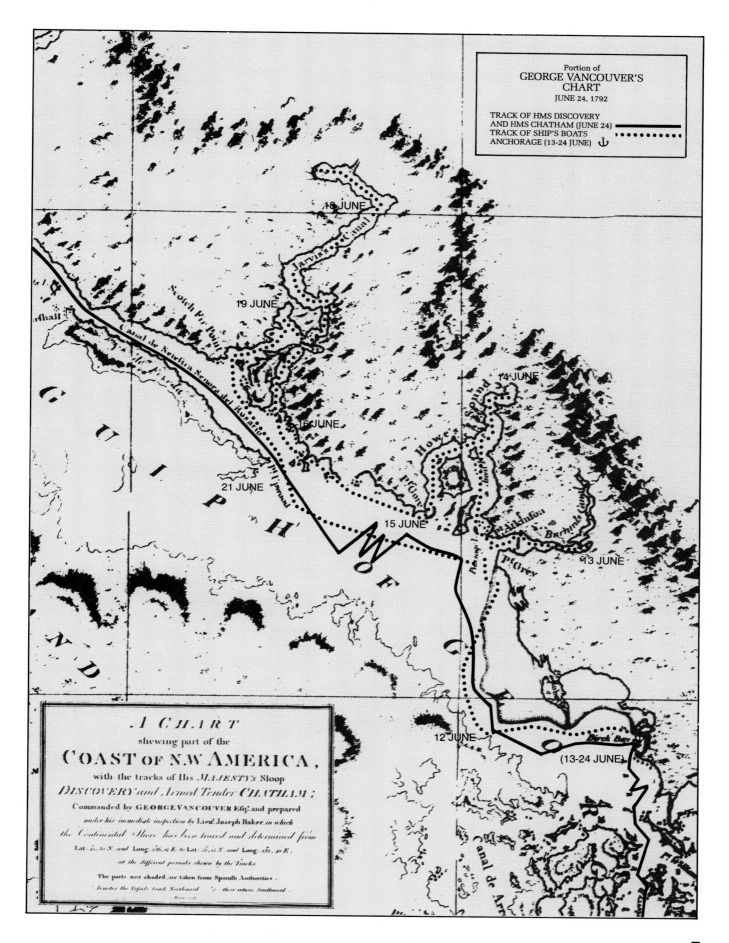

Portion of
GEORGE VANCOUVER'S
CHART
JUNE 24, 1792

TRACK OF HMS DISCOVERY
AND HMS CHATHAM (JUNE 24) ▬▬▬▬
TRACK OF SHIP'S BOATS ••••••••••••
ANCHORAGE (13-24 JUNE) ⚓

18 JUNE

Jarvis's Canal

19 JUNE

Scotch Fir Point

14 JUNE

Howe's Sound

Canal de Nuestra Senora del Rosario

16 JUNE

Pt Gower

21 JUNE

Pt Atkinson

Burrinds Canal

Passage I

15 JUNE

Pt Grey

13 JUNE

G U L P H

O F

G E O R G I A

12 JUNE

Birch Bay

(13-24 JUNE)

A CHART
shewing part of the
COAST OF N.W AMERICA,
with the tracks of His *MAJESTY's* Sloop
DISCOVERY and Armed Tender *CHATHAM*:
Commanded by GEORGE VANCOUVER Esq.' and prepared
under his immediate inspection by Lieu.' Joseph Baker, in which
the Continental Shore has been traced and determined from
Lat: 5. 30 N. and Long. 236. 12 E. to Lat: 52. 15 N. and Long. 231. 30 E.
at the different periods shewn by the Tracks
The parts not shaded, are taken from Spanish Authorities.
Denotes the Vessels track Northward by their return Southward.

Canal de Arro

5

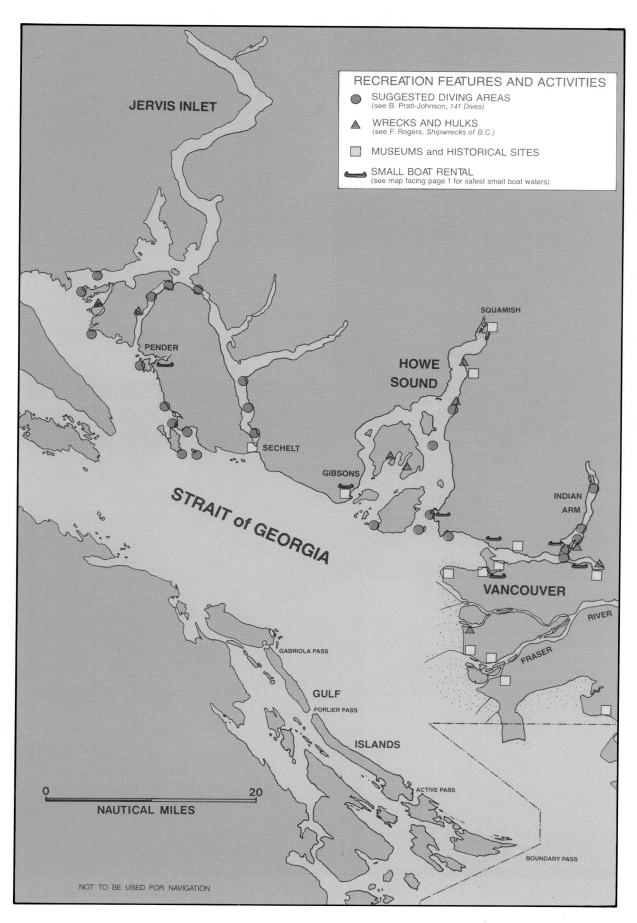

RECREATION FEATURES AND ACTIVITIES

● SUGGESTED DIVING AREAS
(see B. Pratt-Johnson, *141 Dives*)

▲ WRECKS AND HULKS
(see F. Rogers, *Shipwrecks of B.C.*)

▢ MUSEUMS and HISTORICAL SITES

SMALL BOAT RENTAL
(see map facing page 1 for safest small boat waters)

JERVIS INLET

SQUAMISH

HOWE SOUND

PENDER

SECHELT

GIBSONS

INDIAN ARM

STRAIT of GEORGIA

VANCOUVER

RIVER

FRASER

GABRIOLA PASS

GULF

PORLIER PASS

ISLANDS

ACTIVE PASS

0   20

NAUTICAL MILES

BOUNDARY PASS

NOT TO BE USED FOR NAVIGATION

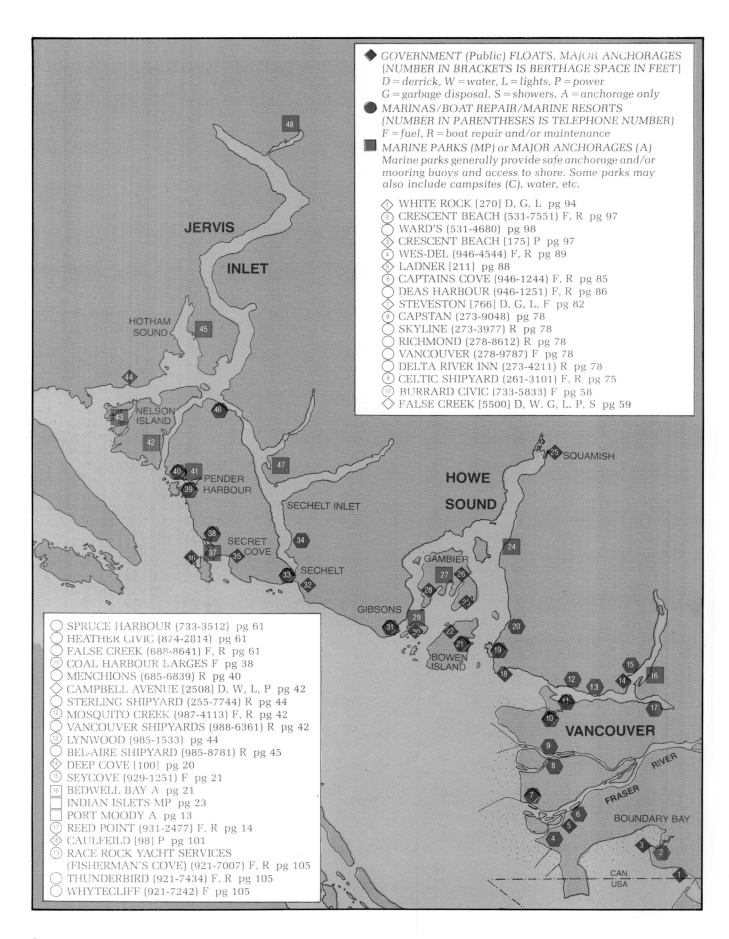

◆ GOVERNMENT (Public) FLOATS, MAJOR ANCHORAGES
[NUMBER IN BRACKETS IS BERTHAGE SPACE IN FEET]
D = derrick, W = water, L = lights, P = power
G = garbage disposal, S = showers, A = anchorage only

● MARINAS/BOAT REPAIR/MARINE RESORTS
(NUMBER IN PARENTHESES IS TELEPHONE NUMBER)
F = fuel, R = boat repair and/or maintenance

■ MARINE PARKS (MP) or MAJOR ANCHORAGES (A)
Marine parks generally provide safe anchorage and/or
mooring buoys and access to shore. Some parks may
also include campsites (C), water, etc.

1 WHITE ROCK [270] D, G, L pg 94
2 CRESCENT BEACH (531-7551) F, R pg 97
○ WARD'S (531-4680) pg 98
3 CRESCENT BEACH [175] P pg 97
4 WES-DEL (946-4544) F, R pg 89
5 LADNER [211] pg 88
6 CAPTAINS COVE (946-1244) F, R pg 85
○ DEAS HARBOUR (946-1251) F, R pg 86
7 STEVESTON [766] D, G, L, F pg 82
8 CAPSTAN (273-9048) pg 78
○ SKYLINE (273-3977) R pg 78
○ RICHMOND (278-8612) R pg 78
○ VANCOUVER (278-9787) F pg 78
○ DELTA RIVER INN (273-4211) R pg 78
9 CELTIC SHIPYARD (261-3101) F, R pg 75
10 BURRARD CIVIC (733-5833) F pg 58
◇ FALSE CREEK [5500] D, W. G, L. P, S pg 59

○ SPRUCE HARBOUR (733-3512) pg 61
○ HEATHER CIVIC (874-2814) pg 61
○ FALSE CREEK (688-8641) F, R pg 61
11 COAL HARBOUR BARGES F pg 38
○ MENCHIONS (685-6839) R pg 40
◇ CAMPBELL AVENUE [2508] D, W, L, P pg 42
○ STERLING SHIPYARD (255-7744) R pg 42
12 MOSQUITO CREEK (987-4113) F, R pg 42
○ VANCOUVER SHIPYARDS (988-6361) R pg 42
13 LYNWOOD (985-1533) pg 44
○ BEL-AIRE SHIPYARD (985-8781) R pg 45
14 DEEP COVE [100] pg 20
15 SEYCOVE (929-1251) F pg 21
16 BEDWELL BAY A pg 21
□ INDIAN ISLETS MP pg 23
□ PORT MOODY A pg 13
17 REED POINT (931-2477) F. R pg 14
18 CAULFEILD [98] P pg 101
19 RACE ROCK YACHT SERVICES
(FISHERMAN'S COVE) (921-7007) F, R pg 105
○ THUNDERBIRD (921-7434) F. R pg 105
○ WHYTECLIFF (921-7242) F pg 105

8

SEWELL'S (921-7461) F, R pg 106
HORSESHOE BAY [520] pg 106
BAY BOAT RENTALS (921-7654) pg 107
20 SUNSET (921-7464) F, R pg 107
NEWMAN CREEK (921-5636) pg 107
LIONS BAY (921-7510) F pg 107
21 SNUG COVE [860] (947-2151) F pg 110
RECONQUISTA (947-9510) F pg 110
22 MT. GARDNER [147] pg 113
23 HALKETT BAY [140] pg 113
24 PORTEAU MP, C pg 120
25 SQUAMISH [1080] L pg 124
26 PORT GRAVES (ARTABAN) [190] pg 133
27 CENTRE BAY moorage on log booms pg 133
28 WEST BAY [120] pg 134
GAMBIER HARBOUR [245] pg 135
NEW BRIGHTON [555] pg 135
29 PLUMPER COVE MP, C pg 137
30 KEATS [100] pg 137
EASTBOURNE [120] pg 131
31 GIBSONS [5700] D pg 137
SMITTY'S (886-7711) F, R pg 137
HYAK (886-9011) F, R pg 137
ALL SPORTS (886-9303) pg 137
32 SELMA PARK A pg 142
33 PORPOISE BAY [1180] D, W, L, P, G pg 146
34 TILLICUM BAY (885-2100) F pg 147
35 HALFMOON BAY [210] pg 151
36 VAUCROFT [72] pg 156
37 SMUGGLER COVE MP, C pg 157
38 SECRET COVE [720] (885-3533) F pg 161
BUCCANEER (885-9563) F, R pg 161
JOLLY ROGER (885-3529) pg 161
LATITUDE 49 (885-2910) pg 161
SMUGGLER'S (885-9617) pg 161
LORD JIM'S (885-2232) pg 161
39 SILVERSANDS (883-2630) pg 166
LOWES (883-2456) pg 171
COHO (883-2248) F, R pg 171
MADEIRA PARK [1575] W, L, P, G pg 170
MADEIRA (883-2266) R pg 170
WHISKEY SLOUGH [490] L, P, G pg 171
LLOYD HANSONS (883-2663) F pg 171
HASSANS (883-2415) pg 171
HEADWATER (883-2406) pg 170
40 IRVINES LANDING [700] G pg 166
IRVINES (883-2296) F, R pg 167
WHITTAKERS (883-2282) pg 168
DUNCAN COVE (883-2424) pg 168
GARDEN BAY SVCS. (883-2722) R pg 168
TAYLOR'S (883-2253) F pg 168
THE FISHERMAN'S (883-2336) pg 169
HOSPITAL BAY [1200] G pg 168
HARBOUR (883-2343) F pg 170
GARDEN BAY (883-2798) F pg 170
PENGA (883-2535) R pg 170
41 GARDEN BAY MP pg 169
GUNBOAT BAY A pg 170
42 QUARRY BAY A 174
BREEN BAY A 176
43 BLIND BAY A pg 186,188
44 SALTERY BAY [1100] L, G pg 212
45 HARMONY ISLANDS A pg 193
46 JERVIS (883-2496) pg 177
EGMONT RESORT (883-2298) F pg 199
EGMONT [1300] D, G pg 199
BATHGATES (883-2222) F pg 199
47 STORM BAY A pg 203
SECHELT INLETS MP pg 202, 204, 206
48 PRINCESS LOUISA MP, C pg 220

FLOATS, ANCHORAGES and MARINAS

Government floats which are available for transient moorage can be identified by their brightly painted red railings and are usually located in coves or harbours which also serve as major anchorages. They provide access to shore, and in some cases (see list) water, power and lights are available on the floats. Garbage disposal facilities and derricks (for lifting masts or engines) are sometimes located on the wharves above the floats. Moorage fees are payable at most government floats. Rafting up alongside other boats is a requirement during busy periods and no obstructions should be placed to hinder other vessels coming alongside. Canadian fishing vessels generally have priority over other vessels at these floats, but in summer when most are away, the floats provide convenient temporary moorage for transient recreational small craft.

Other major anchorages, in isolated coves with little or no facilities, are also listed and identified by blue squares on the map adjacent. Some of these anchorages may be protected by marine park status. The map facing page 7 also gives the location of all provincial parks in this area. In addition to the major anchorages shown here, there are hundreds of places where it is possible to anchor temporarily when wind and tide conditions are suitable. In some places, where log booms are stored along the shore (such as Gambier Island), small craft can moor alongside for short periods of time. These temporary anchorages and log boom storage areas have been described in some detail and located on the maps by asterisks (*) in Part Two of this guide.

Marinas (red circles on map adjacent) offering fuel and other facilities, shipyards for repair or boat maintenance and marine resorts are also described and located on the maps in Part Two.

Cruising Guide to the

SUNSHINE COAST

Vancouver and the Fraser Estuary to Jervis Inlet

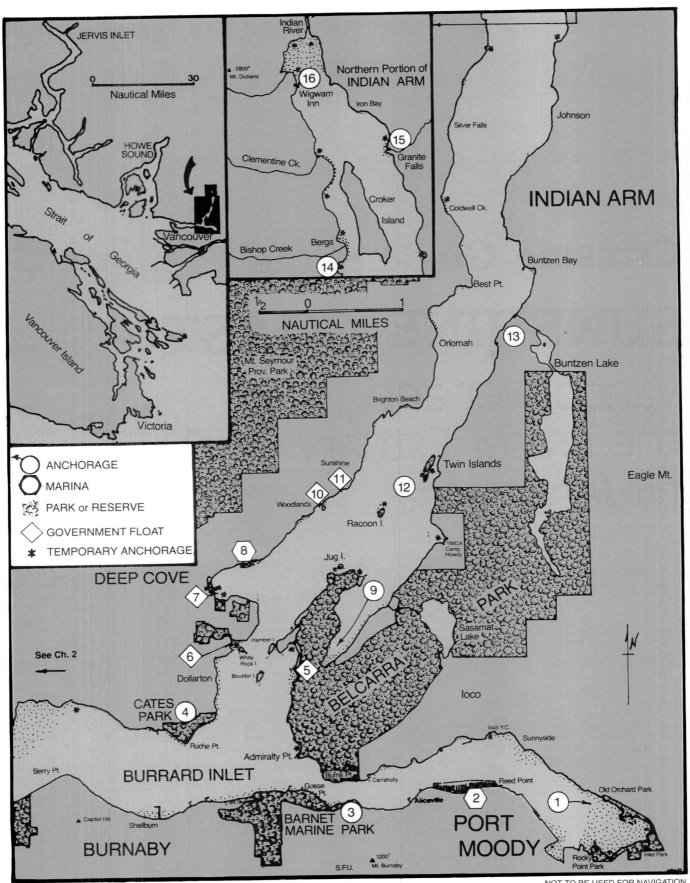

JERVIS INLET

0   30

Nautical Miles

HOWE SOUND

Strait of Georgia

Vancouver

Vancouver Island

Victoria

Indian River

▲ 2800' Mt. Dickens

16

Wigwam Inn

Northern Portion of INDIAN ARM

Iron Bay

Clementine Ck.

15

Granite Falls

Croker Island

Bishop Creek   Bergs

14

Silver Falls

Johnson

Coldwell Ck.

INDIAN ARM

Buntzen Bay

Best Pt.

13

Buntzen Lake

Orlomah

Eagle Mt.

½   0   1

NAUTICAL MILES

Mt. Seymour Prov. Park

Brighton Beach

Sunshine

11

Twin Islands

12

10

Woodlands

Racoon I.

YMCA Camp Howdy

ANCHORAGE

MARINA

PARK or RESERVE

GOVERNMENT FLOAT

TEMPORARY ANCHORAGE

8

DEEP COVE

Jug I.

9

PARK

7

Sasamat Lake

BELCARRA

See Ch. 2

6

Hamber I.

White Rock I.

5

Dollarton   Boulder I.

Ioco

CATES PARK

4

Ioco Y.C.

Sunnyside

Roche Pt.

Admiralty Pt.

Carraholly

Reed Point

Old Orchard Park

Berry Pt.

BURRARD INLET

Gosse Pt.

Burns Pt.

Aliceville

2

1

Capitol Hill

Shellburn

BARNET MARINE PARK

3

PORT MOODY

Rocky Point Park

BURNABY

S.F.U.

▲ 1200' Mt. Burnaby

Inlet Park

NOT TO BE USED FOR NAVIGATION

10

CHAPTER ONE

Port Moody to Indian Arm

Belcarra, Deep Cove, Wigwam Inn

Port Moody and Indian Arm are two placid backwaters, located less than five miles from Vancouver Harbour, one of the busiest ports in North America. These waters provide a cruising area remarkable for their sense of contrast. As the shoreline steepens, the urban-industrial shore of Burrard Inlet gives way quickly to pockets of suburban development, surrounded by trees, hillside-clinging waterfront cottages, and then to Indian Arm — an isolated, forest-covered, mountain-cliffed wilderness fiord that is little changed from when it was sculpted by the glaciers 10,000 years ago. As Malcolm Lowry saw this area, the close contrasts were as striking as those between heaven and hell.

A hundred years ago, a cruise up Indian Arm (known then as the North Arm of Burrard Inlet) evoked strong feelings as described by a curious English explorer, Edward Roper:

"A dream-like magic scene . . . a magnificent spectacle . . . spread before us, grand in the extreme. Around that inland sea the shadows were deepening into gloom. Slowly up the slopes of the mountains they chased the lessening light, whilst beneath the dark reflections of the pines was stretched the shining water, reflecting the brilliant sky, which gleamed in gold and purple overhead . . . The sea, for that it really was, though hard to credit — lay smooth as glass and black as ink, where land and water met. Not a breath disturbed the silence, the mountain walls stretching up to heaven in solemn stillness."

While Indian Arm is beautiful in summer (when Roper saw it), local yachtsmen also love to visit it in autumn, winter or early spring when the rich greens and blues of summer have given way to the diffused lights and darknesses of rain-shrouded mountainsides or the frigid blacks and whites of snow-covered slopes. In winter, when stronger winds and rougher waters discourage small boat cruising out of Burrard Inlet, Indian Arm offers a more protected, easily accessible alternative.

When an exceptionally cold winter hits, it is not unheard of for the Arm to freeze over completely, and in 1936 an oil tanker had to be used to break the ice to get supplies to 30 people marooned at the head of the inlet. In the spring, it is possible to count 50 waterfalls in the Arm, whereas in summer, all but three of these are reduced to a trickle. (D. Lawrence, *Pacific Yachting*, April 1972)

Captain Vancouver did not penetrate the North Arm to any extent when he visited what was to become Port Moody in June 1792; but the Spaniards were more curious and explored this Arm to the end. It was the first of the many fiord-inlets on the west coast of North America and after visiting several more inlets to the north, they noted in their journal (25 June 1792):

"Most of these channels presented an entirely novel aspect (from the country south of here). Following the

CHARTS:
3311 — Strip Chart #1 — PORT MOODY TO HOWE SOUND (1:40,000)
3435 — INDIAN ARM (1:24,330, discontinued)
3495 — VANCOUVER HARBOUR — EASTERN PORTION (1:10,000) includes Indian Arm north of Racoon Island (1:30,000). This chart supercedes 3435 and 3484.

"A dream-like, magic scene . . . the sea lay smooth as glass and black as ink. . . ."

main line of the coast, several gorges are noticed, and if one proceeds into any one of them, an arm is found, generally tortuous, of moderate size, one or two miles broad, formed by the slopes of some rocky mountains, very lofty, cut almost straight, so that they look like a very high wall. In the middle of these channels, bottom cannot be found at eighty fathoms, and on taking soundings near the shore, the line could sometimes be allowed to run out without reaching the bottom. Any one who enters these channels to examine them will be surprised and may well think that he has found the desired entry to the other sea (the Atlantic), or a ready means by which to penetrate for many leagues into the interior of the mainland, but all his hopes will be dissipated when, without having noticed the least indication that the channel was about to end, he finds it closed by a barrier of mountains which form a semicircle round it, and which invariably leave only a narrow beach up which it is impossible to advance for more than a few paces."

(Cecil Jane translation)

Winds

Winds in the Port Moody to Deep Cove area are noticeably less frequent and less troublesome (due to limited fetch) than elsewhere, making these waters suitable for smallcraft exploration by sailing dinghy, canoe, kayak or rowboat. Like most mainland inlets, Indian Arm can also experience good winds with onshore, fair-weather winds blowing most strongly up the Arm on sunny summer afternoons (a north-westerly in the Strait of Georgia will curl through Burrard Inlet to become a stiff southwesterly or southerly wind in Indian Arm), while bad-weather Strait of Georgia southeasterlies make their presence felt in Indian Arm either as gusty northeasterlies or southerlies. In winter, the odd "Squamish" breaks through the Indian River valley and blows down the Arm with considerable force.

1. Port Moody

Because of its strategic location at the head of Burrard Inlet, Port Moody was established in 1859 as an emergency anchorage, the first saltwater port on the Lower Mainland, serving New Westminster — the new capital of British Columbia. The port was charted and named by Captain Richards of H.M.S. *Plumper* in honour of Colonel Richard Clements Moody, officer commanding the Royal Engineers detachment.

Moody was charged with the responsibility for building new roads in the colony and defending it in case of American invasion. He realized that should the Fraser freeze over, Port Moody would offer a convenient backdoor supply route to New Westminster. Moody's duties did not blind him to other uses for the port. According to the Port Moody Gazette (1883), Moody had spent much time on the Inlet:

"He it was who caused the first road to be made, — the North Road — from the Fraser to Port Moody . . . He used to keep his yacht in those placid waters and upon them he spent many, and no doubt, pleasant hours. In short, he

12

Port Moody at low tide. Note dredged channel through drying mud flats to Rocky Point Park.

seemed to be in love with the beautiful sheet of water which has taken his name."

Overland travellers from the East arriving by train first caught sight of Pacific saltwater here at Port Moody where, in 1885, the terms of Confederation binding British Columbia to Canada were physically accomplished with the completion of the transcontinental rail link from Montreal. The port was never developed to its full potential, for two years later the rail terminus was moved ten miles down the Inlet, and Vancouver became Canada's major west coast seaport instead.

Anchorage in what is probably the most placid portion of Burrard Inlet is possible along the northern shore of Port Moody, particularly near Old Orchard Park. An extensive drying mud flat prevents all but shoal draught boats from exploring east of here. Old Orchard Park offers a sandy beach (with water tem-

peratures averaging 18°C (65°F) in summer, the warmest in Burrard Inlet), a picnic ground with tables, and the start of a trail around the head of the port. One can find sawmill ruins, a shingle "midden" and other remnants of past industrial activity. This entire shoreline around to Rocky Point Park is being developed into a park to protect the historic associations and unique natural features of the mudflats. The saltmarsh and mudflats provide habitat for wintering or resting waterfowl. Pigeon Point is noted as the only Lower Mainland nesting site for the relatively rare Band-tailed Pigeon.

Rocky Point Park has a swimming pool, picnic area, and a large boat launching ramp accessible by a

Reed Point Marina was designed to accommodate over 1,000 vessels.

dredged channel through the mud flats with minimum depths of 1 foot below chart datum. The park also serves as the home for the Port Moody Museum — the old CPR station which was moved here from its old location at the foot of Queens Street.

Northwest of Rocky Point Park are the Flavelle Cedar Mill Wharf and the Pacific Coast Bulk Terminals, specialising in coal, potash and sulphur exports and phosphate rock imports.

2. Reed Point Marina

This large marina provides moorage for boats up to 130 feet in length, dry storage, fuel, repairs, marine chandlery, charts, laundry, tidal grid, pumpout station, fishing tackle, rental boats and restaurant. The marina includes a guest float for visiting boats and is ideally situated for Lower Mainland boaters who want to take advantage of the miles of protected cruising waters east of Vancouver Harbour, up Indian Arm.

It was near here, or across the Inlet at Ioco that Captain George Vancouver camped for the night of 13 June 1792 as his journal relates:

"We landed for the night about half a league (1½ miles) from the head of the inlet, and about three leagues (9 miles) from its entrance. Our Indian visitors remained with us until by signs we gave them to understand we were going to rest, and after receiving some acceptable articles, they retired, and by means of the same language, promised an abundant supply of fish the next day; our seine having been tried in their presence with very little success. A great desire was manifested by these people to imitate our actions, especially in the firing of a musket, which one of them performed, though with much fear and trembling. They minutely attended to all our transactions, and examined the color of our skins with infinite curiosity. In other respects they differed little from the generality of the natives we had seen: they possessed no European commodities, or trinkets, excepting some rude ornaments apparently made from sheet copper; this circumstance, and the general tenor of their behavior, gave us reason to conclude that we were the first people from a civilized country they had yet seen. Nor did it appear that they were nearly connected, or had much intercourse with other Indians, who traded with the European or American adventurers.

The shores in this situation were formed by steep rocky cliffs, that afforded no convenient space for pitching our tent, which compelled us to sleep in the boats. Some of the young gentlemen, however, preferring the stony beach for their couch, without duly considering the line of high water mark, found themselves incommoded by the flood tide, of which they were not apprized until they were nearly afloat; and one of them slept so sound, that I believe he might have been conveyed to some distance, had he not been awakened by his companions."

A few hundred yards west of the Reed Point Marina is the deserted site of the nineteenth century resort village of Aliceville.

This was a beauty spot with giant maples throwing a

"delightful shade over a wide green sward and the fresh tang of the evergreen forest mingled with the salt sea breezes which swept up from the ocean . . . Yachting and boating, swimming and bathing . . . isolated yet close at hand from the city (Aliceville was located at the northern terminus of Colonel Moody's North Road, 5 miles north of New Westminster) . . . it was natural that here many picnic parties should enjoy their leisure to the full. Naiads and water nymphs disported in the clear limpid waters in "such a tide as moving, seems asleep," a pleasing contrast to the turbid and swirling Fraser, beside the City." (George Green, Provincial Archives)

Aliceville was named after the youngest daughter of John A. Webster; today nothing remains except the maples and the sea.

The north shore of Port Moody, from Pleasantside, past Sunnyside to what is now Ioco was first settled by "ranchers" and homesteaders around the turn of the century. Ioco is the acronym for Imperial Oil Company, who built the first refinery in British Columbia here in 1914. The first tankerload of Peruvian crude oil to the refinery ended up a victim of one of Germany's few successful torpedo attacks in the Pacific (D. Wood). The Ioco Yacht Club, located in a small bay between the refinery dock and Sunnyside Beach, provides a launching ramp and moorage for members. Immediately west of Ioco is the prominent B.C. Hydro thermal-generating plant which was completed in 1974 and produces up to 900 megawatts of peak power for Vancouver. Carraholly, a former settlement and steamer landing, was named by Judge Bole of Belcarra for the Johnston family, who had two holly trees in front of their homestead here.

3. Third Narrows

Compared to the First and Second Narrows, there is almost no tidal current in the "Third Narrows" between Burns Pt. and Barnet Marine Park although the steep topography does tend to increase any wind which may be blowing. Winds in the summer are usually light and from the west, beginning about

10:30 a.m. and ending about 7:30 p.m. (G. Clay). Gosse Point, at the southern entrance to the narrows is named after Captain Joe Gosse, a Newfoundlander who skippered many boats on the B.C. coast including the S.S. *Tees* to Skagway during the Klondike gold rush, the North Van ferries and for many years was senior Pilot in the B.C. Pilotage.

Due south of Burns Point (named after a former Vancouver Port Manager) is a small cove with a clearing behind it. This was known as Thluk-thluk-way-tun to the Indians who came here to peel cedar bark in the springtime. In the last century it became a place to which Vancouver settlers came for a picnic, travelling on a scow towed by paddlewheel steamer (Matthews).

Between 1900 and 1928, this area served as the site of what was said to be the largest saw mill of its kind in the British Commonwealth, built by a Mr. Barnet McLaren. Today, one can explore the brick ruins of an old saw mill foundation at Gosse Point. From seaward, the ruins resemble the bastion of an old fort, guarding the entrance to Port Moody. Gosse Point or Admiralty Point may well have been considered as potential fort sites in 1860 when Colonel Moody reserved 85 acres further to the east on the south shore and several hundred acres on the north shore as an "Admiralty Reserve" to protect the port approaches from any hostile attack.

These reserves are now largely incorporated in parkland and are commemorated by the naming of Admiralty Point opposite Gosse Point. The land be-hind Admiralty Point was formerly known as Admiralty Park before it was incorporated into Belcarra Regional Park. There is a lovely white shell beach here and the point itself is often visited by picnickers or shipwrecked boaters who have unexpectedly found the seven foot drying rock just off the point. Temporary anchorage can be found on either side of the point in two pretty but exposed coves. Some boats moor alongside the log booms which are occasionally stored north of the point. Cottages, different in a way from others found up Indian Arm, and reminiscent of the colourful squatters shacks of the '30s and '40s can be seen along this shoreline despite a bronze plaque cemented into Admiralty Point. The plaque reads:

"Take Notice that by indenture dated April 13, 1913, the areas outlined on the plan inscribed below (Caraholly to well north of Admiralty Pt.) were leased by the Government of Canada to the City of Vancouver for a term of ninety-nine years, computed from the 1st day of May 1912.

And Further Take Notice that no rights have been given by the City of Vancouver to others to use or occupy the said areas or any portion thereof, and any person so using or occupying the said areas does so without colour of right and at his sole risk and peril.

Dated at Vancouver, B.C. this 25th day of September 1961.

R. Thompson
City Clerk
City of Vancouver."

The white shell beach at Admiralty Point with Barnet Marine Park in background. Ruins of kiln (behind beacon) make exciting castle for kids.

Barnet Marine Park

This park, on the old Kapoor saw mill site, is administered by the Corporation of the District of Burnaby and provides playing fields, change rooms, fishing and observation pier, and an artificial sandy beach protected from the wash of passing boats by a log boom strung between pilings (dols) at the low tide line. Space is also provided for dryland storage of sailing dinghies. Temporary anchorage may be possible with a line to the dolphins east of the pier or in the small cove underneath the power line where one can sit back and listen to the zinging sounds of power lines, passing CPR trains, Barnet Highway traffic and sporadic gunfire from a rifle range echoing out from the base of Mount Burnaby. Simon Fraser University is hidden from view behind the trees atop this steep sloped, 1200-foot high mountain.

Burnaby Foreshore

The south shore of Burrard Inlet might appear to be heavily industrialized but between the docks and log booms, there are a few gaps which might provide temporary anchorage or moorage alongside the booms and some nice beaches for landing a canoe and having a picnic. Much of this shore (below the highway or the railroad tracks) has been reserved for a foreshore walking/hiking path park which will extend west of Barnet Marine Park towards Capitol Hill.

Immediately west of Gosse Point, is the old Texaco Wharf (no longer used) a small beach, and stretching up and around the mountainside — Burnaby Mountain Park and Conservation Area. Further along the shore are Barnet Beach Park and the Trans Mountain Pipeline Westridge terminal and Shellburn Refinery wharves. The view from this shore is splendid with vistas up Indian Arm flanked by Mt. Seymour and Eagle Mountain. Proposals have been made for a new marina-convention centre complex here.

Berry Point is said to be named after Rear Admiral Sir Edward Berry, one of Nelson's captains. This name may have been transferred to this point after Berry Point in Hotham Sound was renamed Elephant Point (see Walbran). North of Berry Pt., on the eastern boundary of the Maplewood flats is the Burrard Indian Reserve village Sieil-wah-tuth, where one can see a native Indian racing war canoe beneath a long cedar boat shed. Close to Cates Park are the Matsumoto Shipyards, specialising in aluminum craft and small-medium boat repairs with haul out facilities of 120 foot., 500-ton capacity and the McKenzie Barge wharves.

Parts of the Burrard Inlet foreshore are still marked by scattered clumps of densely packed pilings. These gaunt sentinels are all that remain of the many squatters' shacks that lined the waterfront during the Depression years. Their demise in the early '50s marked a sad moment in Vancouver's history as many of them were burned to the water line without warning in a single night. Apparently, the citizens of the day objected to their appearance and (probably more accurately) what they represented. And yet, the inhabitants of these dwellings were individuals who had come to have an intimate connection with our coast — "the last truly free people left in the world" — fishermen, loggers, pioneers, boat builders, trappers, artists and one writer in particular who finished writing here what has been claimed as "one of the twentieth century's masterpieces of English literature . . . since it appeared in 1947, no novel has been published to rival it."

Malcolm Lowry, the author of that novel (*Under the Volcano*), whose evocative writings concern the physical and spiritual closeness of heaven and hell, wrote of Vancouver's harbour in the 1940s:

> ". . . you would be sure you were in hell . . . affirmed by the spectacle at first not unpicturesque, of the numerous sawmills relentlessly smoking and champing away like demons, Molochs fed by whole mountainsides of forests . . ." (The Bravest Boat).

Lowry seemed to be haunted by the implications of onrushing civilization and after a year's residence in Vancouver retreated to a squatter's shack on the beach south of Dollarton, in what is now Cates Park. He is reported to have spent the happiest 14 years of his otherwise tormented life here and grew quite attached to his surroundings. He viewed the Shellburn oil refinery across the inlet as a:

> "gleaming open cathedral . . . with the red votive candle of the burning oil wastes flickering ceaselessly all night . . ." Later the refinery decided to "put a great sign over the wharfs . . . But for weeks they never got around to the S, so that it was left HELL. And yet, my own imagination could not have dreamt anything fairer than the heaven from which we perceived this."
> (The Forest Path to the Spring)

4. Cates Park

Cates Park comprises 58 acres around Lowry's "heaven" and includes a paved launching ramp, swimming beach, changing rooms, grass lawn, playground, picnic area and shelter. Although the water is cold, it is much cleaner than elsewhere in Burrard Inlet because of a prevailing current out of Indian Arm and a back eddy on the flood. Temporary anchorage partially exposed to westerlies and the wash of passing waterskiers, powerboats, tugs and barges is possible between the launching ramp and the McKenzie Barge wharves. The park is named after the late Captain Charles Cates, former mayor of North Vancouver and principal of C. H. Cates & Sons Tugboats which handle most of the large freighters entering Vancouver Harbour. The famous "Checkerboard" war canoe, handcarved in 1921 by Chief Henry Peter George and winner of many races on Burrard Inlet, is protected here. There are trails throughout the park including one called the "Malcolm Lowry Walk" which may have been his cherished "Forest Path to the Spring." On returning to his old home a few years before his death he wrote:

> "The path had scarcely changed; nor, here, had the

The entrance to Indian Arm, with ski-slopes of Mount Seymour above, the end of the North Vancouver suburbs at left.

forest. Civilization, creator of deathscapes, like a dull-witted fire of ugliness and ferocious stupidity — so unimaginative it had even almost managed to spoil the architectural beauty of our oil refinery — had spread all down the opposite bank, blown over the water and crept up upon us from the south along it, murdering the trees and taking down the shacks as it went, but it had become baffled by the Indian reserve, and a law that had not been repealed that forbade building too near a lighthouse, so to the south we were miraculously saved by civilization itself (of which a lighthouse is perhaps always the highest symbol) as if it too had become conscious of the futility of pretending that it was advancing by creating the moribund."

Roche Point 'lighthouse' is named after the same Royal Navy officer whose name is honoured in Roche Harbour, San Juan Island (see Walbran). At the northern boundary of the park the ruins of a substantial cement burner foundation with four tunnel-like entrances marks the location of the old Dollar sawmill, built by the Scottish shipping magnate Captain Robert Dollar, in 1917. The Dollarton area was known to the Indians as "See-Mam-ette" or "Land of the lazy people." In Lowry's time, the summer cottages and squatters' shacks along this shore, which have since been replaced with large floating boathouses, carried such descriptive names as "Dunwoiken," "Wywurk" and "Hi-Doubt."

Indian Arm

When Captain Vancouver passed the entrance of Indian Arm after spending the night near Port Moody, he noted in his journal:

"Perfectly satisfied with our researches in this branch of the sound, at four in the morning of Thursday the 14th, we retraced our passage in, leaving on the northern shore a small opening extending to the northward, with two little islets (Boulder and Hamber) before it of little importance, whilst we had a grander object in contemplation (the "northwest passage"); and more particularly so as this arm or channel could not be deemed navigable to shipping. The tide caused no stream; the color of its water, after we had passed the island the day before, was green and perfectly clear, whereas that in the main branch of the sound, extending nearly half over the gulf, and accompanied by a rapid tide, was nearly colorless, which gave us some reason to suppose that the northern branch of the sound might possibly be discovered to terminate in a river of considerable extent."

Vancouver surmised correctly that the lack of tidal flow (maximum ½ knot at springs) and the river outflow meant that this channel could not lead to a navigable route to Europe. In fact, like most west coast

Belcarra Park, on the narrow isthmus between Burrard Inlet and Bedwell Bay just visible at upper left. Wharf allows day stops for recreational craft.

fiords which end in a river, there is a prevailing surface current of fresh water on top of the salt out of the Arm, which only diminishes with a flooding tide, strong southerly wind, or at times of minimum river discharge (January to March, August, September). The strongest outflowing currents (maximum 1 knot) would likely be found at times of peak discharge (May, June, November). In addition, up to 40% of the freshwater input into Indian Arm can come from the Buntzen Power Plants (Thomson, 1981). Water temperatures remain cold except in dry hot summers when there is little fresh water or snow melt runoff.

Indian Arm often experiences swarms of jelly fish — the white ones do not sting, but the larger red ones do. Sunshine penetrates the Arm for only six to twelve hours a day because of the high surrounding mountains, but at night the phosphorescence in the water is a wondrous sight to behold.

The Indians called this Arm "Sasamat," (possibly meaning "cool place"). Lowry describes it:

". . . sailing directly northwards into the snow-covered mountain peaks, past numerous enchanting uninhabited islands of tall pines, down gradually into the narrowing gorge and to the uttermost end of that marvellous region of wilderness known to the Indians as Paradise . . ."

The leader of Edward Roper's expedition in 1887 described it this way:

"This," said he, "is a good example of the innumerable fiords, or inlets, or sounds, which indent this coast, right away up to Alaska. Some run deeper into the land, a few are narrower all the way in, but they are very similar in character, and I think that in this, the North Arm of Burrard Inlet, we have as good a specimen of them as we should have if we went many miles away. It is the nearest to Vancouver City, but it is none the less a typical British Columbia inlet."

"Have you been up many of them?" I asked.

"Yes, very many, and I hope to go up many more; but I think there are better views in this one than in most of them farther up the coast. Higher up this one, where I hope to go with you before we leave, there are some of the most sublime scenes I have looked on anywhere; and I have travelled some, too."

5.   Belcarra Park

The Indians called this place "Tum-ta-mayh-tun," meaning "end of the wind" for it was here that a west wind blowing up the inlet seemed to cease, raise up and pass over (Matthews). It was later known as Hall's Ranch after a John Hall, explorer for Colonel Moody, who preempted 100 acres here in 1870. Judge Boles acquired the property in 1878 in payment for defending Hall, who had been accused of shooting his Indian klootch, and named it Belcarra — Celtic for "the fair land on which the sunshines." Judge Boles' daughter-in-law lived here until recently and nearby, in a tree house, 95 ft above the ground, lived George Dyson — builder of baidarkas (ocean going canoes), son of Freeman Dyson — U.S. starship designer and grandson of Sir George Dyson — director of the Royal College of Music (K. Brower).

Belcarra Regional Park, the largest waterfront park in the Greater Vancouver Regional District, includes 4,450 acres, four miles of marine shoreland and two lakes. At Belcarra Landing there is a wharf extending out over a white shell beach and a float for loading and unloading only (overnight moorage is not permitted). This wharf has been used intermittently by the Harbour Ferries cruises up Indian Arm since the 1920s, by visitors fishing for shiners and crabs, and by scuba divers. Before this, evidence from a nearby midden indicates that Coast Salish Indians had lived here for over 2,000 years. Extensive playing fields, a large picnic area and an old beach house with a refreshment concession are now located here. Temporary anchorage is possible off the shallow beach south of the wharf or north of the wharf in Belcarra Bay.

Hamber Island, connected to Turtle Head at low tide by a rocky tombolo spit is named after a former Lt. Governor of B.C. who had a summer home here.

6.   Strathcona

A tiny municipal float, administered by the District of North Vancouver, is located behind White Rock

Early morning mist in Deep Cove.

Historic view of moored and anchored yachts in Deep Cove from Panorama Park (circa 1976). (Photo: Chris Hatfield)

and Grey Rocks islands. The float dries at low water so is only available for temporary moorage or landing near high tide. This small cove is almost totally surrounded by private homes but Myrtle Park extends down to the water a few hundred feet northeast of the float and temporary anchorage is possible in less than a fathom of water.

7. Deep Cove

This is one of those special coastal settlements which has its own uniquely captivating mood. The "Cove" is connected to Vancouver by road but is really more rural than suburban in nature, and its quiet atmosphere is highly valued by residents and visitors alike.

In the past, the Cove has served as one of the most popular anchorages in the Lower Mainland. Many residents, houseboat dwellers and ocean voyagers have spent happy times here, mooring their vessels on buoys, protected by the steep surrounding cliffs from all but the most ferocious winter northeasterlies and a few "view-conscious" landlubbers.

The view has now been purged of offending vessels and buoys and the National Harbours Board warns that unauthorized (permanent?) anchorage or buoys

are not permitted. Water-skiing is also forbidden and there is a speed limit of 5 knots. Temporary or emergency anchorage for visitors wishing a transitory taste of Elysium may still be possible here however.

The government float here provides about 100 ft of temporary moorage space at the foot of Gallant Avenue with access to grocery stores, restaurants and other facilities serving the Cove community of 5,000. The narrow launching ramp north of the wharf is seldom used because of its steepness. The premises and floats of the Deep Cove Yacht Club are located in front of 6-acre Panorama Park (picnic tables and shelter, changing rooms.)

South of the government float is a small beach and a canoe/rowboat rental establishment. Experienced canoeists can paddle to the head of Indian Arm and back in a day. Although the prevailing outward (southerly) flowing surface current tends to be strongest along the west shore of the inlet, most canoeists are willing to buck this in order to take advantage of the morning sun, returning with the afternoon sun down the east shore of the Arm.

Ten-acre Deep Cove Park is located around the southern shore where Myrtle Creek spills out in a small waterfall, covered at high tide. A four-foot-wide waterfront park reserve for future promenade development connects this park to an extension of 25-acre Wickenden Park in Cove Cliff.

8. Seycove Marina

This marina serves as the last fueling stop for boats en route up Indian Arm (there are no fuel facilities at the head of the Arm). A launching ramp, marine hardware and moorage facilities are also located here.

Indian rock paintings can still be deciphered below Grey Rocks ("Cottonwood" Smiths' bluff) just north of the quarry and the marina. Some people feel these paintings indicate good fishing in the vicinity but J. W Bell, whose family lived in the Cove in 1905, noted that these were "warnings of Se-lala-kum — the evil spirit, devil or mythical being who had the power to frustrate, destroy and cause death to any of his victims. Such places were to be avoided, no fishing, berry picking or trespassing in that vicinity on penalty of death." (*B.C Memories*, Vancouver Archives).

Steep-sided Jug Island, just off the northern tip of the Belcarra Peninsula was so named by Capt. Richards in 1859 "on account of the resemblance to a jug handle formed by a large rock cavity (now crumbled) jutting from its side." Although the island is protected by a recreation reserve, the shoreline is so precipitous that access is almost impossible. A nice pocket beach and picnic area is located south of the island in Belcarra Park. This is a popular scuba diving and waterskiing area and temporary anchorage behind the island is therefore relatively uncongested

Seycove Marina at the north end of Deep Cove offers fuel, moorage, launching and retrieval for smaller craft.

only at night or in the winter months.

Temporary anchorage with less protection from down-inlet winds (infrequent in summer) is possible in the next bay. Charles Reef and Tupper Rock are named after Sir Charles Tupper, a father of Confederation and Prime Minister of Canada for a few weeks in May and June of 1896.

9. Bedwell Bay

Known to the Indians as Chul-whah-ulch (low, shallow beach, covered at high water), this bay offers the best anchorage in Indian Arm. In the winter months, however, the anchorage at the head of the bay is completely exposed to the occasional strong northeasterly. Somewhat more protection from these winds is available in the northwest corner of the bay north of the Vancouver Waterski Club float and jump ramp.

Anchorage with even more protection from winter northeasterlies is possible in Farrer Cove, a mile to the north. Fair protection from southwesterlies is also available in the southern end of this cove near the YMCA Camp Howdy floats at Belvedere, formerly a resort and steamer landing. This is a popular summer weekend anchorage.

Bedwell Bay was used for many years as an unofficial ships' graveyard. Old hulks which were scuttled here made for fascinating exploration. Most have disappeared completely but H.M.S. *Cranbrook*, scuttled by the Federal Government in 1947, lies 100 yards off the Woodhaven shore in 8 fathoms of water and is a popular scuba diving site.

10. Woodlands

A small municipal float provides temporary moorage for access to shore just west of Lone Rock which is joined to the mainland by a catwalk causeway bridge. Woodlands is reputed to be the oldest summer home community in Indian Arm and is connected by road to North Vancouver. The three acres of Lone Rock have been transformed into a spectacular garden by W.H. Hatfield. An earlier resident, J.A. Tepoorten developed his *Samarkand* here with ornamental stonework, lily ponds, archways, a windmill and a miniature lighthouse on a promontory of the island.

There is another tiny municipal float a quarter of a mile north of here at Sunshine (11)

12. Indian Islets Marine Park

Racoon and Twin Islands, first reserved for public recreation use in 1906, were established as a marine park in 1981. Canoeists and other small boat explorers have long used Racoon Island as a favourite picnic stop. Temporary anchorage is possible close to a small beach at the northwest end of the island, taking care to avoid two dangerous rocks which dry about 8 feet less than 200 feet offshore. Although Racoon Island is almost as steep-sided as Jug Island, access is somewhat easier.

The Twin Islands are almost joined at low water by a white shell isthmus and three tiny rocks. Tide pools here are interesting to explore and there are picnic sites and trails around the northernmost island. An old cabin on the south island once served as a base for the Burnaby "Workdodgers Club" and mineral leases on the islands were placed in the vain hope that the mother lode of the rich Brittania mines in Howe Sound might make a reappearance here. Access and shelter between the islands is possible for shoal-draught boats as the tide rises. Mooring buoys are to be placed east of the islands for deeper draught small craft as the waters surrounding these islands are almost everywhere too deep for convenient anchorage.

Temporary anchorage (exposed to southerly winds) might be possible in small indentations in the mainland shore inside the Twin Islands, at Buntzen Bay, or across the arm south of Brighton Beach. There are several small summer home communities along the Arm and several private floats and buoys which should not be used for temporary moorage except in a

Opposite, Bedwell Bay is one of the few reasonably shallow but protected anchorages in Indian Arm. Only northeasters pose any threat, and they are rare in summer.

Above, Twin Islands, part of Indian Islets Marine Park. Below, white shell beaches and tidal pools between the islands are interesting to explore.

Racoon Island, below, is a favourite picnic stop. Temporary anchorage is possible at northwest end.

23

Orlomah Beach, the home of Jubilee Children's Summer Camp, and one of the few relatively flat uplands on Indian Arm.

case of dire emergency. A float near Cascade Cove bears the sign: "PRIVATE — we have cause to shoot at intruders".

Orlomah Beach is the home of the Jubilee Childrens' Summer Camp for dependents of lower mainland labour union members. The name Orlomah is derived from the first letters of former owner Mr. Banfield's family: Orson, Lois, Mae and Mother Harriet. It has also been known as Rainey's Ranch after another former owner, Capt. John Rainey.

13. Buntzen Power Houses

The impressive concrete Buntzen Power Houses, built in 1903 and 1914 to provide the first hydroelectric power to Vancouver, were named after Johannes Buntzen, first general manager of the Vancouver Power Company (1897) which became the B.C. Electric Company (now B.C. Hydro). In 1903, a 2¼ mile tunnel was drilled beneath Eagle Mountain to Lake Coquitlam to provide a continuous supply of water to Lake Beautiful, a popular fishing and picnic area for early wilderness explorers from Vancouver. Lake Beautiful was dammed, flooded, renamed Buntzen

Buntzen Power Houses, supplied with an enormous head of pressure from Buntzen Lake by penstocks, were Vancouver's first hydroelectric power, dating from 1903.

and its augmented waters then travelled by penstock down to the power houses on Indian Arm, 400 ft below the northern end of the reservoir.

Care should be exercised in approaching the Power Houses as the gates may be opened without warning to discharge huge volumes of water. The dock here is for emergency landing only. A road leads from behind Power House No. 1 to a road around the eastern shore of Buntzen Reservoir — the northernmost road access in Indian Arm.

Best Point is named for Wilfred M. Best, killed in action, 17 September, 1944. A few hundred yards north of the point, a small cave opens at the high water mark — the mine shaft of an old prospector's dream for another Britannia? Coldwell Beach is named after C.A. Coldwell, alderman on the first Vancouver City Council, 1886, who had a summer home here.

Temporary anchorage with some protection from southerly winds is possible just north of Seven Mile Point, south of the Johnson summer home settlement and across the arm from Silver Falls.

14. Bishop Creek

Fairly well protected anchorage is possible near high water in indentations around the Bishop Creek and Clementine Creek alluvial fans, particularly between the two fans with Croker Island providing considerable shelter. The Indian Arm Sand and Gravel Company operation at Bergs has left behind some old floats (at the south end of the fan) and what appears to be a tunnel shaft entrance to their old quarry workings. A southern distributary of Bishop Creek widens out to form a miniature lake in an abandoned gravel pit.

Croker Island, the largest within Burrard Inlet, is known to scuba divers as "Paradise" for its good winter underwater visibility (up to 100 feet) and its colourful variety of marine-life (Pratt-Johnson). The island itself is so steep-sided that nearby anchorage or access is extremely difficult. Temporary moorage on log booms is occasionally possible.

15. Granite Falls

Granite Falls (Fairy Falls) is the largest and most conspicuous waterfall in Indian Arm, debouching almost directly into salt water over a wide bare rock surface. While Wigwam Inn was suffering prolonged indignities, this area served as the major resort and terminus of the Harbour Ferries Indian Arm cruise. The site has the advantage of afternoon sun and on summer weekends many small boats anchor temporarily off the Grand Creek delta with the best protection afforded north of the delta or, near high tide, at the base of the falls. One can explore the old quarry operations, picnic and resort sites, or hike the trails

Right, Granite Falls.

Wigwam Inn, with floats for visiting pleasure craft, has been recently refurbished. The Inn now offers a dining room and hotel rooms with antique furniture.

above the falls and 4 miles up the valley to Grand Lake.

Iron Creek recreational reserve protects 3½ acres of shoreline north of Iron Bay. Sheltered anchorage is not available but log booms are occasionally placed here in such a way as to provide fairly well protected temporary moorage.

16. Wigwam Inn

In 1906, an enterprising visionary named B.F. (Benny) Dickens, who started the first advertising agency in Canada, decided to build a first class luxury resort here. The idea was to attract the wealthy and discriminating to a hotel with style and charm where they could sample the natural beauties of the area: "pure mountain air . . . aromas of undefiled nature . . . scenic effects that outclass the famous fiords of Norway." The project ran into financial difficulties and was eventually completed by Count Alvo von Alvensleben in 1910 as a German Luftkurort or "fresh air resort." The grounds were landscaped with rockeries and gazebos to resemble a traditional German beer garden and the resort was internationally and locally popular until war broke out in 1914 and Alvo, faced with internment as an enemy of his adopted country, fled to Seattle. In the '20s, the Inn reopened with an Indian theme replacing the now unpopular German one. In the following years Wigwam Inn changed hands many times. In 1962, the Inn was closed down after an RCMP raid discovered illicit gambling activities, but it has now been restored to some of its former glory. This history of Wigwam Inn is excerpted from a new book by Pam Humphries (1982).

Facilities provided here include moorage (no fee in winter if using Inn's facilities), rooms, lounge, restaurant, games room and weight loss clinic (sauna, etc.). One can explore the grounds and hike up to Spray of Pearls Falls. In summer when there is little runoff, you can hike up the riverbed through Cathedral Can-

A harbour ferry churns away from Wigwam Inn; these excursions usually include both schoolchildren and tourists.

yon (remarkably cool on even the hottest day) to the base of the falls. A longer trail goes up the Indian River over the rock cliffs known as the Palisades to Mount Dickens (2800 feet above sea level). Mt. Felix (3800 feet high) opposite Wigwam Inn, was named after Mr. Francis Bursill who, under the name of "Felix Penne" was a unique literary character in Vancouver for many years (Matthews). This mountain is possibly the one named "Elephanta" in 1887 by Roper.

Temporary anchorage is possible off the Indian River estuary delta but one should be wary of deadheads, stumps and other snags. At high tide it is possible for shallow draught boats to find shelter behind the Wigwam Inn alluvial fan in an isolated nook known as the "lagoon" that is seldom visited. It is also possible to explore up the Indian River as did the Spaniards, Vernaci and Salamanca, a week after Capt. Vancouver had passed by the entrance to Indian Arm. Travelling in shallow draught longboats they noted:

"The northern arm of the channel which we called Floridablanca and which the natives call Sasamat, ends in a river little worthy of notice, which flows down the slopes and through the gorge of a great mountain. Its source appears to be the melting snows, the water from which falls into it. Our officers who explored this chan-

nel wished to go up the river, despite the fact that it was very narrow, and navigating in half a fathom of water they were in danger of finding their boats caught in the trees which were on the banks. These trees formed an attractive wood in which there were some clearings, and near them a number of Indians who were amazed to see vessels so novel in appearance to them, and men even more strange, who appeared in that remote place, the entrance to which was assuredly hidden from all who were not filled with a vehement desire to make discoveries and led on by an unwearied curiosity. But neither the great distance from an inhabited land, nor the complete absence of all trade and means of communication among these people, who live contented with the products of that barren land, nor the darkness and obscurity of the place in which they lived sufficed to preserve for them their lonely peace. The women fled at once and hid themselves among the rocks, while some of the men embarked in a canoe, accompanied by one boy to whom all showed great deference. They approached our boats, observing those who were in them but in a little while returned to land, and went away into the wood"

(Cecil Jane translation)

The Indian River was known as the Mesliloet to the Indians and the head of the Arm was Slail-wah-tuth, reputed to mean "go inside place" (Matthews).

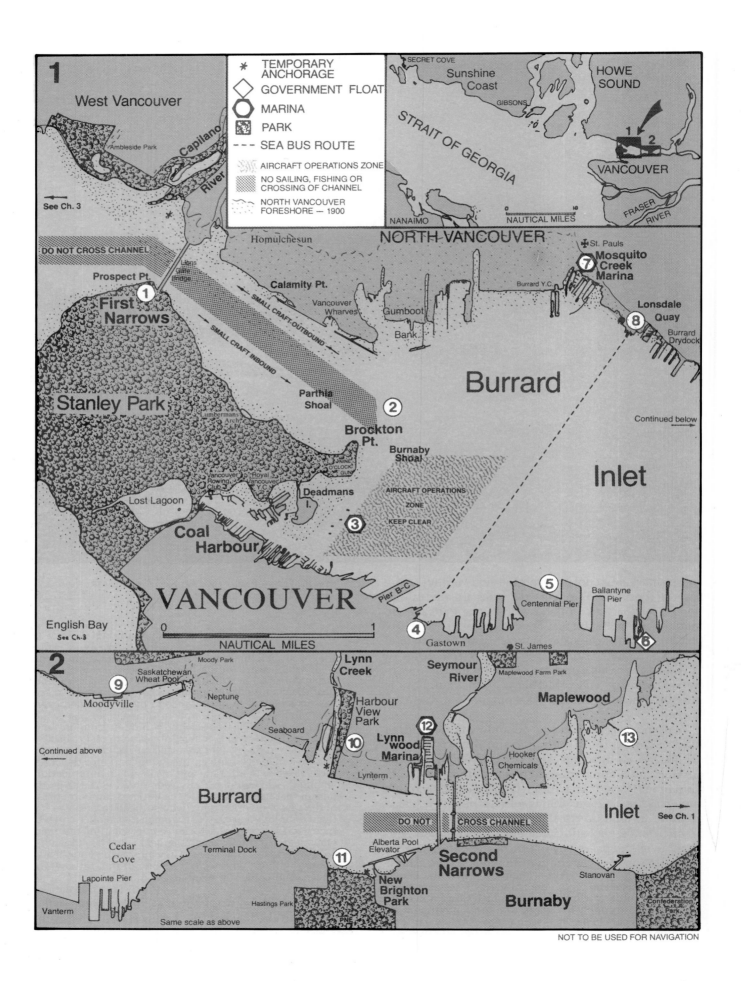

1

TEMPORARY ANCHORAGE
GOVERNMENT FLOAT
MARINA
PARK
SEA BUS ROUTE
AIRCRAFT OPERATIONS ZONE
NO SAILING, FISHING OR CROSSING OF CHANNEL
NORTH VANCOUVER FORESHORE — 1900

SECRET COVE
Sunshine Coast
GIBSONS
HOWE SOUND
STRAIT OF GEORGIA
VANCOUVER
NANAIMO
FRASER RIVER
NAUTICAL MILES

West Vancouver
Ambleside Park
Capilano River
See Ch. 3

DO NOT CROSS CHANNEL

Prospect Pt.
Lions Gate Bridge
Homulchesun
NORTH VANCOUVER
St. Pauls
Mosquito Creek Marina
Burrard Y.C.
Lonsdale Quay
Burrard Drydock

First Narrows
Calamity Pt.
Vancouver Wharves
Gumboot Bank
SMALL CRAFT OUTBOUND
SMALL CRAFT INBOUND

Burrard

Stanley Park
Lumberman's Arch
Parthia Shoal
Brockton Pt.
Burnaby Shoal
Continued below

Vancouver Rowing Club
Royal Vancouver Y.C.
NINE O'CLOCK GUN
Deadmans I.
AIRCRAFT OPERATIONS ZONE KEEP CLEAR
Lost Lagoon

Inlet

Coal Harbour

VANCOUVER

Pier B-C
Centennial Pier
Ballantyne Pier

English Bay
See Ch. 3
0   1
NAUTICAL MILES
Gastown
St. James

2

Moody Park
Saskatchewan Wheat Pool
Lynn Creek
Seymour River
Maplewood Farm Park

Moodyville
Neptune
Harbour View Park
Maplewood

Continued above
Seaboard
Lynnwood Marina
Hooker Chemicals

Burrard
Lynterm
DO NOT   CROSS CHANNEL

Inlet
See Ch. 1

Cedar Cove
Terminal Dock
Alberta Pool Elevator
Second Narrows
Stanovan

Lapointe Pier
New Brighton Park
Burnaby
Confederation Park

Vanterm
Hastings Park
Same scale as above
PNE

CHAPTER TWO

Vancouver Harbour

First Narrows, Coal Harbour, Maplewood Flats

It is hard to believe that a hundred years ago fewer than 300 people lived here. Since that time the primeval forests have been replaced with skyscrapers only slightly taller than the tallest trees in what was probably the finest stand of timber on the coast. Huge deep-sea bulk carriers have replaced the dugout canoe and the natives' potlatch has given way to a marketplace that has made this seaport one of the busiest in the world, second in North America only to New York in volume of foreign cargo handled annually.

Cruising by boat through Burrard Inlet, the view along the waterfront is fascinating. This view changes so rapidly from year to year however, that one is hard pressed to find any trace of the original shoreline, the first settlements or even the comparatively recent pioneering developments of a few decades ago. The haste to modernize, expand, increase efficiency, attract new business and tourists by dredging mudflats, filling marshes, replacing redundant wharves and obliterating small shipyards and other unwanted aspects of our maritime heritage has not yet altered significantly the crowning glory of Vancouver — the mountains, close above the sea.

The view upwards to the mountains on a sunny day is truly spectacular, fully justifying Vancouver's claim to be one of the most beautiful cities in the world. This view is only a little changed from that which Captain George Vancouver first gazed upon almost 200 years ago:

The shores of this channel, which, after Sir Harry Burrard of the navy, I have distinguished by the name of BURRARD'S CHANNEL, may be considered, on the southern side, of a moderate height, and though rocky, well covered with trees of a large growth, principally of the pine tribe. On the northern side, the rugged snowy barrier, whose base we had now nearly approached, rose very abruptly, and was only protected from the wash of the sea by a very narrow border of lowland.

South of Burrard Inlet only Stanley Park remains forested, almost as it was when Colonel Moody and Captain Richards (the next official visitors to the Harbour after Vancouver) recommended its protection as a military reserve in 1859. Walbran notes that before coming to British Columbia, Colonel Moody had served as a professor of military fortifications and as the first governor of the Falkland Islands (1838-49). It is interesting to speculate on whether his experience in the Falklands influenced his selection of the many defensive positions and military reserves around Vancouver. Many of these reserves are now major parks or recreation reserves (Pt. Atkinson, Jericho, Belcarra, Stanley Park).

The close juxtaposition of a modern metropolis beside the near-wilderness surroundings of Stanley Park and the North Shore mountains is an astounding sight, especially when viewed from a boat approaching through the First Narrows.

CHARTS:
3311 — Strip Chart #1 — PORT MOODY TO
        HOWE SOUND (1:40,000)
3482 — Vancouver Harbour — WESTERN
        PORTION (1:10,000)
3483 — Vancouver Harbour — CENTRAL
        PORTION (1:10,000)

The approach to Vancouver through First Narrows and under the Lions' Gate Bridge is flanked by Stanley Park (right) and the Capilano River estuary. Note tide rips as westerly blows against the ebb.

Although there is much of interest in the changing harbour scene, it should be noted that this central portion of Burrard Inlet is primarily a commercial port and not a small boat recreational area. Intensive exploration of Vancouver's waterfront is not encouraged by the port authorities because of potential conflicts with the large volume of coastal and deep sea shipping traffic, ferries, tugs, barges, cruise ships and floatplanes. Visitors may have difficulty finding moorage as there are no designated public wharves or floats for transient small craft within the harbour. Amazing as it may seem, Vancouver is probably the only coastal community in B.C. (or anywhere else, for that matter) which does not have easily accessible public floats or anchorage areas set aside for visiting small craft.

In the summer months, temporary or guest moorage may be found in vacant berths at some of the marinas or yacht clubs by prior arrangement or on an "as available" basis. Temporary anchorage in an emergency or while waiting for a change in weather or tide is possible at a few locations (marked by an asterisk (*) on the accompanying map).

Winds and Fog

Winds in Burrard Inlet are greatly influenced by the east-west trend of the topography and, in summer, by the differential heating and cooling of land and water bodies. Winds recorded at the First Narrows (Lions Gate Bridge) are primarily from the easterly quadrant (NE, E, SE), blowing 50% of the time in summer (mainly at night to a few hours before noon) and 70% in winter. Westerly winds blow 30% of the time in summer (peaking in the afternoon) and 10% in winter. The strongest winds are the easterly in November and December and the westerlies in February, April and May. March is the windiest month with an equal amount of easterlies and westerlies. Average wind speeds decrease markedly through the harbour from Pt. Atkinson (10 mph) to Port Moody (less than 5 mph). Fogs are most frequent in the mornings in the months September to February (6 to 10 days a month).

1. First Narrows

Currents in the First Narrows have changed considerably since Captain Vancouver sailed through with Lt. Peter Puget in the yawl and pinnace from H.M. Ships *Discovery* and *Chatham*. He noted in his journal in 1792:

> we passed to the northward of an island (now Stanley Park) . . . (through) a passage ten to seven fathoms deep, no more than a cable's length (200 yards) in width.

The 1864 *Pilot* noted that maximum currents were 8 knots in the Narrows, with the ebb stream running out for 2 hours after low water by the shore (the flood stream lasted only 4 hours). Captain Charles W. Cates (*Tidal Action in British Columbia Waters*, 1952) has noted that the tide here used to roar like some of the northern narrows at rates up to 10 knots prior to the dredging of the Capilano River shoals in the early part of this century. Dredging has made the Narrows more than twice as wide as they were in Vancouver's time, reduced the strength of the stream to 6 knots (4 knots at neaps) and made slack water coincident with high and low water by the shore.

The authorized approach for inbound small craft is close to the Stanley Park shore. Sailing, fishing or crossing of the central core of the channel are prohibited in both First and Second Narrows (see Port of Vancouver Advisory, Rule 9; *Small Craft Guide*, Vol.2, Ch.III). Sailboats without auxiliary power are advised to arrange for an engine-powered vessel to accompany them through the Narrows.

Passage through the Narrows should be timed to avoid strong contrary currents, tide rips or heavy seas. Slow vessels using the Stanley Park back eddy (see tidal current charts) to make their way up to Prospect Point on an ebbing tide should beware where the back eddy meets the ebb stream as this can cause a vessel to veer toward the north shore into the path of any outgoing vessels (Cates).

The rips extending west of the Narrows, when an ebbing tide meets a westerly wind or swell, can also be uncomfortable. Captain Cates has noted:

> . . . a small vessel coming out with a big ebb is into it almost without warning, and after that there is no turning back . . . it is quite common for small launches to break down in the tide rips, owing to the dirt in fuel tanks being violently stirred-up.

Outbound small craft, close to the north shore, should also be wary of a southerly flowing current at the mouth of the Capilano River which is strongest during the ebb after heavy rainfall or peak runoff (usually in the months of May, November and December). A small cove just east of the mouth of the river could provide emergency anchorage out of the way of passing ship traffic. Half a mile up the river on the west bank in Park Royal is Kapilano 100, a tall dark building, the top floors of which serve as the Vancouver Vessel Traffic Management centre. Radar and VHF communications networks assist in monitoring all ship movements within the harbour and throughout the Strait of Georgia.

The broken remains of the S.S. *Beaver*, "the ship that saved the West" (D. Pethick) rest beneath the deep waters below Prospect Point. The *Beaver* was the first steamship to ply the waters of the Pacific Northeast, arriving on this coast in 1836. Because she could enter and leave many coastal inlets and rivers unbeholden to wind or tide she was able to out-manoeuvre the Russian and American sailing ships in gaining a monopoly of the fur trade for the Hudson's Bay Company. As a well armed naval craft she also carried the Queen's Law into remote coastal areas, served as a survey ship (1863-70), and growing older,

Coal Harbour boating party, circa 1905, painted by the author's grandmother.

MEAN EBB TIDAL CURRENTS IN CENTRAL BURRARD INLET

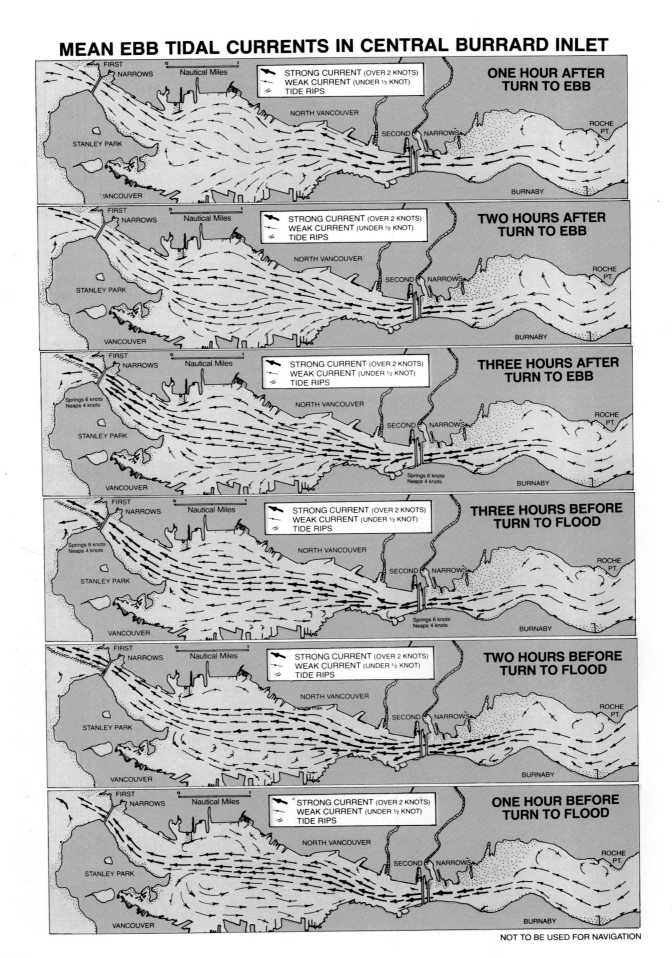

NOT TO BE USED FOR NAVIGATION

MEAN FLOOD TIDAL CURRENTS IN CENTRAL BURRARD INLET

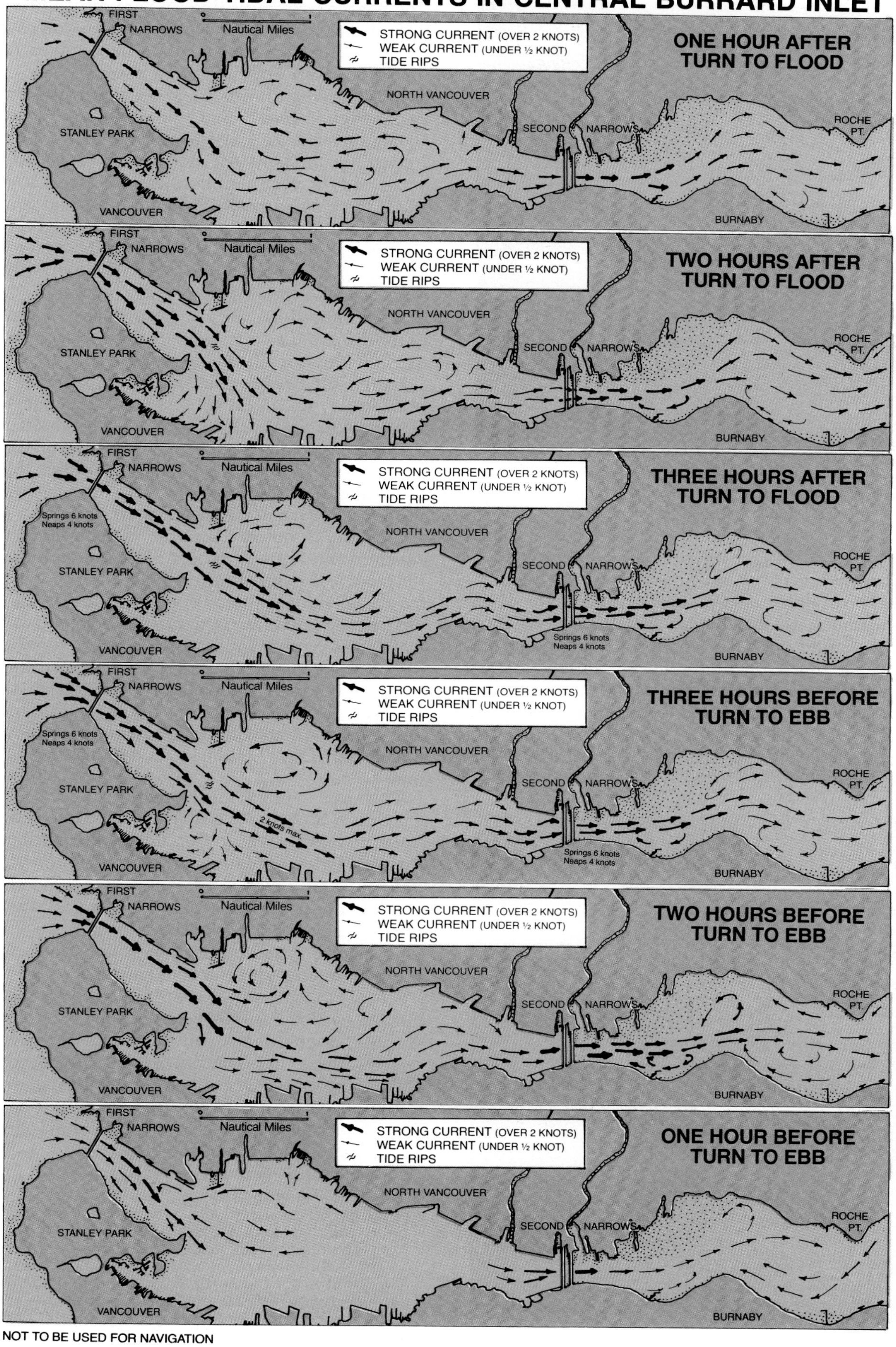

FIRST NARROWS
Nautical Miles
STRONG CURRENT (OVER 2 KNOTS)
WEAK CURRENT (UNDER ½ KNOT)
TIDE RIPS
ONE HOUR AFTER TURN TO FLOOD
NORTH VANCOUVER
STANLEY PARK
SECOND NARROWS
ROCHE PT.
VANCOUVER
BURNABY
FIRST NARROWS
Nautical Miles
STRONG CURRENT (OVER 2 KNOTS)
WEAK CURRENT (UNDER ½ KNOT)
TIDE RIPS
TWO HOURS AFTER TURN TO FLOOD
NORTH VANCOUVER
STANLEY PARK
SECOND NARROWS
ROCHE PT.
VANCOUVER
BURNABY
FIRST NARROWS
Nautical Miles
STRONG CURRENT (OVER 2 KNOTS)
WEAK CURRENT (UNDER ½ KNOT)
TIDE RIPS
THREE HOURS AFTER TURN TO FLOOD
Springs 6 knots
Neaps 4 knots
NORTH VANCOUVER
STANLEY PARK
SECOND NARROWS
ROCHE PT.
Springs 6 knots
Neaps 4 knots
VANCOUVER
BURNABY
FIRST NARROWS
Nautical Miles
STRONG CURRENT (OVER 2 KNOTS)
WEAK CURRENT (UNDER ½ KNOT)
TIDE RIPS
THREE HOURS BEFORE TURN TO EBB
Springs 6 knots
Neaps 4 knots
NORTH VANCOUVER
STANLEY PARK
SECOND NARROWS
ROCHE PT.
2 knots max.
Springs 6 knots
Neaps 4 knots
VANCOUVER
BURNABY
FIRST NARROWS
Nautical Miles
STRONG CURRENT (OVER 2 KNOTS)
WEAK CURRENT (UNDER ½ KNOT)
TIDE RIPS
TWO HOURS BEFORE TURN TO EBB
NORTH VANCOUVER
STANLEY PARK
SECOND NARROWS
ROCHE PT.
VANCOUVER
BURNABY
FIRST NARROWS
Nautical Miles
STRONG CURRENT (OVER 2 KNOTS)
WEAK CURRENT (UNDER ½ KNOT)
TIDE RIPS
ONE HOUR BEFORE TURN TO EBB
NORTH VANCOUVER
STANLEY PARK
SECOND NARROWS
ROCHE PT.
VANCOUVER
BURNABY

NOT TO BE USED FOR NAVIGATION

ADAPTED FROM CANADIAN HYDROGRAPHIC SERVICE, TIDAL CURRENT PUBLICATION No. 30, 1981.
SEE ALSO: CAPT. C.W. CATES, **TIDAL ACTION IN BRITISH COLUMBIA WATERS**, 1952;
and R.E. THOMSON, **OCEANOGRAPHY OF THE BRITISH COLUMBIA COAST**, 1981.

Replica of the historic Beaver, *moored below Gastown. Original was wrecked at Prospect Point in 1888, after over 50 years' service.*

as a freighter, passenger vessel, tugboat and tower of log booms and becalmed sailing vessels into the first sawmill berths of British Columbia. The Indians were so impressed with the *Beaver* that they were convinced she could not have been built without the aid of the Great Spirit, *Saghalie Tyee.* Calling on the assistance of their shamans, they made rock paintings of the *Beaver* and attempted to duplicate it by model-

Mount Baker rises in the distance; the city has long since fulfilled an Indian warrior's horrified vision of an endless village of newcomers.

ling a large tree into a dugout version, painted black and decked over with cedar planks. Motive power was provided by concealed Indian braves turning bright red paddles.

After serving on this coast for over fifty years, she met an ignominious end while attempting to leave Vancouver Harbour about midnight, July 26, 1888. According to Captain Cates' father "the crew were sober and therefore not normal", and were unable to avoid the backeddy which caught the boat when she attempted to steer south of the tide rips, west of the Narrows. According to Joe Simson, however, it was not the tide rips or backeddy, but a sudden realization that the ship's liquor supply had been left in Gastown that prompted an abrupt U-turn and unexpected grounding. "The crew were, in actual fact, quite normal" (*Raincoast Chronicles, #9*).

Lions Gate Bridge was built by the Guinness brewing family of Dublin in 1938 in exchange for the acquisition and subsequent development of the British Properties residential subdivision in West Vancouver. The bridge is named after the twin mountain domes above the Capilano headwaters, formerly known as The Sisters, or "Shebas's paps".

Calamity Point on the north shore is so named because of the large numbers of vessels which had a propensity for stranding on the shoals which formerly extended halfway across to Stanley Park from where they are now. Care must be taken on an ebb to watch out for a set to the north (Cates). Coming in on the south shore, while it is important to keep out of the fairway for large vessels, one should also take care to avoid backeddies on the flood (particularly one hour after LW and before HW) and large boulder reefs jutting out from Stanley Park just east of Lumberman's Arch.

The chart symbol "Mon" marks the location of the "Girl in a Wetsuit" perched on a foreshore boulder; Vancouver's answer to Copenhagen's mermaid. The Empress of Japan figurehead, a replica from the original steamship looks out above the seawall here. Further along, the Park opens up to reveal the Cricket Grounds, claimed by Sir Donald Bradman to be the most beautiful in the world, with the downtown skyscrapers looming in the background.

Parthia Shoal was named after the CPR steamer *Parthia*, which grounded on it in 1890 when the shoal was 3½ fathoms deep in mid-channel. At that time the deepest water for inbound vessels lay south of the shoal. There was not much manoeuvring room for outbound vessels between this shoal and Gumboot Bank (marked by a gumboot on top of a pole) to the north and the North Shore back eddy was much stronger than it is today.

Captain Cates recalls:

One day in the summer of, I think, 1906, I was sitting on our verandah with a good pair of glasses watching the tug *Chehalis* which had left Larsons wharf in North Vancouver with a picnic party for Bowen Island. The tug went out in the big north eddy to where it met the flood stream (west of Gumboot Bank). Just at this point the *Princess Victoria* was slowly bucking out against the

34

The head of Coal Harbour is almost linked to English Bay by Lost Lagoon. A hundred years ago, Indians pulled their canoes into the harbour through the lagoon.

strong flood stream. The *Chehalis* came out of the eddy and the flood tide struck her starboard bow. It seemed that in an instant the *Chehalis* shot out and came flat against the Princess Victoria, right under the flare of the starboard bow. There was just a crash and the *Chehalis* was gone, never to be found...

The *Chehalis* was actually bound for Gowland Harbour. A memorial cross behind Brockton Pt. honours the eight who drowned; one of them was Dr. Hutton of the Columbia Coast Mission (see (1), Ch. 11).

2. Indians and Vancouver

As Captain Vancouver sailed by what is now Brockton Point in 1792, he looked back to the southwest:

This island [Stanley Park] lying exactly across the channel, appeared to form a similar passage [through Lost Lagoon?] to the South of it, with a small island [Deadman's I.] lying before it. From these islands, the channel, in width about half a mile, continued its direction about east. Here we were met by about fifty Indians, in their canoes, who conducted themselves with the greatest decorum and civility, presenting us with several fish cooked, and undressed, of the sort already mentioned as resembling the smelt. These good people, finding we were inclined to make some return for their hospitality, shewed much understanding in preferring iron to copper.

For the sake of the company of our new friends, we stood on under an easy sail, which encouraged them to attend us some little distance up the arm. The major part of the canoes twice paddled forward, assembled before us, and each time a conference was held. Our visit and appearance were most likely the objects of their consultation, as our motions on these occasions seemed to engage the whole of their attention. The subject matter, which remained a profound secret to us, did not appear of an unfriendly nature to us, as they soon returned, and, if possible, expressed additional cordiality and respect. This sort of conduct always creates a degree of suspicion, and should ever be regarded with a watchful eye. In our short intercourse with the people of this country, we have generally found these consultations take place, whether their number were great or small; and though I have ever considered it prudent to be cautiously attentive on such occasions, they ought by no means to be considered as indicating at all times a positive intention of concerting hostile measures; having witnessed many of these conferences, without our experiencing afterwards any alteration in their friendly disposition. This was now the case with our numerous attendants, who gradually dispersed as we advanced from the station where we had first met them, and three or four canoes only accompanied us up a navigation which, in some places, does not exceed an hundred and fifty yards in width.

After spending the night near Port Moody, Vancouver returned back down Burrard Inlet:

As we passed the situation from whence the Indians had first visited us the preceding day, which is a small border of low marshy land on the northern shore, intersected by several creeks of fresh water, we were in expectation of their company, but were disappointed, owing to our travelling so soon in the morning. Most of their canoes were hauled up into the creeks, and two or three only of the natives were seen straggling about on the beach. None of their habitations could be discovered whence we concluded that their village was within the forest. Two canoes came off as we passed the island, but our boats being under sail, with a fresh favorable breeze, I was not inclined to halt, and they almost immediately returned.

The Indians who met Vancouver were probably of the Squamish tribe from the village of Homulcheson at the mouth of the Capilano River. Chief Joe Capilano (*Legends of Vancouver*, Pauline Johnson, 1911) recalls that some time after Vancouver left, an Indian brave . . . "the strongest man on all the North Pacific Coast" dreamed that "some day a great camp for palefaces would lie between False Creek and the Inlet". This dream haunted him for he knew that with the growth of this camp, the Indians would adopt some of the newcomers' customs and lose "all bravery, all courage, all confidence." He paddled his canoe far up the North Arm (now called Indian Arm) where the Saghalie Tyee (God) took his strength away from him and placed it on an island (the "Lost Island") where it is preserved until a time when the Indian children will find the island and regain their lost courage and bravery.

Another legend tells of the coming of certain vices which were despised as deplorable things: ". . . the Indian looks upon greed of gain, miserliness, avariciousness and wealth accumulated above the head of his poorer neighbour as one of the lowest degradations he can fall to . . ." When the first gold-hunters came in 1858, many Indians guided them, as guests to their country, far up the Fraser River. All of the Indians returned as they went, except one "Shak-Shak" who came back entranced with his hoard of gold nuggets and chickimin (money), which he refused to share in a potlatch.

Then the Saghalie Tyee spoke out of the sky and said, Shak-Shak, you have made of yourself a loathsome thing; you will not listen to the cry of the hungry, to the call of the old and sick; you will not share your possessions; you have made of yourself an outcast from your tribe and disobeyed the ancient laws of your people . . .

Shak-Shak was turned into a hideous two-headed sea-serpent with one head resting on the bluffs at Brockton Point, the other on a group of rocks below Calamity Point. The body of the serpent blocked all entrance through the Narrows. Only after a great battle did a young brave, generous and pure, kill the sea-serpent.

It is interesting to note that most histories of Vancouver state that the second visit of the white man into Burrard Inlet (after Vancouver, Galiano and Valdez in 1792) occurred in 1859. Akrigg (*B.C. Chronicles, 1847-1871*) notes, however that in 1858:

one sloop containing twelve miners mistook the en-

trance to Burrard Inlet for the mouth of the Fraser, had their vessel looted, and were themselves massacred by the Indians.

This incident is one of the few recorded of early B.C. coastal-mainland Indian hostility to whites. Akrigg also notes that the Indians had been encouraged by Governor Sir James Douglas and the Hudson's Bay Company to find gold on the Fraser:

. . . unfortunately word of their discoveries was gradually percolating down into American territory. This year (1858) a few American miners moved north of the international boundary. The Indians, angered at seeing these white men coming for the gold which they regarded as their own inheritance, and superstitiously believing their presence would drive the salmon from the river, decided to keep the newcomers out of the gold areas. Their decision elicited from Douglas a comment that "I cannot help admiring the wisdom and foresight of the Indians."

Coal Harbour

On June 13, 1859, Captain Richards, H.M.S. *Plumper*, entered the Inlet. The Indians told him

Aerial view of Coal Harbour, Lions Gate and English Bay beyond, shows Lost Lagoon (upper left) and Stanley Park, Vancouver Rowing Club (left centre), RVYC station (centre), H.M.C.S. Discovery (right centre) and gas barges (lower right); on a bright summer day the area is thronged with pleasurecraft.

about a coal seam on the shore, south of Deadman's Island and Richards sent his chief engineer, Francis Brockton (after whom Brockton Point is named) to investigate. A favourable report led to more detailed exploration in August by Robert Burnaby (secretary to Col. Richard Moody, after whom Burnaby Shoal is named) and Walter Moberly, engineer and explorer. The increased activity and excitement seemed to upset the Indians who assumed a menacing attitude. The apprehensive whites called for help . . .

> The *Plumper* was hurried around to the Inlet, and that night, says Moberly, "the presence of the bluejackets enabled us to spend a jolly time. They landed, as we had done, at the foot of what is now Bute Street, and later brought a keg ashore. Then we lit a roaring fire of logs, as night came on, and our party and the English sailors spent one of the jolliest nights I remember. Before he left next day, Commander Richards named Coal Harbour." (Creighton, 1936)

Expectations that the coal seam might prove substantial led to the first settlers. "The Three Greenhorns" John Morton, Samuel Brighouse and William Hailstone preempting 550 acres (the West End) in

1862. The coal never proved up and settlement within the inlet was slow for the next 25 years.

Boats entering Coal Harbour on a summer evening should be prepared for the loud boom of the Nine O'Clock Gun thundering out its time check from the shoreline 300 yards south of Brockton Point. This naval 12 pound muzzle loader was cast in 1816 and bears the crests of King George III and the Earl of Mulgrave, Master General of Ordnance. Occasionally, the boom can be heard 12 miles away in Port Moody (at about one minute after 9 o'clock). The gun was originally fired only on Sundays at 6 o'clock as a time check for fishermen. Early mariners visiting Vancouver Harbour used it to calibrate their ship's chronometers (adding 5 seconds for each mile away from the gun they were anchored).

Deadman's Island

There are several explanations for this island's name. One claim is that hundreds of years ago Indian

37

Large concentration of pleasure craft in Coal Harbour include those at Vancouver Rowing Club floats (foreground), RVYC, and recent Bayshore Marina at right.

Unusual view across Coal Harbour to North Shore, the whole scene under a dusting of winter snow.

tribes from the south captured the women, children and old of their enemies, the Northerners, and held them on this island. They were only released when two hundred northern braves gave themselves up as a sacrifice, in exchange. The morning after, their dead bodies were transformed into flaming fire-flowers, which so terrified the southerners that they slipped away, "... turned their canoes southwards and this coastline knew them no more." (P. Johnson). In later years the island was used as a cemetery. The dead were wrapped in cedar mats, put in boxes or canoes and suspended in the lower branches of trees growing on the island. The island is now attached to Stanley Park by a causeway and serves as a naval training base, H.M.C.S. *Discovery*.

3.   Coal Harbour Fuel Barges

These barges (Texaco, Shell, Chevron, Gulf and Esso) provide fuel, ice, water and bait. Barges and boats moored alongside have, on occasion, exploded due to patrons failing to heed the NO SMOKING signs or standard safety precautions. Only sea cadet training vessels are allowed to sail in Coal Harbour, there is a 5 knot speed limit and no anchorage (strictly enforced by Harbour Police who seem to spend considerable time in chasing boats away from "unauthorized areas").

Small craft entering or leaving Coal Harbour must pass fairly close to the barges as drying rocks and shoals extend out from Deadman's Island to within 200 feet of the barges; and to the east, an aircraft operations zone should be kept clear. Over 100 float planes land and take off in this zone every day. The planes are controlled from an Air Traffic Centre atop Granville Square, just south of Pier B-C.

In 1915, one of the first airplanes in British Columbia was built and flown from here by the Hoffar Brothers, builders of classic yachts in Coal Harbour. The design was based on a picture in *Flight* magazine and used a speedboat's marine engine for propulsion. Since no one knew how to fly it, the Hoffars decided to teach themselves, tossed a coin, and were horrified when the plane took off on its first taxi trial, carrying its terrified pilot (Jim Hoffar) on a tour over the harbour. (S.Burke, *Vancouver Courier; Raincoast Chronicles #9*).

Behind Deadman's Island are the floats and boathouses of the Royal Vancouver Yacht Club and the Vancouver Rowing Club. In the early days of Vancouver, sailing and rowing were popular activities both as recreation and as a means of getting from one part of the harbour to another. Jones and Burdis had a boat house and salt water swimming pool (the first "aquatic centre" in Vancouver) at the foot of Thurlow. The Burrard Inlet Sailing Club was founded in 1887 with the first regatta held on Dominion Day in honour of the Queen's Jubilee. The R.V.Y.C. was established in 1903 with a floating clubhouse just west of the foot of Bute Street. In 1905 it was moved over to Stanley

Park and in 1927 an outstation for sailing yachts was established at Jericho in English Bay. At the head of Coal Harbour are the facilities of the Vancouver Rowing Club. A charming clubhouse, built in 1911, nestles on piles only a few yards from the busy highway entrance to Stanley Park and the North Shore. In 1921 the moorage fees here were $15 per year. In 1932 members with motorboats formed the Burrard Yacht Club (now located in North Vancouver). V.R.C. crews have won many Olympic and Commonwealth Games medals for Canada and the placid waters of the harbour are still occasionally used for training.

The south shore of Coal Harbour grew into prominence as the centre for B.C.'s major marine industries after the Union Steamship Company constructed the first shipyard at the foot of Bidwell Street in 1891. Within six months the first steel ships assembled in B.C. were launched. Other ship and engine builders who established yards here included Hoffar, Easthope, Menchion and Benson. The harbour became a hub of local fishing, rum-running, yachting and towing activities. These industries are almost all gone now, replaced by charter and tour boat operators, yacht brokerages, hotels, highrises, car parks and a vacant lot — the open space park at the entrance to Stanley Park. Harbour Ferries operates excursion and tour boats from the foot of Denman Street. They also provide moorage for approximately 180 boats. The tours of the inner harbour which allow visitors to

"The Old Waterfront, Vancouver, 1898," a painting by the exacting marine artist John M. Horton.

Full moon over the Coal Harbour skyline (photo: Peter Tough).

39

Sailing regatta, Vancouver Harbour, circa 1890.

become knowledgeable about port activities and the excursions to Indian Arm have become major tourist attractions in Vancouver.

Extending west from Harbour Ferries are Trilight Yacht Services (boat maintenance and repair), the Bayshore Inn (brokerage, charters and moorage), Bristol Yachts (brokerage), Menchions (boat building and repairs), The Boathouse (Chandlery) and Keg Restaurant, *Boating News*, Coal Harbour Marina (brokerage), Van Anchor Marine (brokerage), Bute Marina (brokerage), Air B.C. (float plane service to various coastal locations), Tradewinds (brokerage and charter boats), Barbary Coast Yacht Basin (charter boats), Malibu Yacht Charters and Sailing Beyond.

Moorage for visiting yachtsmen may be difficult to find in Coal Harbour unless you have made prior arrangements, are willing to *pay*, or know someone ... If the opportunity arises, temporary moorage here is very convenient for exploration of downtown Vancouver. A copy of Walbran (*B.C. Coast Names*) is useful in determining the origin of street names, as most are named after early explorers or naval heroes. Some street names have been mispelled from the original: Bidwell, Barclay and Cardero should be Bedwell, Barkley and Cordero.

Just west of the foot of Burrard Street is the CPR dock for freight car ferries. Pier B-C, originally built as a passenger liner terminal in 1927 is slated to become a cruise ship-convention centre for Vancouver's *EXPO 86*. Along this shore trans-Pacific steamers first met the western terminus of the CPR in 1887 to bring Vancouver into world prominence as a port. For many years the elegant *Empresses* sailed from here across the Pacific and coastal ferries of almost equal gracefulness served Vancouver Island and northern ports. As Donald Stainsby notes:

> These passenger vessels were so important to Vancouver, for sentimental as well as commercial reasons, that when the old *Aorangi* made her first trip after the Second World War thousands of people on shore and aboard small boats were on hand to greet her, a welcome accorded each of her several successors.

In 1925, when the *Aorangi* began operating out of Vancouver, she was the largest motorliner in the world with a gross tonnage of 17,491 tons.

4 Gastown

In 1867, John Deighton ("Gassy Jack"), a Fraser River pilot, opened a saloon here to service thirsty workers from the nearby Stamp's Mill. A small community quickly grew to become "Gastown" (officially after 1870 it was "Granville") and then ... Vancouver. All of the buildings fronted onto the water, many were on pilings and had log float landings. These

were all destroyed by the great fire of Sunday, July 13th, 1886.

Exactly one year later, the *SS Abyssinia* brought her cargo of silk, tea and passengers from the Orient to a newly constructed trestle-wharf which extended into deep water, paralleling the Vancouver shore from Cambie to west of Burrard Street. In later years, the foreshore between the trestle and the shoreline was filled in to accommodate railyards serving the many new wharves and piers along this waterfront. Today, most of these wharves are abandoned or have disappeared completely and all one can see from the water of the birthplace of Vancouver beyond the Sea Bus Terminal, a nearly empty riprap shoreline and railyards are the backs of brick warehouses fronting onto the new "Gastown", facing inwards, away from the sea.

At the foot of Carrall Street, next to the City Wharf, Andy Linton had his boathouse in 1885 (the finest sailing yachts and rowing boats on the coast for sale or rent). During the high tide months of June and December it was possible to paddle a canoe from here into False Creek along what is now Columbia Street. This area now houses National Harbours Board offices, Harbour police, Kingcome Navigation, Grand Trunk Pacific (Canadian National), and the home for a replica of the *S.S. Beaver* (charters and harbour excursion tours).

Dominating Vancouver Harbour, the new Canada Place served as the Canadian Pavilion for Expo 86, after which it was converted into a major cruise ship facility, convention centre and luxury hotel.

The National Harbours Board Master Plan envisages future "comprehensive development" for this area to include canneries, fisherman's market, heliport, ALRT station, restaurants, pubs, mooring for fishboats, service boats, tugs, barges and water taxis and the possiblity of public moorage for visiting small boats.

St. James Church stands like a beacon, rebuilt on the corner of Cordova and Gore after the 1886 fire destroyed the original church on the waterfront in Gastown. Although the present church, rebuilt about 1936, is well back from the water now, its distinctive dome is visible behind the masts of the *Beaver*, and it remains the "guardian of pilgrims" and other unfortunates in this area. An early rector of this parish, the Rev. Henry Fiennes-Clinton set up Vancouver's first fire department, first hospital, first library and first seamen's institute.

5 Centennial Pier

In 1865, the first industrial enterprise on the south shore of Burrard Inlet was established here as Stamp's Mill. In 1870, it was renamed Hastings Mill, in honour of Admiral Hastings, commanding the Royal

Campbell Avenue Fishermen's docks handle much of the incoming catch. Simple restaurant serves fresh seafood.

Naval squadron at Esquimalt. The mill operated until 1925 when:

> the great band saws ceased their screaming and the huge sawdust burner whose flames and sparks had been a signal beacon for ships in the Gulf for nearly sixty years . . . grew cold. (Hacking)

The Hastings Mill Office building (1906) at the foot of Dunlevy Avenue now serves as the Mission to Seamen "Flying Angel Club". Centennial Pier (1958) is now a container and general cargo terminal distinguishable by its huge bright red cranes. The Harbour Master's offices and the harbour fireboat are also located here.

Visiting cruise ships tie up at Ballantyne Pier pending reconstruction of Pier B-C. When Ballantyne Pier was completed in 1923, it was claimed to be the "ne plus ultra of pier construction . . . the finest on the Pacific Coast . . . an artistic addition to the waterfront".

6   Campbell Avenue Fish Dock

Temporary moorage for small craft may be available here when space is not taken up by fishboats engaged in unloading fish and taking on supplies. The Marine View Coffee Shop provides excellent seafood meals and a view of the docks.

A private marina tucked between commercial vessels beside Rogers Sugar Refinery.

Immediately next door is the B.C. Sugar Refinery, where a few small craft moor at private floats. This company was established in 1890 by Benjamin Rogers and a museum here describes the arrival of the first raw sugar aboard the former Cunard steamship *Parthia*.

North Vancouver

The tall twin silver spires of St. Paul's Mission Church have long served as a waterfront landmark for captains checking their compass deviation. The first church in the Vancouver area was built on this site when it was known as *Ustlawn*, and the present church, St. Paul's, replaced it in 1884. At that time you could paddle right to the door as the Mosquito Creek estuary had not been filled in.

On Sunday, June 13th, 1886, exactly 94 years to the day after Vancouver had recorded his entrance into the Inlet, five thousand natives from up the coast were gathered for the consecration of the church. Attention was drawn across the Inlet as the faint clang of the bell of St. James Anglican in Vancouver sounded the alarm for a huge fire which consumed the entire city in forty minutes. Slash fires at the western edge of the city had blown out of control, fanned by an increasing afternoon westerly breeze. By the time people from the Mission had paddled across the Inlet to pull a few survivors out of the water, St. James Church bell was a molten mass and only twelve buildings remained standing out of an estimated total of over 800.

7   Mosquito Creek Marina

This facility is also known as the North Shore Marine Basin and provides fuel, moorage, dry storage with do-it-yourself work areas, boat repairs, brokerage, chandlery and a mobile marine 9 ton hoist for haulouts. Moorage for visiting small craft is usually available in the summer (Phone 987-4113) and it is a short walk to the North Shore Sea Bus Terminal. A floating concrete breakwater provides fair protection from southeasterly seas.

The floats and boathouses of the Burrard Yacht Club and tiny Bewicke Waterfront Park are located on the western shore of the outlet of Mosquito Creek. During World War I, Lyall Shipbuilding built top-sail schooners here.

8   Lonsdale Quay

This new waterfront development includes plans for a six acre park, a promenade, and a pier to provide temporary moorage for visiting boats and to serve as the home of the tall ship *Maple Leaf*. The Pacific Marine Training Institute and the Sea Bus Terminal are also located here. A few blocks up the hill, at the corner of Third and Chesterfield, in the old City Hall, are the North Shore Museum and Archives. Martin Marine chandlery is located at 121 West 1st Street.

In 1892, Tom Turner's Ranch was a popular resort

for picnic boating parties from Vancouver. In 1911, Andy Linton moved his small boat buiding operation here in order to build the tug *Gaviota* (still operating as the *C.H. Cates III*) for the Cates towing firm. These distinctive pale orange trimmed tugboats are moored at the foot of Lonsdale when they are not bustling about the harbour, providing berthing assistance for vessels entering and leaving the Inlet. Next door, the Seven Seas Restaurant is housed in the old North Van Ferry No. 5. Moorage for guests is available behind the Ferry.

Burrard Yarrows

Alfred Wallace, principal shipwright with the Union Steamship yard in Coal Harbour (1891-94) moved his small boat building firm here from False Creek in 1908. Since that time, the firm has grown to become one of the largest shipbuilders in Canada. Ships turned out included the *Princess Louise* (1920), a superbly finished luxury coastwise steamer; the *Mabel Brown*, a five masted schooner; North Van Ferries; fireboats, the *RCMP St. Roch*; and over 100 naval and wartime cargo vessels. A huge floating drydock capable of accommodating some of the largest vessels afloat was introduced in 1981.

9 Moodyville

The first pioneering settlement in Burrard Inlet was established here in 1863. Abundant timber and water-power provided the resource for the Pioneer Mills. The first shipment of lumber was carried to New Westminster on the steamboat *Flying Dutchman* in August; and the first foreign cargo was carried to Australia by the *Ellen Lewis* in November 1864. A year later, an enterprising State of Mainer — Sewell P. Moody (no relation to Col. Moody) bought the mill. He expanded and modernized it using the boilers and machinery from *H.M.S. Sparrowhawk* and provided docking facilities for a dozen ships. A few pilings and flumes projecting out from the bank are all that remain visible today. Moody Park, "Saghalie Illahee", (high land) rises behind the Saskatchewan Wheat Pool Elevators.

The bulk terminals built over the estuary of Lynn Creek are interesting operations to watch: the loading of coal (Neptune), lumber (Seaboard — probably the largest forest products terminal in the world), bulk timber, steel, general cargo (Lynterm).

10 Harbour View Park

In 1871, John Linn, a sapper with the Royal Engineers, preempted the east bank of the creek which came to bear his name (now spelled Lynn). Four years later, the *S.S. Beaver* landed 15 men at Linn's farm to build a cattle trail through to Lillooet. The trail was used only once and is now commemorated by a cairn at the north end of the Second Narrows Bridge.

Sheltered temporary anchorage is possible in the mouth of Lynn Creek in water depths somewhat de-

Campbell Avenue Fishermen's docks house the offices of several fish buying and processing concerns.

Above, Mosquito Creek Marina and the Burrard Yacht Club floats (centre left) on the North Shore. Below, Burrard Dry Dock is called on to maintain and repair large vessels.

The mouth of Lynn Creek. Harbour View Park, with viewing tower at lower right.

The Lions from New Brighton Park.

eper than charted. There is a deep channel through the drying banks which does not dry out completely at low tide. At highwater, small shoaldraft boats can navigate a short distance upstream beyond the railway bridge. The eastern shore is protected as a linear park and there is a wooded trail from the railway bridge to a viewing tower at the southwestern tip of Lynterm.

Vancouver Shore

Vanterm, on the south shore of Burrard Inlet, serves as a modern container terminal for deep sea vessels. There is a special viewing area here for those interested in a close look at ship-loading activities. Immediately east of Lapointe Pier is the first grain elevator, built in 1914 by the Dominion government and known for the first eight years of its life as "Stevens' Folly" after Harry H. Stevens, M.P., who had arranged for it to be built. By 1924, it was handling more grain annually than any other facility of similar size in the world. There are now ten active grain berths in the harbour making Vancouver the world's most important wheat shipping port (Hacking).

B.C. Marine Shipbuilders, Sterling Shipyards, and a number of other marine industries are also located in Cedar Cove, or "Hup-Hah-Pai" (a lot of cedar trees here). Arrangements for temporary moorage at Riv Tow Straits, McMillan Fisheries or B.C. Ice floats can usually be made for patrons of the Cannery Seafood Restaurant (254-9606).

11 New Brighton Park

In 1865, the Douglas road was built from New Westminster to here. The terminus of the road was at a natural clearing known as "Kah-nah-moot". It also became known as "Road End" or "Hockings", "Maxies" and "Blacks" over the years after different hotel proprietors. The hotel here also served as the first customs, revenue, telegraph and post office in the Inlet. It was called "Hastings" in 1869, but being on the seashore, oldtimers say that the name "Brighton" seemed particularly appropriate to those who knew the English resort by that name. Today, broken stone rip-rap conceals a beach which was described by a New Westminster newspaper in the 1870's as "the most fashionable watering place in British Columbia".

Temporary anchorage is possible off the park shore or in a fairly protected nook behind the Alberta Wheat Pool Dock, out of the way of harbour traffic. Facilities at the park include a field house, picnic tables, playground, swimming pool, refreshment stand and soccer pitch.

12 Lynwood Marina

This marina tucked below the Second Narrows Bridge on the North Shore provides moorage (space may be available for visiting boats in the summer months) and a 9 ton capacity hoist for repairs. A

At Second Narrows, railway bridge must be raised for masts to pass through.
Right, Lynwood Marina and mouth of Seymour River, upper right, flank the north end of the Second Narrows bridge.

floating log breakwater provides some protection from the wash of passing vessels. Between the bridges is the Bel-Aire Shipyard and Noble Towing.

Second Narrows

The tide tables indicate that the change in the Second Narrows may be up to ten minutes before the change at First Narrows. If transit of the Narrows must be made at a low tide below seven feet, it is least uncomfortable if the passage can be timed exactly for slack water (refer to Tide Tables and *Small Craft Guide*). Captain Cates notes however that:

> The second narrows is not so close as to time of change. I think a great deal of this error is caused by the volume of fresh water which is poured into the upper inlet by the rivers in the winter time. I have found it safer to be a little late when coming down on the last of a big ebb as sometimes at low slack by the book the run out will still be quite strong.

There is considerable turbulence east of the Narrows at the beginning of most floods and west of the bridges at the end of an ebb. For this reason, transit of

the Narrows is preferable close to HW slack, but special care is still necessary as this is usually the time when all large vessels also use the Narrows. As at First Narrows, no sailing, fishing or crossing of the channel is permitted here.

The railway bridge is usually left open, except when rail traffic is expected. If the bridge is down (clearance 35 feet at HW), sailboats can wait out of the fairway off New Brighton Park (inbound) or Hooker Chemical (outbound). The bridge can also be phoned (666-3226) or radioed (Ch. 11,12) to determine bridge closing times.

When Vancouver passed here in 1792, he noted that the narrowest part of the channel did not exceed 150 yards in width. Since then, dredging of the Seymour estuary has widened the distance at low tide to 300 yards but the navigable channel between bridge piers remains close to the original width — 150 yards.

The first plan to span the Narrows (1911) involved a dam with locks to allow shipping to pass into a raised, fresh water, upper Inlet. A three mile canal across Coquitlam would link Port Moody to the Fraser River. Another plan (1914) called for a wide road/rail bridge with the longest swing span (581 feet) in the world. Unfortunately, this was not built, and the bridge that was eventually built (1925) was a continual hazard to shipping. Sixteen serious shipping accidents were recorded until the bridge was put out of commission completely in a spectacular crash in 1930. The bridge has since been continually replaced or repaired over the years with the most recent accident (1979) putting the bridge out of commission for six months. The latest mishap occurred in a nightime fog when the outbound *Japan Erica* mistook the Seymour estuary transmission tower for the north pier of the bridge. This accident resulted in stringent regulations for ship passage of the Narrows and attempts to set up an elaborate underwater lighting scheme to keep vessels pointed in the right direction.

It may be that these Narrows are jinxed, as the Second Narrows Highway Bridge also collapsed during construction in 1958, with the loss of 18 lives. When this bridge, the second largest cantilever span in Canada, was eventually opened in 1960, a total of 23 men had been killed in the course of its construction.

Hugh Barr established the first farm on the North Shore when he homesteaded the east side of the mouth of Seymour River in 1864. Rowboats were used to supply Moodyville, Hastings and Granville with fresh milk and cream... or butter (when the weather or tide was rough). Cutters Island and the estuary of both Seymour and Lynn Creeks were fashionable places for boating picnics and fishing.

13 Maplewood Flats

In 1930, there were still approximately 350 acres of marshland left in Burrard Inlet. Today, there is less than 25 acres, most located in the Maplewood area east of the Seymour. Marshland is critically important habitat providing food and shelter for many species of fish and birds. A 1972-73 survey indicated that over 10,000 birds (53 species) use the Maplewood estuaries area. Some of the birds sighted include mergansers, buffleheads, mallards, widgeon, green-winged teal, geese, cormorants, grebes, loons, gulls, great blue herons, scaup, goldeneye and scoters.

An enclosed small boat harbour has been proposed for the existing dredged log pond north of Stanovan. The marina as proposed would include berths for visiting boats, tour boats and any future harbour water-bus service. Ecological reserves to protect the last remaining salt marsh in Burrard Inlet, waterfront parks and trails have also been proposed for this still beautiful area.

Captain Charles W. Cates, who knew Vancouver harbour like the back of his hand, may have been thinking of Maplewood flats when he wrote:

The ebb tide always seems to me to have the same characteristics as the fall of the year or the later years of a person's life. When the tide is ebbing all the creatures of the sea and those creatures that live near the sea become listless. The crabs which you may catch in 40 to 50 feet of water and which have been coming constantly to the bait during the flood tide, will cease to feed during the ebb. It seems queer that they would know the difference in that depth of water but such is the case. Even though the tide is still high and the flats are well covered, all the crabs and small fish will disappear as soon as the ebb starts.

...Along the edge of the receding sea the ducks and gulls feed and the herons wade out quietly on their long legs to catch the unwary small fish with a lightning swift dart of their long pointed beaks. The crows, while not true sea birds, also are around in large numbers. It is comical to watch these wise birds pick up clams and fly up over a large rock or even take them to nearby concrete pavement where they drop them so that their shells will be smashed.

It always seemed to me that all this activity is carried out in a very leisurely manner, without haste, for it is like the autumn and peace is in the air.

Now, as a big ebb reaches near its extreme low, a tension seems to come in the air. I have asked many sailors and they say that they can feel it. Certainly the fish and birds and crustaceans know that the flood is coming. A little before low water all these creatures reappear and become very active. Any fisherman will tell you that at the low slack and as the flood starts is the time to catch salmon as they race around in the little eddys and snap up the little fish to be found there. The crabs reappear and wait just at the tide lines ready to scurry over the flats in countless numbers as soon as there is barely sufficient water for them to travel in. All along the shore the gulls and ducks swoop and dive for there is renewed life in the sea. The flood tide is starting. The old Indians smile and say Kwa-Kwatts, the tide is rising. *(Tidal Action in B.C. Waters).* □

Sunset over Vancouver Harbour.

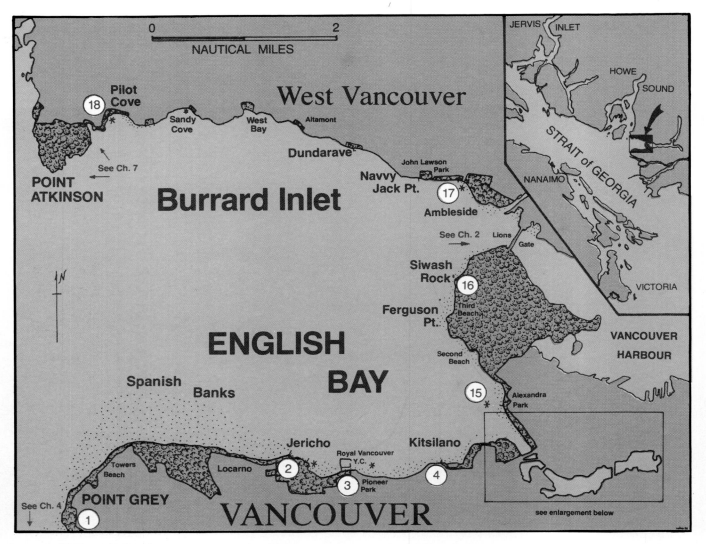

Upper map

0 2
NAUTICAL MILES

Pilot Cove

West Vancouver

⑱

Sandy Cove
West Bay
Altamont

Dundarave

John Lawson Park

Navvy Jack Pt.

⑰

POINT ATKINSON

See Ch. 7 ←

Burrard Inlet

Ambleside

See Ch. 2 →

Lions Gate

Siwash Rock

⑯

Third Beach

ENGLISH BAY

Ferguson Pt.

Second Beach

Spanish Banks

⑮

Alexandra Park

VANCOUVER HARBOUR

Towers Beach

Jericho

Locarno

Royal Vancouver Y.C.

Kitsilano

②

③

④

Pioneer Park

POINT GREY

See Ch. 4 ↓

①

VANCOUVER

see enlargement below

Inset (top right)

JERVIS INLET

HOWE SOUND

STRAIT of GEORGIA

NANAIMO

VICTORIA

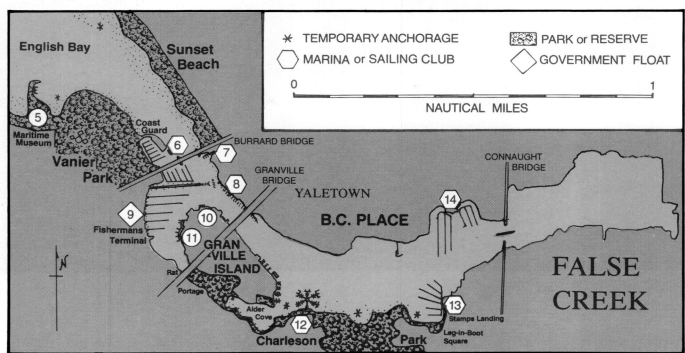

Lower map (enlargement)

English Bay

Sunset Beach

⑤

Maritime Museum

Vanier Park

Coast Guard

⑥

BURRARD BRIDGE

⑦

⑧

GRANVILLE BRIDGE

YALETOWN

B.C. PLACE

CONNAUGHT BRIDGE

⑨

⑩

⑪

Fishermans Terminal

GRANVILLE ISLAND

Rat Portage

Alder Cove

⑫

Charleson Park

⑬

Stamps Landing

Leg-in-Boot Square

⑭

FALSE CREEK

Legend

⚹ TEMPORARY ANCHORAGE   PARK or RESERVE

⬡ MARINA or SAILING CLUB   ◇ GOVERNMENT FLOAT

0 1
NAUTICAL MILES

NOT TO BE USED FOR NAVIGATION

48

CHAPTER THREE

English Bay

Point Grey, False Creek, West Vancouver

For cruising boats, the ideal time to enter Burrard Inlet is early on a summer evening, assisted by a flooding tide and a westerly wind. The setting sun glistens off towering white-yellow skyscrapers which seem to loom out of the water close beside the deep blue greens of Stanley Park and the rising, rugged peaks to the north. All around, the city begins to hum and throb and far away, the pink-hued cone of Mount Baker materializes. Entering Vancouver by boat is an unforgettable experience. The city, for all its cosmopolitan modernity, bounds on the primeval sea and the mountain wilderness.

The English Bay portion of Burrard Inlet is probably the most intensively used marine recreational area in Canada. The Bay is used year round by local yacht clubs, marinas, sailing associations and schools with a full range of racing and training activities underway. On a busy summer weekend the waters teem with thousands of boats, tacking, paddling, powering or puttering between anchored freighters. Along the shore, strollers line the promenades while sunbathers disport themselves on the surrounding beaches and grassy banks. How many gaze longingly out to sea, dreaming of the far horizon?

Winds

Wind patterns along the West Vancouver shore are somewhat similar to those inside First Narrows, blowing mainly from the east or west. A notable exception is that calms are more frequent along this shore. Winds recorded at the Pacific Environment Centre in Sandy Cove are primarily from the easterly

quadrant in the winter (50% frequency) or are calm (40%). In summer, winds are either SE (30%), SW (20%), or calm (50%).

Because of the lower topography along the south shore of English Bay, winds here tend to follow the SE - NW trend of the Strait of Georgia. Calms and periods of persistently light winds are most prevalent in autumn and winter because the daytime heating of the landmass in spring and summer almost invariably attracts a daily onshore breeze. The onshore "westerly" averages more than 15 mph but seldom blows over 30 mph in the summer months, and is usually followed at sunset by a light nighttime easterly offshore landbreeze which may last through to mid-morning.

This pattern generally holds throughout the summer when low pressure systems are infrequent. Jack Emslie (*Pacific Yachting*, June, 1971) has noted that there are four rules of thumb to follow regarding the sea breeze:
(1) Light easterly overnight — expect sea breeze 3 to 5 hours after sunrise;
(2) Strong easterly overnight — if cloudy, no sea breeze the next day;
(3) Strong easterly overnight — if sunny, weak sea breeze, late in the day;

3311 — Strip Chart #1 - PORT MOODY to
      HOWE SOUND (1:40,000)
3481 — Approaches to VANCOUVER
      HARBOUR (1:20,000)
3482 — VANCOUVER HARBOUR - Western
      Portion (1:10,000)

49

(4) Westerly overnight — stronger westerly during the afternoon.

Currents

Currents at the entrance to Burrard Inlet are not always what one might expect. The normal tidal flood-in, ebb-out does not always hold, especially near the two points which guard the entrance or when strong winds are blowing. Another influence is the current resulting from freshwater flowing out of the Fraser River (maximum in June) or rivers entering from the north shore (maximums in May and November).

Captain Cates has noted:
> At practically all stages of the tide, flood or ebb, the flow is to the westward at Point Atkinson, while the reverse is the case along the Point Grey shore. I presume that this flow is what brings the enormous quantity of sand out of the North Arm of the Fraser, to form Spanish Banks along the northwest shore of Point Grey. (*Tidal Action in B.C. Waters*)

Off Point Grey, the prevailing current is actually to the northeast or north only during the flood; on the ebb it is to the northwest. This north flowing current is strongest during the Fraser freshet in June and July and is reinforced by southerly winds which prevail along the Fraser Estuary shore.

The prevailing current along the south shore of English Bay, from Kitsilano to Spanish Banks, is generally to the west on the flood (as a weak backeddy) as well as the ebb. Another backeddy off Stanley Park, north of Ferguson Point, results in a northeasterly flowing current on both flood and ebb (strongest at

The drying sand flats of Spanish Banks are exposed at low tide as silty Fraser River water is pushed north around Point Grey into English Bay.

springs). See page 32 for currents inside First Narrows.

From First Narrows to Point Atkinson, there is a strong westerly flowing current which is almost "river-like" on the ebb, becoming a weak backeddy close along the West Vancouver shore on the flood (strongest at neaps). At spring tides, the ebb streaming out through First Narrows and past Point Atkinson, can be particularly uncomfortable for small boats, when it is heaped up against an incoming westerly wind.

Freighters at anchor in English Bay serve as useful indicators of local current direction. It is not unusual for freighters at either end of the bay to be pointing in almost opposite directions and only a fairly strong wind will align them in the same direction. Detailed information on Burrard Inlet winds and currents is available in R.E. Thomson's *Oceanography of the B.C. Coast* (1981).

1) Point Grey

The Point Grey shoreline has proved strangely attractive to a wide variety of explorers for hundreds of years. In native mythology, this area was known as "The Battle Ground of the West Wind". A local chief who ruled these waters once attempted to prove himself stronger than the winds, the seas . . . and the great Tyee (God) himself. For his pains, he was turned into a great boulder on the beach called *Homolsom* and was commanded to assist passing voyagers who desired a favourable wind. Indians in canoes or fishermen whose sails were idle could paddle up to the rock, touch it with their paddle and wait for a wind which would soon arise, blowing them in which ever direction they wished to go (Pauline Johnson, *Legends of Vancouver*).

It is not known whether *Homolsom* has survived the efforts of modern man to prove himself stronger than the elements. There have been various schemes to "protect" the beaches and the Point Grey cliffs from wind and weather by bulldozing the foreshore and other, less subtle techniques.

The first explorer known to have visited here was Jose Maria Narvaez in July, 1791. He anchored his schooner, the *Santa Saturnina* just outside the 4 fathom line southwest of what he called the *Is. de Langara* (Point Grey), while he explored English Bay by small boat, trying to find the source of the "sweet water" from a mysterious river he had named *Boca de Florida Blanca* (mouth of the Fraser River). It is an easy mistake to make. The outer portion of Burrard Inlet is often so full of the fresh but muddy Fraser River water that a number of explorers mistook the entrance for the mouth of the Fraser.

Exactly a year later, the Spaniards Galiano and Valdez were back searching for the same river with no greater success. They anchored in almost the same place as Narvaez after a perilous night dodging the shallows at the edge of the estuary and huge trees which were being swept into the Strait by the Fraser in flood.

The next morning, they noticed seven canoes ap-

proaching them from Punta de Langara (Point Grey). Their journal relates:

> Each (canoe) carried two or three Indians, who had taken off their blankets, and were consequently entirely naked. A few wore hats and most of them were painted in various colours. The appearance of these natives was better than that of the other Indians whom we had seen all along that channel . . . Their muscles, if not more developed, were of better form than those of the inhabitants of Nutka and they were not so white, but their liveliness, grace and talent angaged all our attention . . .

It may be possible for modern voyagers to paddle in close to shore here in calm weather to chance a similar greeting to that which was bestowed on the Spaniards 200 years ago. Although Wreck Beach is covered in Chapter 4, Ginny and Beth Evans note:

> This section of the shoreline will appeal to those who prefer to do their sunbathing in the buff. It used to be located discreetly around the corner (south of Point Grey) until the Parks Board decided to attack the erosion problem. New sand was poured over a foundation of cobblestones to hold the old sand in place. One winter's weather blew it all away — down towards Spanish Banks — leaving the cobblestones bare. Faithfull sun worshippers have followed their sand. (*The Vancouver Guide Book*)

Galiano and Valdez later re-anchored their vessels *Sutil* and *Mexicana* in 10 fathoms of water northwest of Point Grey, off Tower Beach in order to avoid an onshore wind, shallow depths and stronger currents (4½ knots) coming out of the Fraser River.

At seven in the morning of June 21, 1792, a small boat approached the *Sutil*. It was Captain Vancouver

Captain Vancouver and crew back at Point Grey from their nine day charting of the coast from Boundary Bay to Jervis Inlet. Vessel in background is either Sutil or Mexicana. (painting: courtesy of Confederation Life)

who was returning to Birch Bay (where H.M.S. *Discovery* and *Chatham* were at anchor) after completing a detailed nine-day small boat survey of the coastline from Boundary Bay to the head of Jervis Inlet.

Vancouver showed the Spaniards his charts and a decision was made to coordinate their future explorations. Four days later, after the Spaniards had explored Indian Arm (missed by Vancouver), the two Spanish and two British vessels together sailed up Georgia and Malaspina Straits and into Desolation Sound (see page 171). Spanish Banks and English Bay were named to commemorate this meeting. Point Grey had been named by Vancouver on June 13 after his friend Captain George Grey, who five years later commanded H.M.S. *Victory* at the Battle of Cape St. Vincent.

In World War II, gun batteries were located atop Point Grey and today, two search light towers still remain on the foreshore of Towers Beach.

Spanish Banks, (known also to the Coast Guard as the "flytrap" or the "Jericho Triangle") have proved to be a particularly troublesome stretch of shoal. Almost every weekend some boat finds the Banks and the Coast Guard have noted that on one particular

52

weekend, (Bathtub Race), 30 boats were stranded at one time. A grounding may not be a problem with a rising tide and an offshore wind, but some measure of unpleasantness can be expected if conditions are otherwise.

Locarno Park is a peaceful park which can be approached by shoal draught boat near high tide. The park is named after the pact, supposed to outlaw war, which was signed in Locarno, Switzerland in 1925.

2 Jericho Park

A huge Indian lodge or potlatch house 300 feet long by 30 feet wide once stood at *Eyalmu* (good camping ground), a native village at the edge of a swamp. In 1859, it became Admiralty Reserve and in 1864, it served as the base for Jeremiah (Jerry) Rogers' logging camp, thus becoming "Jerry's Cove", now corrupted to "Jericho". Jericho Park has also served as a golf and country club, RCAF station for flying boats, and site for the Habitat '76 Forum on Human Settlements. It is now used for the annual summer Folk Festival — one of the largest in North America.

The last air force hangar remaining at Jericho serves as the base for the Jericho Sailing Centre, said to be the largest, most active small-craft public sailing centre in Canada. Over twenty sailing organizations make use of the facilities here for boat storage and launching, training, and racing activities. The storage of boats which are not actively used is discouraged, but small boat voyagers are welcome to land and store their boat here for a nominal fee. The Canadian Hostel at Jericho provides accommodation for visitors, making this location ideal for cruising canoeists and kayakers as a stopover while visiting the city.

The westernmost pier at Jericho is used for fishing and as a public promenade. It also provides shelter for small craft landing. The most protected location for temporary anchorage along this shore is just east of the eastern log-piling pier off the sandy Jericho Beach shallows.

3 Royal Vancouver Yacht Club

The Jericho Station of the Royal Vancouver Yacht Club provides moorage for 350 of the members' sailboats. In 1903, H.O. Alexander proposed that the club rooms and yacht moorings in Coal Harbour should be moved to Jericho because "the anchorage is fine and the position sheltered and far from the turmoil of city life". The move was accomplished in 1927 and a substantial breakwater now provides year-round protection from north-westerly seas. The beautiful mermaid figurehead leaning out from the club's balcony is from the yacht *Syrene*. It was given to the club by the Columbia Coast Mission when the *Syrene* was converted to a new life as the hospital ship *John Antle* in 1934 (Anderson, *The Columbia is Coming!*). Today the yacht is back in the club, resuming her life of

English Bay, looking east: in foreground, Jericho Sailing Centre, Jericho Beach, and Royal Vancouver Yacht Club. City seems to rise out of the bay, flanked by Stanley Park at left.

Anchorage off Jericho Beach, West End in background.

leisure after a career which included a stint as a Forestry Service vessel.

Directly behind the Yacht Club moorings is 2½ acre Pioneer Park, home of the old Hastings Mill Store, the oldest building in Vancouver. The store was built in 1865, survived the Great Fire of 1886 and was towed on a barge from its original site (Centennial Pier (5), Ch. 2) in 1930. It now serves as a museum of pioneer artifacts operated by the Native Daughters of Vancouver.

4 Kitsilano Yacht Club

The Kitsilano Yacht Club, founded in 1934, leases land for their club house and dry storage (150 boats) from the Vancouver Parks Board. The Club has served as the centre for local sailboat racing activities and host for many provincial, national, and international regattas. Although charts have indicated a "mooring area" off the club, boats no longer are moored here because of the open northwest exposure.

Kitsilano Beach was formerly known as Sam Greer's Beach after an early pioneer who fired buckshot at officials attempting to evict him so that the CPR could build railyards and ocean docks here. The eviction succeeded, but fortunately the railway didn't, and in the 1890s Greer's Beach became a fashionable weekend or summer holiday retreat. Vacationers rowed across False Creek to tent among the trees. Dredging of the False Creek shallows has provided sand for the beach. The central part of a salt water pool is staged over for summertime "Showboat" performances in the open air.

The Gulf Yacht Club, for active cruising sailors, holds meetings every second Monday of the month in the Billy Bishop Legion on Laburnum Street, behind Kitsilano Beach.

Princess of Vancouver *approaching the First Narrows.*
Painting by T.F.R. Thompson courtesy of Richard Beard
Gallery, of West Vancouver. (photo: N. Jill Newby)

False Creek

For the visiting yachtsman, False Creek is an ideal harbour, conveniently located in the centre of the city, with a continually increasing array of marine services and other surprises.

False Creek was named by Captain Richards during his survey of 1859. The muddy waters of English Bay and the low topography of the surrounding shores may have deceived Richards into believing that the Creek was either another arm of the Fraser or another passage into the upper portions of Burrard Inlet. Captain Vancouver's chart (which Richards was probably using) shows such a passage to the south of Stanley Park (shown as an island in the middle of Burrard Inlet).

At this time the Creek was actually three times the size it is now (at high tide), but only half its present size at chart datum (low tide). The uppermost mile of the Creek — a wide expanse of drying mud flat, and much of the surrounding foreshore have now been filled in, and the lower navigable channels have been widened and deepened.

Over the years the Creek gradually changed from a pristine wilderness with six trout-bearing streams to

Vancouver in 1986, showing Expo 86, B.C. Place Stadium, Canada Place, Vancouver Harbour and the north shore mountains.

become the centre for Vancouver's waterfront industries. There were over forty sawmills, shipbuilding yards, warehouses, woodproducts and furniture factories, piggeries, slaughterhouses and a creosote mill. In the depression, the Creek was also home for hundreds of houseboats and foreshore squatters living in tarpaper shacks. The increasing pollution lessened the attractiveness of this otherwise perfect harbour for yachtsmen, and it was referred to as a "crud-strewn stretch of smelly water surrounded by decrepit and depressing industrial ghetto". (*Vancouver Province*, Oct. 1975)

Starting in the early 1970s, False Creek has been undergoing another transformation or rebirth, in a process which is not yet complete. The old industries are almost all gone, being replaced with grassy parks, seafront promenades, open-air markets, marinas and innovative community housing developments. With the change from urban blight to dynamic waterfront community, there have been suggestions that the Creek should be renamed. Some suggestions have included "Van Horne", "Pleasant" or "Kitsilano" Inlet. The late city archivist, Major J.S. Matthews spoofed these by suggesting the most elegant name of all: "Ensenada del Elgano" (Spanish for "False Creek"). Whatever it may be called, False Creek is beginning to realize its tremendous potential as the major small boat haven for local and visiting boats and as the west coast centre for sail training and other marine-recreation industry activities. Two of the largest sailing school/charter boat companies in Canada operate out of False Creek.

Redevelopment of the north shore of False Creek into B.C. Place in conjunction with Expo 86 will also bring a new look to this part of the city. Expo 86, an international exposition or "world's fair" with a transportation-communications theme, will commemorate the centenary of the founding of the city of Vancouver.

5   Vancouver Maritime Museum

The maritime museum, at the entrance to False Creek, was developed after a determined drive by Major Matthews to save the R.C.M.P. Arctic Patrol vessel *St. Roch* in 1958. This two-masted schooner, built in North Vancouver, was the first ship to circumnavigate North America and the first to traverse the Northwest Passage from west to east. She was declared a National Historic Monument, restored to her 1944 condition, and is now on display in the main museum building — a distinctive A-Frame with glass apex roof.

The museum also includes many intricate ship models, relics, uniforms, navigation equipment, photographs, documents and a marine reference library. In June 1982, Captain George Vancouver's chronometer was added to the museum collection.

The 100-foot-high totem pole in the museum grounds is a duplicate of the Centennial Totem Pole which was specially carved by Chief Mungo Martin for Her Majesty, Queen Elizabeth in 1958. The original now stands at Virginia Water, Surrey, England.

A breakwater extending out from the museum provides protected moorage for several historic vessels. These include the *Thomas F. Bayard* — a 96-foot pilot schooner, freighter, sealing ship and former Sandheads lightship; and the S.S. *Master* — the only surviving wood-hulled, steam-engine-powered tug on the B.C. Coast, built in 1922 by Arthur Moscrop at False Creek Shipyards.

For visitors to the museum, temporary anchorage or landing by dinghy may be possible off "Indian" Beach between the breakwater and Vanier Park.

Vanier Park

This 30-acre park is named after Canada's first French-Canadian Governor-General, Georges P. Vanier, who served with great distinction and dignity from 1959-1967. The Park site was originally the Kitsilano Indian Reserve but was purchased by the Provincial Government in 1911. Over the years, it was proposed as the location for ocean terminal docks, a civic stadium, ship-building plant, railyards, grain terminal and a Ford motor car assembly plant.

The prominent white domed building in the centre of the park is the Vancouver Museum-Observatory-Planetarium complex. A huge stainless steel sculpture of a crab at the entrance represents the crab that traditionally guards harbour entrances in Indian mythology. Inside the museum, there are historical

A fleet of Jib Set Sailing School Cal 20s sail out of False Creek off Kitsilano. (photo: Clementien Wolferstan)

Vanier Park, with city's museum, planetarium, and archives; the Maritime Museum, with St. Roch housed in A-frame at left, Kitsilano Coast Guard station, and Burrard Civic Marina are all close neighbors.

exhibits and Indian artifacts. The Lipsett collection is one of the best displays in Canada of native Indian tools, baskets, rattles, clothing and masks. There is also a diorama-model of Vancouver as it looked over 100 years ago (99% forest). Nearby, partly hidden under the wide grassy lawns surrounding the museum, is the City Archives, dedicated to the memory of Major J.S. Matthews who did so much to preserve the history of this city.

The entrance to False Creek seems deceptively straight forward, but there are a few hazards to beware of. The navigable channel narrows to less than half its width at low tide. The sector light at the base of the northern bridge pier is particularly useful in keeping outbound vessels off the shoal which extends halfway across the entrance from Sunset Beach. Tidal streams can be quite rapid (maximum 2 knots). One must be prepared for large concentrations of tugs, barges, fish boats and other vessels entering and leaving False Creek and small boats hovering off the launching ramps west of the Coast Guard wharf or the fuel barge near the Bridge.

The huge Vancouver Aquatic Centre Building on the Sunset Beach shore close to the North end of the Burrard Bridge is on the site of George E. Cates 1896 boatyard and marine railway.

6   Burrard Bridge Civic Marina

The Burrard Bridge Civic Marina occasionally provides temporary moorage space on an "as available" basis. Since this is one of the most conveniently located marinas in the city, there is a multi-year waiting list for permanent moorage. Visiting boats can sometimes tie up on the outside of the long float between the Bridge and the Kitsilano Trestle. Hazards here include the occasional sideswipe and wash from passing barges, log booms and other vessels; and droppings from birds and others from above.

7   The Jib Set

The Jib Set Sailing School, probably the largest in Canada, was founded in 1967 by Les Alfreds, and is located below the inside east end of the Burrard Bridge. Courses offered include: day sailing, coastal cruising, racing, heavy weather, seamanship, navigation, five day cruise'n learn (to the Gulf Islands). Rental and charter boats and flotilla cruises out of Maple Bay are also available. Students, graduates and Jib Set charterers are welcome to use the Club facilities which include the "Prospect of Bowen" lounge, with a fantastic view across English Bay to Bowen Island, the HMCS "Sailfish" bar, library, chart room, European sauna, showers and laundry. When moorage space is available, visitors are very welcome.

The S.S. Essington, now permanently moored above the high tide line behind the Jib Set as a restaurant, was formerly a Fraser River paddlewheeler.

The Kitsilano Trestle Railway Bridge was originally built in 1886 to serve a proposed rail and deepsea shipping terminal in English Bay. The trestle has survived countless attacks by sparks from nearby sawmills and passing trains, oversize barges and sailboat masts. It is scheduled for removal by 1983, thereby simplifying access into the Creek.

8   Boaters Village

There is a travelift here for lifting boats out of the water for repair or maintenance. Maximum capacity is 60 ft./30 tons. Some of the marine services available include: Sea Wing Sailing (formerly the North Shore Sailing School, founded by Brian Morse) offering a complete range of CYA courses and a large fleet of charter boats; Hood Sails and Pak-a-boat rentals. The entire north shore of False Creek is at this writing undergoing a massive redevelopment. Some of the marine facilities at Boaters Village will be relocating to Granville Island or elsewhere in False Creek as leases expire.

In 1894, Alfred Wallace had his shipyard here. He built the west coast's first fishery protection vessel, the *Kestrel*, many lifeboats, fishboats, a sternwheeler and the first North Van ferry before moving to the foot of Lonsdale in 1908 (see (8), Ch. 2). The first Granville Street Bridge was built on trestles in 1889 and in 1892 carried Vancouver's first streetcar across the Creek. East of the bridge is Yaletown, a former settlement for CPR workers in the 1880's. It was here, in a pile of logging slash, that the great fire which destroyed Vancouver in 1886 started. In 1890, a blacksmith, furniture factory and sawmill were located here. B.C. Place plans development of a 400 berth marina with temporary moorage space for visitors, seafront promenades, parks, islands and restaurants along this shore.

9   Fisherman's Terminal

South of the Kitsilano Trestle and west of Granville Island is the Vancouver Fisherman's Terminal, comprising one of the larger concentrations of public float space in the province. These floats are primarily for use by fishing boats, but in the summer when most boats are away fishing, some temporary moorage space will be available. The Terminal is an ideal location for cruising yachtsmen who are content with a more informal moorage than that provided at commercial marinas. One can relax with a beer, moot the weather with the retired fisherman moored alongside, feed the family of Canada geese which make a daily circuit of the Creek looking for handouts, row across to the island for a morning cappucino in the

False Creek government floats hold the fishing fleet. There is occasional transient moorage available when the fleet is at sea.

False Creek before Expo 86 — concrete distribution plant, log booms and sawdust barges of major industries mingle with yachts, floating homes and public recreation spaces.

market, or watch the sun set on the Bridge's bistro's brilliant yellow facade. Moorage fees are reasonable and showers are provided.

10 Granville Island

Granville Island was once a wide expanse of mud flat, prime clam bed and Indian net fishing area. Residents of the Village of *Snauq*, formerly located beneath the south end of the Burrard Bridge, also erected traps across the flats to catch salmon and speared sturgeon in the shallows. From 1913 to 1915, sand dredged from the Creek was used to create a new 35-acre island which eventually accommodated over 50 industries. Today, only four of these industries remain active, while many of the old warehouses have been recycled to create a dynamic new commercial-entertainment area. There are several theatres, restaurants, art and craft galleries and open

"Snowflake crystal" layout of Floating Home Cooperative allows liveaboard residents quick access to central hub which houses services. Granville Island Hotel (right centre) provides transient moorage with luxury hotel facilities.

space parks and pubs. The Granville Island Market with a multitude of open stalls selling everything from fresh fish and local produce to breads, bagels, meats, cheese, imported delicacies, fudge and other health foods is located at the northeast end of the island.

Although large signs around the island warn that moorage is prohibited, these are intended to discourage long-term berthage. Visiting yachtsmen are generally welcome to tie up for a few hours while shopping on the island. If you leave your boat any longer, you risk a heavy fine or removal.

There are a number of small False Creek ferries providing regular commuter service between the island and various moorages in the Creek, the West End (Hornby St.) and the Maritime Museum.

11 Maritime Market

Granville Island's Maritime Market incorporates a wide range of haulout; engine-sail-mast-boat building, repair and maintenance; brokerage and chandlery services. Sea-Wing Sailing (also at Boaters Village) have an office here. Red and White Boat Rentals provide rowboats and canoes for leisurely exploration of the creek. John Dowd (author of *Ocean Kayaking*) has his Eco-marine store here — the west coast marine centre for all types of kayaks and practical advice on this unique method for exploring the coast. There are plans for a Maritime Academy with facilities for instruction and building of small boats at the east end of the basin.

One of the first sawmills in the Creek, later known as the Rat Portage Mill, was built on the isthmus of land which linked Granville Island to the south shore. Harold Clay operated one of the first "marinas" in Vancouver here from 1932 to 1974.

On the east side of the island under the Granville Bridge, the Ocean Cement company is still operating with a lease to the end of the century. If one has the time to poke around, one can find other industries where wire cables, chains and nails are made. Right next door to Ocean Cement is the Emily Carr School of Art with bizarre sculptures and other creations arresting the attention of passing mariners.

The Sea Village community of houseboats near the east end of the island is continuing the historic coastal tradition of waterfront living. In the 1930s, houseboats provided an inexpensive, tax-free and romantic alternative to land-bound accommodation. By 1947, there were about 1500 people living in float houses along Vancouver's waterfront or perched on piles above the foreshore and thousands more up the coast lived in logging camps on rafts which were towed from bay to bay. The few houseboats here and the Cold Mountain Institute Barge are modern examples of this coastal lifestyle.

Mariners Inn, a "boatel" at the eastern tip of the Island, provides accommodation, health club, restaurant, lounge and moorage for visiting yachts. The southern tip of the Island includes an open park, amphitheatre and miniature "mountain" to climb. Alder Bay might appear to be a perfect anchorage, but is reserved for small boat use. There is a community dock at the head of the bay for use by Sea Scouts and the False Creek Sailing and Rowing Society. Visiting yachtsmen can purchase memberships in the False Creek Community Centre for a nominal fee permitting use of the Centre with showers and sauna. There is a children's playground with fire hydrants that work and running water to splash in on a hot summer day. Alder Bay is also known as Brigantine bay for it is here that the Small Ship Society, store, maintain and test-sail their Sabot fighting ships. Early industries which operated near Alder Bay included Electric Turpentine, Empire Manufacturing, iron foundries, Imperial Shingle and the world famous Vivian Engine Works (See *Raincoast Chronicle #9*).

12   Spruce Harbour Marina

This marina is known officially as the Greater Vancouver Floating Home Co-operative. Temporary moorage may be available here while resident boats are out cruising in the summer months. Facilities at the "hub" of the floats include laundry, showers sauna and informal lounge.

Temporary anchorage may be available in this section of the creek for those willing to hazard the shallow depths close to shore and the occasional annoyance of passing barges, booms, vessels and "patrol" boats.

Charleson Park, named after the man who originally logged this area for the CPR in the 1880's, is a 28-acre area that includes a playground, playing field, seawall promenade and extensive grassy lawns, hidden glades and enclosed meadows, pools, gardens and a huge rockery with a tumbling waterfall visible from the Creek.

13   Heather Civic Marina

This marina is the home for another contingent of False Creek's liveaboard community. Although they are often away cruising, temporary moorage for visitors is scarce even in the summer months. There are plans for expanded moorage facilities in the direction of Johnston Terminals. Temporary anchorage may be possible southwest of the marina in a small basin that was originally scheduled for a visitors boat dock. Leg-in-Boot Square, modelled on a Mediterranean courtyard plaza, is named to commemorate the finding of a knee boat with a leg still in it at the turn of the century. In spite of the efforts of the police, it was never claimed.

This is the site of what was said to be the earliest industry on the south shore of False Creek, but there is some dispute as to whether the sawmill was Stamp's, Cassidy's, or Leamy and Kyles. J. Coughlan and Sons (pioneers in steel shipbuilding) and Vancouver Engineering Works were located east of here. A variety of stores, restaurants, sidewalk cafe and a pub (Stamp's Landing) are found around the Square.

Immediately northwest of Stamp's Landing, across the creek, is The Old Fireboat House, where the False Creek Fireboat (No. 16) was kept. In the days of heavy

No, these are not 12-Metres fighting it out in English Bay, but model yachts, their sheets and rudders radio controlled, in the Vanier Park pond. (photo: C. Wolferstan)

industry, with scores of beehive burners, saw, planing and shingle mills, there was an alarm almost everyday. The only 5 alarm fire in Vancouver's history occurred in 1960 when the B.C. Forest Products mill burned down in a spectacular waterfront blaze (Alex Matches).

14   False Creek Marina

This huge facility can easily be located by noticing that it is due southeast of the headquarters for *Pacific Yachting* magazine at 1132 Hamilton Street. All moorage is permanent or private so it may be hard for visitors to find a berth here. There are several boat brokerages, a fuel dock, a chandlery, haulout (20-ton elevator), repair and maintenance facilities, sail training (D.G. Sail West), restaurants (Ondines, Clam and Rib) and Hilda's Galley.

Although the Connaught Bridge (known locally as

Heather Civic Marina (foreground) provides liveaboard but no transient moorage. B.C. Place Stadium under construction (upper right). After Expo 86 all False Creek north shore land developed for housing.

the Cambie Bridge) swing span is shown in an open position on Chart 3482, (1982), it is actually closed most of the time. The bridge, which was completed in 1912 and named after the Governor-General, The Duke of Connaught, is scheduled to be replaced by 1986. Four hours notice is required to open the bridge which happens about two or three times a week. The closed clearance at high tide is 39 feet, with opened clearance 69 feet, to overhead wires. The deeper northern channel is the preferred passage.

Industry continues to churn away in the uppermost basin of False Creek although it is gradually being phased out to make way for Expo 86 and B.C. Place. Sweeney's Cooperage was still building wooden barrels here until 1981, and Bay Forest Products, the last sawmill operating in the Creek, is due to go before 1986. Parts of this basin may be dyked and turned into another "lost" lagoon with man-made islands, bridges and catwalks. There have been other proposals to rejoin the Creek with Burrard Inlet by constructing a canal along Columbia Street.

The terminus of False Creek in 1900 was actually another mile beyond where it ends now. In 1876, the Westminster Bridge (now Main Street) was built to link Gastown with the south shore of False Creek and the trail to New Westminster (now Kingsway). The Creek narrowed here, and the Indians called the passage *Ke-wah-usks* or "two points exactly opposite".

The only other way to cross was at low tide on boulders rolled into the Creek by a bridge-hating eccentric called Julius Ceasar who lived there. The eastern tidal flats had a noxious reputation . . . foul smells, rowdy drinking parties, an opium factory, shanty towns, and . . . many houseboats. From 1915 to 1921, the squatters were evicted and the flats were filled in for industry, railyards and the Canadian National and Great Northern rail terminus.

Vancouver Sea Festival

Yachtsmen fortunate enough to be visiting Vancouver during the annual Sea Festival (usually mid-July) should not miss the opportunity to partake in this unique Vancouver happening. The opening night festivities are particularly impressive as hundreds of boats anchor out in English Bay and tens of thousands of spectators throng the shores while spectacular fireworks overhead bring collective expressions of approval from the multitudes. Other activities include Sabot-Brigantine Battles by the Small Ship Society, Zodiac Football, salmon barbecues, and

As many as 1,000 boats anchor off English Bay beach and Kitsilano to watch Sea Festival fireworks (there goes one now, below right).

A closer look reveals beneath the fighting brigantines, 8 foot Sabot dinghies rigged out in eighteenth century gear.
(photos: B. Cedroff)

63

the arrival of any Tall Ships in the vicinity and Bathtub Race Survivors from Nanaimo.

A winter version of the Vancouver Sea Festival is reenacted every New Years Day when hundreds of boats raft up together off English Bay Beach to observe the annual "Polar Bear Swim". Thousands of hardy souls rush into the water together to celebrate their delight and solidarity with the west coast marine environment and to recover from the previous evenings revelry.

15 English Bay Beach

Although daytime winds in English Bay are more likely to be calm in the winter months, there is also a much higher probability of occasional, very strong winds from the southeast or west.

In the summer months, English Bay is a reasonably good temporary anchorage. Moderately strong westerly onshore winds may make the anchorage somewhat uncomfortable in the afternoon. At night with offshore winds or calms prevailing, the only hindrance to anchorage would be the city noise from the West End and the odd swell from passing tugs and deep sea traffic. More security is available in False Creek.

The beach here, which was called *Ayyulshun* (soft under feet) by the Indians, has become the most popular in Vancouver. Alexandra Park above it was named in honour of Queen Alexandra who, with King Edward VII, reigned when this park was acquired. The park was home for Seraphim (Joe) Fortes of Barbados, Vancouver's first lifeguard, who patrolled the beach in the early part of this century by boat, on foot, and in the water, He rescued hundreds from drowning and taught thousands of children (including my mother) to swim. Alan Morley has noted:

> Every morning all year round, he swam in the bay and drank his "medicine" — a cup of sea water . . . Joe belonged to the beach, and the beach to Joe. From dawn to dark and long after dark, he was host to picnickers, chaperone to courting couples and a terror to the bum and hoodlum. His cottage was spick and span within and without . . . beside his bed was his only book, Thomas a Kempis 'Imitation of Christ', and he left the bay only on Sunday morning to attend Mass, for he was a devout Catholic. The City gave him the authority of a special constable . . . Joe took his duties seriously. When — as was bound occasionally to happen — his utmost efforts (in trying to rescue someone from the water) failed, his grief was shattering to behold . . . He died in 1922. In the quiet little park where he had lived and served so long, there is a simple granite monument — a drinking fountain, low enough for the smallest of the children that play nearby, and over it a modest bronze plaque with the head and shoulders of a cheerful, heavy-set brown man and three just such rowdy youngsters below, as Joe delighted in. On the granite is carved only: *"Little Children Loved him"*. (from *Vancouver: From Milltown to Metropolis*)

A rock groyne at the foot of Gilford is all that remains of the old English Bay Pier, built in 1908. A pavilion at the end served as concert hall, dance hall, tea room and roller skating rink before it was demolished in 1939.

According to the late City Archivist, Major J.S. Matthews, Stanley Park was originally an island at high tide: "When the tide was not full, it required little effort for Indians to drag their dugout canoes out of harms way from rough seas at *Staitwouk* (Second Beach) to the sheltered calm of *Chul-wah-ulch* (Lost Lagoon)."

Between Second Beach and Siwash Rock there is often a "dead spot" in the wind, although a strong westerly may be blowing onto English Bay Beach or through First Narrows. This "dead spot" often traps local sailors. It is caused by the dense cool forest of Stanley Park preventing heating of the ground and hence, allows little convection. The sea breeze mechanism does not operate just west of Stanley Park. In fact, there will be cold air drainage out from the Park and over the water, resulting in practically calm winds offshore (J. Emsley, *Pacific Yachting*).

Behind Ferguson Point, where a 4.7 inch gun battery was located during World War II, stands the Ferguson Point Tea Rooms and a monument to the Indian Poet E. Pauline Johnson.

16 Siwash Rock

Jose Maria Narvaez named Ferguson Point "Punta de la Bodega" in 1791, and missed discovering Vancouver Harbour because he did not pass north of Siwash Rock. Major Matthews notes:

> Originally, both north and south shores were so heavily forested that they blended one into another. One early navigator, following on Indian canoe, was astounded when the canoe suddenly disappeared. Narvaez was deceived in like manner, but Captain Vancouver was more fortunate.

As the 1898 *Pilot* notes: "FIRST NARROWS . . . to a stranger, the entrance is not easily made out until close in".

Although Matthews felt that Narvaez was the first European to gaze on the future site of Vancouver, it may have been possible that others were here 200 years before him. Indian legend and the recent research of Robert Ward (July 1981 *Geographical Journal*) indicate that Sir Francis Drake and a captured pilot "John the Greek" (Juan de Fuca) may have discovered the Strait of Georgia, believing it to be the North West Passage in 1579.

Sailing for many days through a large inlet near 48°N, they passed 'diverse islands' until, 'on the north coast thereof, they came to a great headland, or island (Stanley Park?), with a pinnacle or spired rock, like a pillar thereupon' (Siwash Rock?).

A plaque at the base of Siwash Rock notes:

> Indian legend tells us that this 50 foot high pinnacle of rock stands as an imperishable monument to Sklash, 'the unselfish' who is turned into stone by Q'uas, the transformer as a reward for his unselfishness.

Siwash Rock was also known as "Ninepin Rock" to early Vancouver settlers.

West Vancouver

Water transport has played a vital role in the development of West Vancouver. In 1866, Navvy Jack (John Thomas), a Welshman, established the first ferry service from Granville (later Gastown) to Navvy Jack Point. Thomas was given the nickname "Navvy" Jack to distinguish him from the other Jack ("Gassy")

Is this the view that Sir Francis Drake saw 400 years ago? Siwash Rock and Stanley Park from English Bay.

resident within the harbour. Besides running the ferry service, Thomas established a gravel hole on his beach from which early Vancouver residents got their gravel for building purposes. The quality of this gravel was so good that to this very day construction firms continue to use the term "Navvy Jack" when ordering gravel.

Navvy Jack's rooster was said to have been one of the first navigational aids in Burrard Inet. In 1888, the *Charmer* was bringing a party of excursionists from Victoria to celebrate the Queen's Birthday holiday in Vancouver. When they entered Burrard Inlet, a thick fog prevented them from finding the entrance to the First Narrows. With the engines stopped, the crow of a rooster came out of the mist, allowing the Captain to establish his bearings and take the *Charmer* safely through the Narrows.

17 Hollyburn Sailing Club

The Hollyburn Sailing Club store their boats at the west end of Ambleside Park. Immediately next door is Ambleside boat rentals with small boats for rent, dry

Above, Hollyburn Sailing Club at the west end of Ambleside Park in West Vancouver. Opposite page, Dun- *darave Pier with Peppi's restaurant has entertained generations of Vancouverites.*

storage and day charters. Launching is partially protected by the old ferry terminal pier. The West Vancouver Municipal Transportation Office is housed in the original ferry terminal building.

From Ambleside Park, it is possible to walk up the Capilano Trail, parallel to the river, as far as Canyon Park and the Cleveland Dam. It is also possible to walk west along the shoreline, past John Lawson Park and Navvy Jack Point to Dundarave. Ambleside Park has playing fields, gardens, and a bird sanctuary in a marsh beside the river. A cairn above the beach commemorates the visit to Burrard Inlet of Pilot Commander Don Jose Maria Narvaez in 1791.

John Lawson Park at the foot of 17th Street was formerly the ferry terminus (1909). This terminus had to be abandoned because the current was so strong that passengers had to occasionally be landed by

lifeboat. A spring ebb tide tends to run straight towards Navvy Jack Point from the First Narrows before being deflected towards Point Atkinson.

At Dundarave Park, there is a substantial pier, also known as the "Government Wharf" which serves as a starting mark for local yacht races. At the head of the pier is Peppi's restaurant, formerly St. Mawes Inn where Cornish teas were served in the 1950s. This area is named after Dundarave Castle in Scotland. The origin of Dundarave (should rhyme with "have") comes from the Gaellic for a two-oared boat.

Further along the West Vancouver shore is Altamont Beach Park, West Bay Park, Sandy Cove Park and Cypress Beach Park in Pilot Cove. Although most of this shoreline is residential, access above the shore is possible in a few of the coves where there are public parks. West Bay served as the fire command post

during World War II when Burrard Inlet was defended by four gun batteries.

The earliest known settlement in West Vancouver was an Indian village in Sandy Cove. The only major industry, the Great Northern Cannery, was also located here in 1891 and operated from 1922 until 1967 by the Millerd family. This site is now the home for the Pacific Environment Institute of the Federal Government.

18 Pilot Cove

In 1890, a permanent pilotage station was established at Skunk Cove, also known as Pilot Cove or Claymore Cove after the official pilot boat, the 50 foot sailing cutter *Claymore*. Pilots for deep sea traffic into Vancouver now board at Victoria. The rest of the West Vancouver shoreline, west and north of Pilot Cove, is covered in Chapter 7.

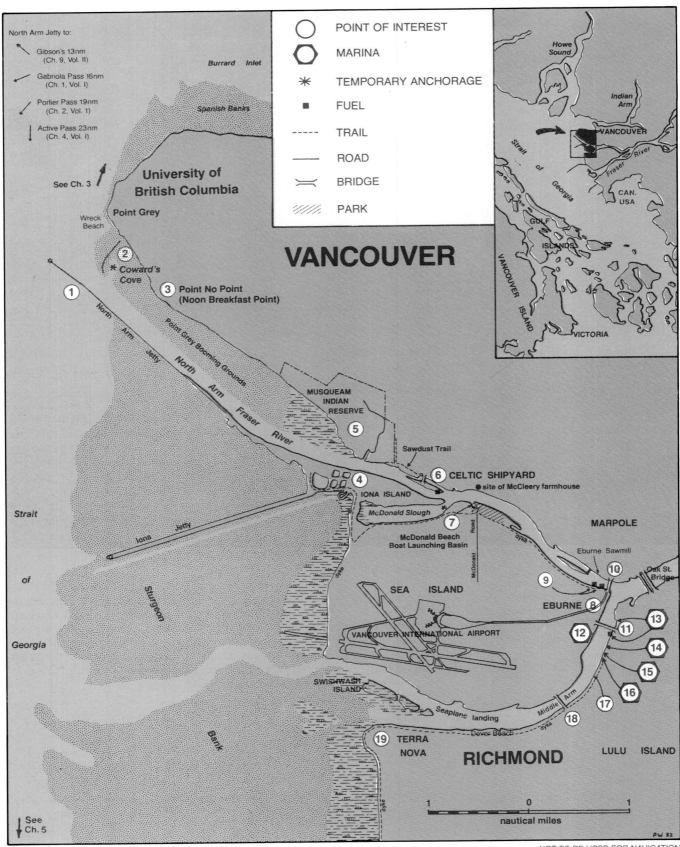

VANCOUVER

Legend:
- ○ POINT OF INTEREST
- ⬡ MARINA
- ✳ TEMPORARY ANCHORAGE
- ■ FUEL
- --- TRAIL
- — ROAD
- ⟫⟪ BRIDGE
- ▨ PARK

North Arm Jetty to:

Gibson's 13nm
(Ch. 9, Vol. II)

Gabriola Pass 16nm
(Ch. 1, Vol. I)

Porlier Pass 19nm
(Ch. 2, Vol. 1)

Active Pass 23nm
(Ch. 4, Vol. I)

See Ch. 3

Burrard Inlet

Spanish Banks

University of British Columbia

Point Grey

Wreck Beach

② Coward's Cove

① ③ Point No Point (Noon Breakfast Point)

North Arm Jetty

North Arm Fraser River

Point Grey Booming Grounds

MUSQUEAM INDIAN RESERVE

⑤

Sawdust Trail

④ ⑥ CELTIC SHIPYARD

site of McCleery farmhouse

IONA ISLAND

McDonald Slough

⑦

McDonald Beach Boat Launching Basin

MARPOLE

Eburne Sawmill

⑩

Oak St. Bridge

⑨

McDonald Road

dyke

Strait

Iona Jetty

of

Georgia

Sturgeon

SEA ISLAND

VANCOUVER INTERNATIONAL AIRPORT

EBURNE ⑧

⑬

⑫ ⑪

⑭

⑮

⑯

SWISHWASH ISLAND

Seaplane landing

Middle Arm dyke

⑰

⑱

Bank

Dever Beach

⑲ TERRA NOVA

RICHMOND

LULU ISLAND

dyke

See Ch. 5

1 0 1
nautical miles

PW 82

NOT TO BE USED FOR NAVIGATION

(Inset map, upper right): Howe Sound, Indian Arm, VANCOUVER, Fraser River, Strait of Georgia, GULF ISLANDS, CAN. USA, VANCOUVER ISLAND, VICTORIA

68

CHAPTER FOUR

The Fraser River Estuary

(1) The North and Middle Arms

by Peggy and Bill Ward

To many, rivers are simply a convenient route to more rewarding cruising grounds. To others, inland waterways provide unique and fascinating cruising with challenges differing only in kind from those of the more open waters. As the original highways of commerce, rivers provide a chance to explore communities from a different perspective. Man has always respected rivers, for their utility if not for their beauty or ecology; an industrial shoreline has a story to tell that reflects the diversity and dependency of the citizens who dwell and work along its banks. The sights along the Fraser, for example, are a constant reminder of the logging, milling, fishing and canning that have long been integral parts of the area's economy.

The Fraser River estuary is truly an interesting place to explore: tens of thousands of people live, work and play along its banks; millions of tons of cargo pass through its ports; and wildlife abounds in the less developed areas. Unfortunately, most people merely catch a glimpse of the river as they pass high overhead on the various bridges. The more fortunate yachtsman, on the other hand, has access to the entire estuary.

Virtually any vessel can cruise on the river, but it is no surprise that in the early days sternwheelers were the predominant type of vessel to stem the river currents. Power to make good at least four knots against the current, and shallow draft to allow exploration of the shallow reaches and landing at the beaches and banks are the two most desirable characteristics for pleasure craft using this river. Failing shallow draft, a good anchor and dinghy, canoe or kayak are essential if you want to explore the more remote and unspoiled reaches of the estuary. Vessels with deeper draft are confined to the deeper channels and must look for floats or wharves to come alongside.

Sailing is not prohibited on the river, but the volume of traffic in some reaches makes it rather awkward for all. If the wind is fair, however, motorsailing can provide an extra few knots and better steerage way.

Depths

Each year, the Fraser River deposits over 20 million tons of sand, silt and clay at the river's mouth, forming the largest estuary/delta on Canada's west coast ('estuary' refers to the water adjacent to the delta where river and sea water mix). At the approaches to the river, the deposition of this river-borne material has resulted in the build-up of a broad expanse of tidal flats which extend up to 6 nautical miles seaward of the dykes (see air photo). Sturgeon Bank is marked only by the lights at the western end of the North Arm, Iona and Steveston jetties; Roberts Bank is marked by the western extent of the Roberts Bank Superport jetty and the Tsawwassen Ferry Terminal jetty. The Canadian Coast Guard hovercraft unit responds to almost

---

CHART
3491 — FRASER RIVER, NORTH ARM
    (1:20,000)
        Replaces 3489

---

100 distress situations annually from small craft which have gone aground on these banks. Maintenance of a good DR position is essential, especially on hazy days; there are few visible landmarks on the distant flat delta from which to obtain a fix. If you do run aground and are waiting for the incoming tide to refloat you, put out an anchor to prevent your boat from being washed further inshore.

In the river, clearly marked navigation channels are maintained by dredging; however, outside of these dredged channels, conditions constantly change due to silting and scouring. For this reason the Department of Public Works conducts surveys every two years in the North Arm and annually in the Main Arm. They recommend that boaters obtain copies of these sounding charts to use in conjunction with the Hydrographic Charts. They are available only from the Canadian Hydrographic Service, P.O. Box 6000, 9860 West Saanich Road, Sidney, B.C. V8L 4B2, telephone (604) 656-8358. Hydrographic chart 3490 covers the Main Arm of the Fraser, and chart 3491 (new edition 1982) replaces chart 3489 which covers the North Arm.

Water Quality

The brownish colour of the river water is caused by large amounts of suspended sediment which is often mistaken for pollution. However, the quality of the water is generally good at present, although there is evidence of a long-term build up of contaminants in the estuary which may lead to problems in the future. The water is not toxic to fish, but shellfish harvesting is prohibited throughout the estuary (Fraser River Estuary Study, 1981). Swimming is allowed at the beaches in Boundary Bay and at Tsawwassen but is prohibited at the Fraser River beaches for several reasons, including swift river currents, heavy river traffic, high water turbidity and high levels of fecal coliforms.

The sediment in the river water can act as an abrasive on certain water pump parts, noticeably those using rubber impellors, so it is wise to check the engine temperature and/or the flow of the cooling water frequently.

Tides and Currents

The estuary is tidal and it is well worth timing your arrival or departure according to the tides. However, one should be aware of more than the tide tables in order to be able to predict river currents and depths with any accuracy. Variations in river discharge and the relative shallowness of the river also affect the movement of water in the estuary.

River discharge varies greatly from season to season. Due to snow-melt, about 80% of the annual runoff occurs between May and July; this period is known as spring freshet. The greatly increased flow at this time causes more discoloration of the water because of increased erosion and sedimentation and brings with it large amounts of floating debris in the form of logs, deadheads, sinkers, tree roots, etc., which are a particular hazard to small craft.

River currents are at their greatest during freshet. Maximum outflow speeds occur about 2-3 hours before the low stage of a large ebb tide and may reach 5½ knots at the mouth of the Main Arm and 4 knots at the mouth of the North Arm. At more constricted places speeds of at least 6 knots can be reached, for example, off Celtic Island in the North Arm, in the Main Arm in Woodward Reach and at the No. 10 and 12 buoys by the bend in the Steveston jetty. Lesser velocities can be found closer to the banks of the river or on the inside of a bend in the river. During freshet currents will slow to one knot or less at high tide. Outside of the freshet season, from August to April, the greatest current occurs about 1½ hrs before local low water and is seldom greater than 3 knots in both the Main Arm and the North Arm.

River flow is downstream at all stages of the tide during a normal freshet, although during a small freshet the current can still reverse for a short period on the flood. Beginning in August and continuing to the end of April, the current in the river reverses for most of the flood on all large tides. The speed of this reversed current is about one knot on average, but may be greater at times of low discharge (December to March). The yachtsman can take advantage of this reversal by timing his upstream trip accordingly; and since the flooding tide will reverse the current in the middle of the channel first, he can take this route if inbound or use the sides of the channel if outbound. However, he should also make allowances for the swing of his vessel when anchoring for any length of time (over a tidal cycle, for example).

Another important tidal feature of the estuary is that the tide turn in the river is considerably delayed relative to the Strait of Georgia, due to the shallowness of the river; low tides are delayed even more than the highs (Thomson, *Oceanography of the British Columbia Coast*, 1981). Relative to Point Atkinson, the tide turn in the North Arm (at the Arthur Laing Bridge) is one hour later on a flood tide and 1½ hrs later on a large ebb tide. During freshet, add another half-hour to the delays. For the Main Arm, see Table 5 in the Tide and Current Tables for specific information on tidal heights and time differences at Steveston, Deas Island and New Westminster.

Winds

Calm conditions occur less than 10% of the time over the estuary. The strongest winds are associated with the stormy winter season when easterly winds predominate. There are also strong cold outflows of arctic air which flow down the Harrison and Fraser valleys and affect the more exposed southern portion of the estuary. The North and Middle Arms are partially protected from these strong northeasterlies by the Burrard Peninsula. In summer, under lighter

wind conditions, the land-sea breeze pattern dominates. A westerly sea breeze begins about 10 a.m., strengthening to 10-15 knots by mid afternoon and dying away before sunset when a lighter easterly land breeze blows out onto the Strait of Georgia until early morning. Onshore winds tend to enhance the effect of the flooding tide and to decrease the effect of an ebbing tide and of river outflow.

Waves

Seas at the mouth of the river are quite hazardous during certain conditions; according to the Coast Guard, these areas are potentially the most dangerous for small craft. High standing waves occur where

Sea Island with Vancouver International Airport separates the North and Middle Arms of the Fraser. Silt feeds growth of Sturgeon Bank. (photo: Canada Dept. of Energy, Mines and Resources).

strong river currents oppose wind waves generated by strong winds. Seaward of the North Arm and Steveston jetties, during a strong west or northwest wind, extremely dangerous rips are created during periods of high runoff or near low tide, when currents are at their greatest. Shallow waters over the delta front further increase wave heights, making these areas much rougher than adjacent portions of the Strait (Thomson). These waves are noticeable as far upstream as Steveston in the Main Arm, but are neg-

ligible in the North Arm. However in the narrower North Arm, a substantial chop can develop from the large numbers of vessels using this channel.

Hazards

There are three search and rescue hovercraft in the Strait of Georgia with crews who are trained in first aid to ambulance-attendant level, and an additional core of about 12 Coast Guard Auxiliary craft. In an emergency a hovercraft could be on its way within 3 minutes of receiving a call. VHF Channel 16 is the emergency channel to be used. The majority of marine incidents responded to by the Coast Guard are caused either by an ignorance of good seamanship or a lack of knowledge about the area (people have actually used road maps to navigate by) or about the equipment being used (lack of fuel is a major cause of marine distress).

As a first pinciple of good seamanship, a vessel which cannot be readily propelled by hand should have the anchor ready for letting go in case of engine failure. Smaller boats and particularly inflatables should carry a suitable anchor (the folding grapnel type is good) with the rode ready to run. It can be flaked or coiled in the bailing bucket.

An occasional grounding can be expected by those who venture away from dredged channels, since the charted depths in areas outside these channels are subject to change. These are nothing to worry about provided the tide is flooding. A powerful engine helps, as does a kedge, dinghy and powerful sheet winch or anchor windlass; however, the first effort should probably be at heeling the boat which can immediately and dramatically reduce draft. Use of the boom and a heavy crew member can work wonders on many sailboats.

Fog seldom occurs in the estuary between March and August. It is most likely to develop between October and February on clear calm nights and is most dense just before sunrise. The frequency and density of fog in the Lower Mainland has decreased drastically since the 1940s. One contributing factor is thought to be the change from sawdust to natural gas for home heating. Visibilities of less than 1 mile occur on about 35 days of the year; in the 1940s they occurred on more than 100 days a year.

There is considerable traffic in the estuary, ranging from deep sea vessels to tugboats towing lengthy log booms and barges which may be on a lengthy offshore scope. Skippers should be aware of the usual Rules of the Road and give way to larger vessels which can

Opposite, the curving breakwater of Coward's Cove creates a refuge at the mouth of the North Arm. Cove is at the eastern end of Wreck Beach. For low tide view of dredged basin see page 50.

Right, the North Arm channel, with boom storage port and starboard, viewed from upriver.

only manoeuvre in the middle of the fairway. It would also be wise to give log booms in tow a wide berth when passing as the pushing and towing can often force a log to project down and out beneath the surface from the edge of the boom; this also applies to booms moored along the shoreline. In addition, many people work on the river, on booms, dredges, pile drivers, floats, tugs, etc., so although there is no speed limit, it would be best to slow down when approaching them because damage and injuries can be caused easily by excessive bow-waves and wash.

Bridges

For the sailor who is also a bridge buff, rivers and waterways give him a chance to look at these engineering marvels in a different and unhurried way. For those who aren't, the bridge is a reminder of the more frantic world of the motorway and deepens the satisfaction to be found cruising the relatively tranquil river. If your mast height from the charted water level exceeds the bridge clearance then the bridge may be opened for you. In some cases the bridge opens on demand, in other cases it is normally left open. Specific information for each bridge is given later in the chapter. The current will increase in velocity and eddies will form under a constricted bridge span so a little extra power will be required to maintain speed when travelling against the current.

The North Arm

The North Arm is one of the busiest industrial areas on the Fraser River. There is constant activity on this narrow, winding and relatively shallow river channel, where fishboats and tugs towing their log booms, scows and barges are commonplace. For the pleasure boater, there are excellent marine facilities and many points of interest along the way. This chapter deals only with the lower part of the North Arm and with the Middle Arm.

The North and Middle Arms comprise the North Fraser Harbour, and are under the jurisdiction of the North Fraser Harbour Commission. Their patrol boat, NF Patrol #2, operates daily between 0800-1600 hours and 2000-0400 hours and can be contacted by VHF radio channel 6. In case of an emergency they work closely with the Coast Guard; however, the Coast Guard should be contacted first.

The North Arm is entered between Point Grey and the western tip of the North Arm Jetty. When entering from the north, give the tidal flats at Wreck Beach a wide berth, even though this popular nudist beach might tempt you to take a closer look. When approaching from the south, along Sturgeon Bank, it is useful to remember the help that can be provided by the nearshore current of about 1 to 2 knots which runs northward about ½ nautical mile off the edge of the bank; it is most prevalent between May and September.

1 The North Arm Jetty

The North Arm Jetty is only one of the many river training structures in the Fraser estuary; it was built originally between 1914-1917 by the federal Department of Public Works, with a westerly addition of 750m built in 1935. It is now the most probable contender for the location of a new B.C. Ferries Terminal which would link the Mainland to Vancouver Island via Gabriola Island.

2 Coward's Cove

An additional river training structure — the breakwater to port — was built in 1951 to funnel the river flow into the main channel and to help decrease the deposition of sediment at the river mouth. Upstream of the southwestern end of the breakwater there is a dredged basin (to about 10 feet at local low water) which provides a safe anchorage for small craft during inclement weather in the Strait of Georgia. When anchoring, stay clear of the pilings and booms as there may not be sufficient water there at all stages of the tide. On charts the area is called Fisherman's Mooring

McDonald Slough can provide anchorage and access by dinghy to Iona and Sea Island.

Wildflowers grow in the tidal marsh along the delta front. (photo: M. Dunn)

Basin although it is more graphically known as Coward's Cove.

Extending about 3 miles upstream from this basin, are the large Point Grey Booming Grounds which have been in use since the North Arm Jetty was built; they provide nearly one half of the total available log storage space in the North Fraser Harbour. This is the first fresh water mooring site for log booms in-transit from salt water sorting areas up the coast, en route to the various mills in the North Fraser and Fraser River harbours. All along the banks of the North Arm you will notice other in-transit facilities for scows and log tows as well as other log storage areas.

3 Noon Breakfast Point

The name "Noon Breakfast Point" may soon be assigned to a place near Point Grey (perhaps at Point No Point) in order to commemorate the landing of Captain George Vancouver's fourth boat expedition of 13 June, 1792. The author of this proposal, J.E. Roberts, of Victoria, B.C. suggests that this would honour "the hardships and efforts of 'the people' who manned the boats of the survey expedition". The name originated with Lieutenant Peter Puget, who recorded that after leaving the main ship at Birch Bay to chart the coast line to the north, the men had lunch at Point Roberts at noon, June 12. The seamen then spent the next 24 hours without proper rest or food; they could not find a suitable landing spot due to the extensive shoals along the delta front and to the strong tidal stream against them. They slept in their boats (possibly near Mayne or Galiano islands) and the next morning "again visited the shoals whose edge we traced to a bluff (which for distinction sake we shall call Noon Breakfast Point)". Later, however, Capt. Vancouver preferred to assign the name of this friend Capt. George Grey to this point.

4 Iona Island

Iona Island was named by an early settler after an island in the Inner Hebrides, where St. Columbia first preached Christianity to the Scots, in 563 A.D. It is privately owned by Canadian Forest Products and the Greater Vancouver Sewerage and Drainage District (for their sewage treatment plant). However, an undeveloped Regional Park, which includes the sandy beach between the jetties and the area of sand dunes to the north of the beach and east of the log barrier, is open to the public for picnicking, sunbathing, beachcombing and walking — toilets and picnic tables have been installed recently. Bring your binoculars if you are interested in wildlife. The tidal marshes of Sturgeon Bank, the water overlying the tidal flats, the upland fields and sewage lagoons all attract numerous bird species. In fact, Iona Island is most famous as a concentration area for songbirds and sandpipers and is the place where the largest number of rare birds is seen in B.C. (August is the best time to see the shorebirds).

The safest and nearest temporary anchorage from which to visit Iona Island is in McDonald Slough. It looks like a good anchorage on the hydrographic chart, but although there is sufficient depth in the navigable channel running the length of the slough, there is a considerable bottom debris problem due to all the booming activity (the channel is not maintained by dredging, except at its mouth). Access to the shoreline is obstructed by a continuous band of log booms; and it is mostly swampy and unsuitable for landing, except at the eastern end of Iona Island. The North Fraser Harbour Commission discourages temporary anchorage in the slough because it may interfere with the primary purpose of the area which is log boom storage. If you do anchor or secure alongside a boom, do not leave your vessel unattended, and be prepared to move at short notice.

5   Musqueam Indian Reserve

The Musqueam Indian Reserve can be seen to port, where the floodplain extends out from the base of the Point Grey uplands. The area was the home of Vancouver's earliest inhabitants; ancestors of the present Musqueam Indian Band have lived here for the last thousand years. It is somehow fitting that in 1808 Simon Fraser's closest landing spot to the mouth of the Fraser River was here. He apparently beached his

Celtic Island shelters a commercial fishboat harbour, while B.C. Forestry Department maintains and repairs its vessels in the yard to the left.

canoe in a bay while he went ashore to look around, only to find it left high and dry by the ebbing tide when he returned. It is probable that this bay is the one in the southeastern shoreline of the reserve. The creek flowing into the bay, Tin Can or Musqueam Creek, is the last salmon supporting stream in Vancouver.

For the next 2½ miles the view to port is mostly peaceful and scenic. Known as Southlands, it is an important equestrian area and has four beautifully landscaped golf courses. The large estates along Southwest Marine Drive can be seen above these lowlands, reminding you that the city is not that far away. Immediately upstream of the Musqueam Indian Reserve you may notice a number of people and horses walking along the popular "Sawdust Trail".

6   Celtic Shipyard

Deering Island (better known as Celtic Island) is located about 1 mile upstream of the bay where Fraser landed. Celtic Island and slough is the site of B.C. Packers commercial fishboat marina and net repair depot. This is your first reminder of the historical importance of the Fraser River fishery. In 1897, the

McDonald Beach Launching Basin is one of the rare recreational boat launching ramps in the Fraser estuary.

Celtic Cannery began operations here. Merging with B.C. Packers in 1902, it continued to operate as a cannery until 1917. It was then used as a fish camp until 1927 when it became a shipyard for B.C. Packers. (Marlene Parsons, *Fraser River Estuary Heritage Resource Inventory*, Heritage Conservation Branch, Province of B.C., April 1981). For those with a large boat in need of repair, this shipyard has a 500-ton hoist. There is also a Shell fuelling float near the upstream end of the island which is open from 0800-1630, Monday to Friday.

7   McDonald Beach Launching Basin

Across the river and about ¼ mile upstream from Celtic Island is the entrance to the McDonald Beach Boat Launching Basin. This is part of a municipal park which has washroom facilities, bait for sale, picnic tables, a large grassy playing field and a sandy beach for sunbathing, beachcombing or bar fishing. There is a paved boat launching ramp and floats for use only by boats using the ramp. Richmond Muncipality discourages temporary anchorage here; however, when it is not busy you could secure alongside the pilings along the western shore of the basin (there is about 10 ft here at low water), as long as you do not leave your vessel unattended and are prepared to leave at short notice. If you feel like stretching your legs ashore a bit, there are several interesting routes you can take. Walk westward along the dyke and visit Iona Island beach or walk eastward and enjoy the birdlife in the open fields to the south and the planes taking off and landing at Vancouver International Airport.

Nearly all of Sea Island is owned by the Ministry of Transport (MOT) and the airport covers most of this property. The airport has been operating now for 50 years and is the third busiest in Canada with over seven million passengers using it each year.

If you walk toward the airport, along McDonald Road, you will pass the abandoned Cora Brown subdivision which was expropriated by MOT between 1963-73 in order to build a third major runway and expand present airport facilities. The proposed expansion is highly controversial and the third runway has not yet been built; it was mentioned as a future option in the Vancouver International Airport Master Plan which was published in 1980. Most of the houses are gone from the area, but the lots are still distinguishable by the presence of paved driveways and old fences and hedges. Songbirds abound in the trees and shrubs and throughout the area is found one of the densest wintering populations of hawks and owls in B.C.

On the western side of the road, about a half mile south of the launching ramp, you will see the Grauer Farm, one of the oldest remaining farms on Sea Island, dating from about 1910. It is a reminder of the island's early thriving farming community which began in 1861 when Hugh McRoberts bought nearly half the island and began cultivating and harvesting fruit and wheat; he also established a cattle ranch and built the first dyke. Other farmers soon followed and by the turn of the century dairy farming was one of the area's major industries, supplying Vancouver's growing market. It has been said that at one time the largest farm in the British Empire was located on Sea Island.

Across the river from the launching ramp basin is the site of the home of the first settlers on the Vancouver side of the North Arm. The McCleery brothers established their farm there in 1862; unfortunately their 1873 farmhouse was recently destroyed and the only reminder of these pioneers is the golf course which bears their name. (Parsons).

8 Eburne

As you approach the Arthur Laing Bridge (10) there are two fuelling floats (9) to starboard, operated by Gulf and Chevron; Chevron is open from 0800-1700 Monday to Friday and 0800-1200 Saturday. Gulf is open for business between 0600-1700 Monday to Friday and 0600-1200 Saturday. Behind the Chevron station there is a large willow tree growing next to one of the bridge supports. It stands where one of the earliest Sea Island farmers' family homes used to be, and is all that is left of a once bustling community called Eburne. The first general store was built here in the 1880s by Harry Eburne and other businesses soon followed to serve the growing farming communities on both Sea and Lulu islands. Between 1889 and 1891, bridges were built connecting Sea Island to Marpole (on the same alignment as the Arthur Laing Bridge) and Lulu Island to Sea Island. Thus, all the agricultural goods from Sea and Lulu islands passed through Eburne on their way to Vancouver markets (Parsons). In fact, the first Granville Street Bridge over False Creek was built at the same time to give access to the Marpole/Eburne area. Eburne remained an important commercial area until it was bypassed in 1957 by the Oak Street Bridge. This, as well as land exprop-

riation for airport development, caused business in Eburne to dwindle and in 1976, the last business (Grauer's store) closed.

Lulu Island was named in 1862 by Colonel Moody, R.E., in command of a detachment of the Royal Engineers then stationed in New Westminster, after Lulu Sweet, a young actress belonging to the first theatrical troupe that ever acted in that city. Her conduct, acting and graceful manners gave great satisfaction, and were appreciated to such an extent by her friends and patrons that the island was named after her. (Walbran)

Also reminiscent of this earlier period is the Eburne Sawmill, immediately downstream of the Arthur Laing Bridge, on the right bank. It was built in the 1890s to process local timber (before this, settlers who logged their land had to send their timber all the way upstream to New Westminster for processing). Some of the original buildings remain although many newer and larger structures have since been built (Parsons).

10 Arthur Laing Bridge

The Arthur Laing Bridge was built in 1975 to serve Vancouver International Airport. It has a minimum clearance of 66 ft on a 12 ft tide, under the center portion of the main span.

Snow geese flock over the river. Area has a dense population of wintering fowl. (photo: B.R. Gates).

The Middle Arm

The Middle Arm is used mostly for recreational boating, with an array of modern marine facilities most of which are located between the Middle Arm Bridge (11) and the Dinsmore Bridge (18). After entering the Middle Arm there are privately operated floats to starboard which are home to a number of interesting converted and restored tugs. The Middle Arm is entered and left via the North Arm. There is no navigable channel downstream of the Dinsmore Bridge due to seaplane landing operations and the low clearance under the bridge; neither is there a navigable channel at the mouth of the Middle Arm because Sturgeon Bank dries completely at low water. This would have been useful information for a local dinghy racing association which sent its members off on a circumnavigation of Sea Island — at low water! So intent were the racers on dragging their dinghies across the sand flats at the mouth of the Middle Arm, to the Middle Arm channel, that they barely took time to explain to the Coast Guard what they were doing.

11   The Middle Arm Bridge

When closed, the Middle Arm Swing Bridge has a minimum clearance of 18 ft on a 12 ft tide; it may be less than this during freshet. The bridge will open on demand — four long horn or whistle blasts followed by one short one — except between 0700-0900 and 1600-1800, seven days a week.

12   Delta's River Inn Marina

There are 5 marinas lining the Middle Arm, with a total of 1000 berths and a large variety of facilities.

Delta's River Inn Marina, at 3500 Cessna Drive, 273-4211, the only marina on Sea Island, is just downstream of the Middle Arm Bridge. It has six or seven visitors' berths which can accommodate boats up to 70 ft; visitors' facilities include all hotel

Terra Nova and Swishwash Island at the mouth of the Middle Arm. Mount Baker is just visible 60 miles away.

facilities, such as showers, sauna, pool and even room service! Power and sail, bareboat or crewed charters are also available. It is a convenient place for out-of-town yachtsmen as there is a shuttle bus service from the hotel to the airport. The marina operators recently acquired Delta Shipyard across the river and now can provide all repairs and a lift capacity of 40 ft and 10 tons. The other four marinas are on the Lulu Island side of the river.

13   Vancouver Marina

Vancouver Marina, 8331 River Road, 278-9787, is located on both sides of the Middle Arm Bridge and has the only fuelling float in the Middle Arm. Located downstream of the bridge, the Texaco float is open from 0700 to dark in the summer and 0900 to 1700 in winter.

14   Richmond Marina

Richmond Marina, 8191 River road, 278-8612, has a few visitors' berths for yachts up to 30 ft and provides showers and a laundromat. The Airport Yacht Club is a tenant of the marina and welcomes visitors in their modern clubhouse. There are facilities for mechanical repairs and a lift capacity up to 25' in length. Delta Shipyard (see No. 12) is adjacent to Richmond Marina at 8051 River Road.

15   Skyline Marina

Skyline Marina, 8031 River Road, 273-3977, has a Travelift with a capacity of 30 tons and does all types of repair.

16   Capstan Marina

Capstan Marina, 7951 River Road, 273-9048, is the next downstream but has no visitors' facilities. Next is Skyline Marina's annex with additional long term moorage. A few hundred yards downstream is the Richmond Yacht Club (17), 7471 River Road, 278-1013. This is a private club which has reciprocal visitors rights with a number of other clubs including the Nanaimo Yacht Club.

18   Dinsmore Bridge

The Dinsmore Bridge is a fixed bridge with a clearance of 13 ft on a 12 ft tide; clearance may be less during freshet. Use the span to port, when travelling downstream, as shoaling occurs along the Sea Island side of the channel.

19   Terra Nova and Swishwash Island

Take a trip by dinghy, canoe or kayak to Terra Nova and Swishwash Island, at the mouth of the Middle Arm. Despite its proximity to the airport and urban Richmond, this part of the Midddle Arm is one of the most beautiful, out-of-the-way reaches in the Fraser estuary. Leave your boat in one of the marinas, but

The Middle Arm marinas have one of the largest concentrations of pleasure craft moorage in the region.

take your binoculars because this is also an excellent birdwatching area. Stay close to the south side of the river to avoid the seaplane landing area and watch for shoal patches (see chart). To the north watch the jets landing and taking off. You may want to stop at sandy Dover Beach, about half a mile downstream from Dinsmore Bridge — this is a popular local spot for bar fishing, sunbathing, picnicking and beachcombing. Watch also for great blue heron feeding along the shoreline and for various species of ducks.

Terra Nova was the name given to the farming community established at the northwestern tip of Lulu Island in 1890, when five families from New-foundland settled here. You will know when you have reached Terra Nova, by the presence of some old pilings and bits of wood debris left from the demolition, in 1978, of the old Terra Nova cannery. There were two original canneries here — Terra Nova, built in 1892 and Alliance cannery in 1895 — but they began operating as one in 1902, when B.C. Packers absorbed them. It·was closed in 1928 and became a fish station and net storage shed. If you go ashore in this area, you will see, immediately inside the dike behind the cannery pilings, a house at 2760 River Road, which is typical of the narrow floating houses associated with the Fraser River canneries. The barge sides were probably removed when the house was moved onto land (Parsons).

By now, you will have noticed the tidal marshes seaward of Terra Nova, which are part of one of the largest and most productive areas of marsh in the Fraser Estuary. Cattail, sedge, and bulrush grow out onto Sturgeon Bank in a strip up to one kilometre wide. These marshes provide an abundance of food which attracts a large variety of birdlife; mallard, pintail, gadwall, American widgeon, and green-winged teal are seen close to the dyke; diving ducks such as canvasback and scaup are seen in more open waters; snow geese are seen during their spring and fall migrations; and herons, shorebirds, songbirds and raptors are seen at various times throughout the year.

Sturgeon Bank was named by Capt. George Vancouver on Friday, 22 June 1792 (after his visit with Galiano and Valdez off Point Grey; see Chapter 3),

> "in consequence of our having purchased of the natives some excellent fish of that kind weighing from fourteen to two hundred pounds each."

These were small in comparison to the largest sturgeon caught in the Fraser which was reported to have weighed over 1800 pounds.

To fully appreciate the marsh with its wildlife, cross over to Swishwash Island and glide quietly along its shoreline; it is fascinating and peaceful and on clear days you get a magnificent panoramic view of the Strait of Georgia and the surrounding mountain ranges. Do watch out for the Coast Guard Hovercraft as its base is just north of the island; its normal approach is from the southwest around the western tip of Swishwash.

The current through the Middle Arm is only slightly less than in the North Arm, so time your return trip, especially during freshet, to coincide with a flooding tide which will stem the outflowing current somewhat, making your return to the marina a bit easier.

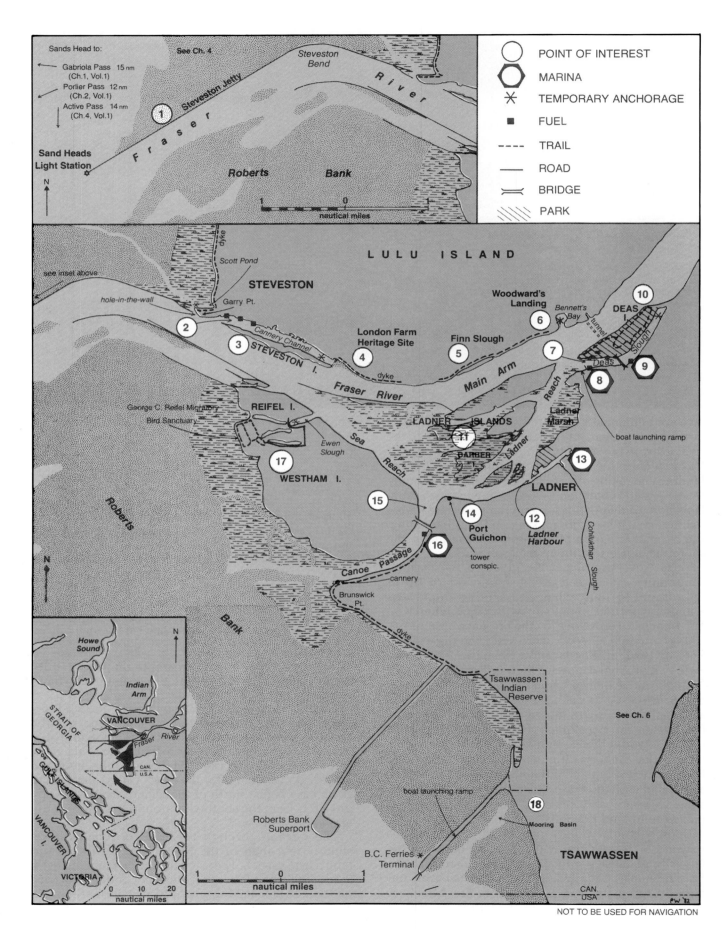

Sands Head to:
→ Gabriola Pass 15 nm
(Ch.1, Vol.1)
Porlier Pass 12 nm
(Ch.2, Vol.1)
↓ Active Pass 14 nm
(Ch.4, Vol.1)

See Ch. 4

Steveston Bend

Fraser River

Steveston Jetty

Sand Heads
Light Station

N

Roberts Bank

nautical miles

POINT OF INTEREST
MARINA
TEMPORARY ANCHORAGE
FUEL
TRAIL
ROAD
BRIDGE
PARK

L U L U   I S L A N D

dyke
Scott Pond
see inset above
hole-in-the-wall
STEVESTON
Garry Pt.
Cannery Channel
STEVESTON I.

Woodward's Landing
Bennett's Bay
DEAS I.
tunnel
Slough

London Farm
Heritage Site
Finn Slough
Deas

Fraser River
Main Arm
Reach

George C. Reifel Migratory
Bird Sanctuary
REIFEL I.
Ewen Slough
WESTHAM I.
Sea Reach
LADNER ISLANDS
BARBER
Ladner Marsh
Ladner
LADNER
boat launching ramp

Roberts
Bank

Port Guichon
tower conspic.
Ladner Harbour
Cohilukthan Slough

Canoe Passage
cannery

Brunswick Pt.
dyke

N

Howe Sound
Indian Arm
STRAIT OF GEORGIA
VANCOUVER
Fraser River
CAN.
U.S.A.
GULF ISLANDS
VANCOUVER I.
VICTORIA
nautical miles

Tsawwassen
Indian
Reserve

See Ch. 6

boat launching ramp
Mooring Basin

Roberts Bank
Superport

B.C. Ferries
Terminal

TSAWWASSEN

CAN
USA

nautical miles

PW '82

80

CHAPTER FIVE

The Fraser River Estuary

(2) THE MAIN ARM
SAND HEADS TO DEAS SLOUGH

by Peggy Ward

On first approaching the Fraser River delta in 1859, Colonel R. C. Moody, of the Royal Engineers, wrote that it was:

> quite impossible to exaggerate the beauty of the country. Extending miles to the right and left are low marshlands (apparently of very rich qualities) and yet from the Background of Superb Mountains — Swiss in outline, dark in woods, grandly towering into the Clouds there is a sublimity that deeply impresses you. Everything is large and magnificent worthy of the entrance to the Queen of England's dominions on the Pacific Mainland. I scarcely ever enjoyed a scene so much in my life.

Today, along with the same magnificent scenery Moody marvelled at, the Main Arm of the Fraser estuary has one of Canada's busiest deepsea ports, fishboat harbours and a variety of facilities for the cruising yachtsman. In addition, large areas of undisturbed marsh still teem with wildlife and provide excellent birdwatching, canoeing, kayaking, fishing, and photography.

Hydrographic Chart 3490 (the new metric chart superseding 3488) covers the Main Arm, but gives soundings only for the main navigational channel. Therefore, the Department of Public Works (DPW) charts which also show soundings for areas outside of the main channel should be obtained. They are updated annually, but they do not give soundings for every reach each year, so when ordering them, specify the area you are interested in, for example: Sea Reach, Ladner Reach, Ladner Harbour, or Deas Slough. They are available only from the Canadian Hydrographic Service (P.O. Box 6000, 9860 West Saanich Road, Sidney, B.C., V8L 4B2, telephone (604) 656-8358).

Detailed information on tides and currents, river depths, winds, waves and hazards in the Fraser estuary is included at the beginning of Chapter 4. Suffice to say here that the yachtsman should time his river trip according to the ebb or flood of the river and should avoid approaching or leaving the estuary when peak outflows are met by strong opposing winds at the river mouth for these conditions result in a very short, steep and dangerous sea. Currents reach their maximum speed of about 6 knots during freshet and spring tides; at other times, the current reaches only about 3 knots on the ebb.

One of the concerns of small craft operators should be the commercial traffic on the Main Arm. The large deepsea ships, with drafts of up to 35 feet, cannot stop quickly, have little manoeuvrability, and in many cases, are restricted to the centre of the relatively narrow channel. Small craft are advised to keep well over to the starboard side of the channel at all times, but especially at dusk or at night, when a small boat is barely visible to the larger vessels.

Something else to watch for is the large number of

CHARTS
3490 — FRASER RIVER — Sand Heads to Douglas Island (1:20,000) Replaces 3488
3480 — ACTIVE PASS to BURRARD INLET (1:50,000) (especially for Canoe Passage)
3450 — EAST POINT to SAND HEADS (1:80,000)
DPW Charts, Sheets 1 to 3: Fraser River (1:12,500)

Hole-in-the-Wall gives access to Scott Pond and Garry Point Channel.

gillnetters in the river (as many as 125 at a time) during the salmon fishery. The season extends from about July 25 to about September 4 and is open again for one week at the beginning of October. Since the fishery has been restricted in recent times to one day a week (usually from 0800 Monday to 0800 Tuesday) it would be worthwhile for the yachtsman to avoid leaving or entering the Main Arm during this time, or go via the North Arm. If you must use the river, note that the end of the gill nets are marked with orange buoys and that, by gentlemen's agreement, the fishermen leave a 12 to 14 foot channel adjacent to the Steveston Jetty for boats to pass through. For specific times of the fishery openings contact the Fisheries and Oceans field office at Steveston, 247-7217 or New Westminster, 524-7181.

The Main Arm

The Main Arm is entered between the buoyed northwestern extremity of Roberts Bank and the Sand Heads Light Station, about 4 nautical miles southwest of Garry Point. It is under the jurisdiction of the Fraser River Harbour Commission.

Watch for herds of sea lions which can be seen at the Sand Heads Light Station during the eulachon run, from about March 15 to about May 30, reaching maximum numbers around the beginning of May; in 1981, 550 were counted at one time. Killer whales have also been seen following the run up the river as far as Steveston.

1   The Steveston Jetty

This is the oldest and largest single river training structure in the Faser estuary, built in stages between 1911 and 1932. At Steveston Bend the channel narrows and during peak outflows currents reach at least 6 knots. In addition, the flow will set across the jetty, drawing with it underpowered vessels. At Garry Point there is an opening in the jetty commonly known as the 'hole-in-the-wall' which was opened by Canadian Fish Ltd. in the 1930s. They also dredged a channel (Garry Point Channel) across Sturgeon Bank which is now used at high water by fishermen and others with small shoal draft boats and local knowledge of the area. This opening also gives access to Scott Pond, a private fishboat harbour, north of Garry Point, where a well-protected temporary anchorage may be found in an emergency; otherwise it makes for a pleasant dinghy trip, in calm or southwesterly weather.

2   Steveston Harbour

This large commercial fishing harbour is entered between Garry Point and the western end of Steveston Island. Its northern shore is lined with hundreds of fishboats and a mixture of old and new wharves and fish processing facilities. Steveston Island on the south of the harbour is undeveloped and a popular, though unofficial, outdoor education and recreation area (see #3). Cannery Channel is dredged to 15 feet at local low water and is protected from the main river channel by Steveston Island and by a rock dam (which is submerged at high water) connecting Lulu Island and the eastern end of Steveston Island. Temporary anchorage is possible in the eastern part of the harbour along the Steveston Island side of the channel on a short scope with a line to a dolphin or ashore if possible, to avoid blocking the channel. From this anchorage, you can visit Steveston Island (see #3), London Farm (see #4), or the town of Steveston.

Facilities of interest to the yachtsman and suitable dinghy landings are situated near the western end of the channel, the rest being occupied by private fishing facilities. The Steveston Chevron Marine gas float, at the foot of Sixth Avenue, 277-4712, is open daily between 0700 and 1700 during the winter and for 24 hours a day from May to September. Their new facilities include temporary overnight berthage for a few boats, electrical plug-ins, showers, washrooms, laundromat, water, ice, fishing supplies and facilities for oil changes and pumping out holding tanks. Just upstream of the Chevron float is the Gulf barge, at the foot of Third Avenue, 277-7744, which sells fuel to pleasure boats only between 0800 and 0900 daily. Further upstream is the Esso barge, at the foot of First Avenue, 277-7626, which is open from 0800 to 1700

daily and has showers, toilets and oil change facilities.

If you feel like going ashore to look around Steveston and are looking for an overnight berth, you might be able to arrange with the harbour manager to stay at a temporarily unoccupied float in the large government fishing vessel marina, adjacent to the Gulf barge. Whether you stay here or not, if you visit their floats on a weekend morning you can buy fresh seafood right from the fishboats. Salmon is available from the end of July to the beginning of September; crab is best in summer and fall, beginning in the middle of June; tuna is sometimes available; and shrimp and bottom fish are usually available all year round.

The simultaneous development of Cannery Channel as fishing and canning centre, and of the town of Steveston as a commercial center dates back to the 1880s. Between 1882 and 1897, fourteen canneries were built along Cannery Channel, while other small canneries were built along the various other reaches of the Fraser. Fierce competition between the many small independent firms resulted in mergers and the eventual formation, in 1902, of B.C. Packers Ltd. This

Steveston Harbour, protected from the main river channel by Steveston Island.

company absorbed 22 smaller firms and from then on concentrated their efforts at Steveston, thus enhancing the area's importance as a canning center. (Marlene Parsons, *Fraser River Estuary Heritage Resource Inventory*, Heritage Conservation Branch, Province of B.C., April 1981)

The town of Steveston was founded around 1880 by a New Brunswick farmer, Manoah Steves, and grew quickly, serving the local farmers, fishermen and cannery workers. By 1906, 10,000 people lived here; there was a large Chinatown and even an opera house!

In 1918, however, most of the town burned down, leaving homeless over 600 Chinese and Japanese families. This fire, as well as several others, destroyed most of the original structures in Cannery Row, and although several canneries remain, all but one is used for other purposes such as net and gear storage. The one remaining operating cannery on the Fraser, the Imperial Cannery (built in 1893), is located just upstream of No. 1 Road and is considered to be one of the largest fish processing plants in the British Commonwealth. The old white and red building — formerly the Gulf of Georgia Cannery — behind the government fishboat marina at the foot of Third Avenue is owned by the federal government. There are plans to develop it as a National Historic Park with a public interpretive centre dealing with the Fraser's fishing and canning industries. If all goes well, it should open in 1986-87.

In addition to exploring Cannery Channel, go ashore and take a stroll along Moncton Street, the main street of the original town. It has restaurants, a hotel pub, a museum and one of the most popular chandleries in the lower mainland at the corner of Second and Moncton — the Steveston Marine and Hardware Store.

3   Steveston (Shady) Island

This 1½ mile long, undeveloped, undyked island is a popular outdoor education and recreation area because of the variety of its plant and animal life and its sandy beaches. In the late 1800s Steveston Island was only a small sand bar, however, its natural evolution was accelerated by building a rock groyne down part of it, dumping dredged river sand onto it, and by

The unique lifestyle of Finn Slough is reflected in its own waters.

building two wing dams out from its southern shoreline to prevent the sand from being washed back out into the main channel.

The educational attraction of Steveston Island lies in the fact that the natural process of "plant succession" is so well demonstrated. There are over 100 plant species here, representing the development of vegetation over time; they include sand dune and marsh plants, herbs, shrubs, and floodplain forest. Over sixty bird species are present; look for waterfowl, shorebirds, songbirds, raptors and pheasants. A booklet entitled *Shady Island: A Natural History* by Don Watmough is available from the Richmond Nature Park and is recommended to all those who wish to explore the island.

Access to the island is normally by boat, although some people do walk across the rock dam at the eastern end of the island at low water.

4   London Farm Historic Site

The London Farmhouse, just inside the dyke and west of Gilbert Road, was built in 1898 and is being restored by the Richmond Historical and Museum Society. It is well worth a visit. Although the river is deep along the shoreline east of Gilbert Road, the current is very strong there, so a preferable anchorage would be in Cannery Channel. Access to the farm would then be by dinghy to the eastern end of the channel and then by foot along the dyke for a few hundred feet; or at high water you could take the dinghy over the southern portion of the rock dam where there is a bit of a depression and go ashore at the unpaved small boat launching ramp which is just upstream.

Lulu Island's first farm and dykes were built here in 1865. In the 1880s, the London brothers acquired the land between No. 2 Road and Gilbert Road and built a cannery and steamer landing at the western end of their property. In 1886, London's Landing became one of the main stopping places for steamers en route from Victoria to New Westminster; it was also the terminus for the ferry to Ladner's Landing until 1913, when the Lulu Island terminus moved to Woodward's landing (#6). At present (spring 1982), the restored farmhouse and picnic area are only open on Sundays, 1:00 p.m. - 4:00 p.m. with free guided tours available. The society hopes to open on a full-time basis by the summer of 1982, when a small admission charge will be made. Plans for this heritage farm and park include a barn with small animals and farm machinery, a chicken coop and a restaurant. Further in the future, the society envisages a heritage village at this site.

5   Finn Slough

Further upstream is another area of historical interest. Finn Slough, (Gilmour Slough on the charts) separates Gilmour and Lulu Islands and was settled in 1890 by Finnish fishermen and cannery workers. Their wooden houses were built on pilings or floats and some are still intact and occupied. The fishermen

Deas Slough provides the yachtsman with two marinas, protected anchorage, and easy access to Deas Island Regional Park.

moor their boats at their front doors, even though the slough is gradually silting up. Passage into the slough is possible only at high water, while at low water the boats are left high and dry, leaning against the floats or pilings.

6　Woodward's Landing

Woodward's Landing, at the foot of No. 5 Road, was settled in 1874 by the Woodward family, builders of fishing skiffs. In 1894, the landing became a stopover point for people travelling up river and in 1913 ferry service began between here and Ladner's Landing (which was then located in Ladner Harbour). This major connection between Delta and Richmond continued till 1959 when the Deas Island Tunnel was built. A few of the old wharf pilings remain on the foreshore.

Just upstream is the large B.C. Ferries vessel maintenance and storage basin (sometimes known as Bennett's Bay). It has ample water and the western shore could probably be used for temporary anchorage if someone were in the boat at all times in order to move on short notice.

7　Deas Slough

Deas Slough is entered between the starboard hand light beacon and the western tip of Deas Island. The pilings and unused ferry wharf at the entrance are the remnants of Ladner's Landing which was used from 1933 until the Deas Island Tunnel opened in 1959. Immediately downstream of the ferry wharf is a free, concrete boat launching ramp with space for parking a couple of dozen cars and trailers. There are two marinas on the south side of the slough (see #8 and #9) and Deas Island Regional Park (see #10) on the north side. A fixed freeway bridge with a minimum clearance of 8 feet restricts access to the eastern part although boats requiring up to 20 feet have been known to go through at low water.

The channel upstream of Deas Harbour Marina is not surveyed regularly; nevertheless, there is probably good depth right up to the head of the slough because this was the route used by smaller craft travelling up river before the upstream end of the channel was filled in, prior to construction of the Deas Island Tunnel, in the 1950s. A well protected temporary anchorage is possible near the head of the slough or alongside a log boom. There will be additional space for anchoring once the log booms, pilings and deadheads are removed from the northern shore after the booming lease expires on July 1, 1982.

If you can't fit under the bridge, a trip by dinghy up the slough is worthwhile — tall cottonwoods along the banks are good habitat for raptors and songbirds, and the slough itself attracts many species of waterfowl. Access to the park is at the head of the slough.

8　Captain's Cove Marina

Captain's Cove Marina, 6100 Ferry Road, Delta, V4K 3M9, 946-1244, lies downstream of the bridge.

The head of Deas Slough welcomes boaters with a gentle sloping beach and a mountain backdrop. (photo: Bill Ward).

Opposite: the Ladner Harbour Yacht Club occupies the uppermost basin in Ladner Harbour.

They have visitor's moorage for boats up to 30 feet, but for larger boats, prior arrangements should be made. Facilities include showers, washrooms, restaurant, land storage and a small chandlery. They have a travellift for up to 30 tons and a Chevron gas float which operates between 0830 - 1700 Monday - Friday, 0900 - 1700 Saturday and Sunday in winter and in the summer daily from 0800 - 1800.

9   Deas Harbour Marina

Deas Harbour Marina, 5825 Sixtieth Avenue, Delta, V4K 4E2, 946-1251, is used mainly by power boats because of the bridge. This attractive and well kept marina has visitors' berths for boats up to 38 feet, washrooms, a well stocked chandlery, charts, full service facilities, haulout facilities for up to 32 feet and land storage. The Chevron gas float (no diesel) at the western end of the floats is open daily from 0800 - 2000 April to November and from 0800 - 1600 the rest of the time. A waterfront pub (the first of its kind, on the Fraser), a restaurant, showers and a laundromat are scheduled to open by mid-summer, 1982.

10   Deas Island Regional Park

Deas Island was named after John Sullivan Deas, one of the founders of the B.C. canning industry. He was a tinsmith from the United States, who preempted the island in 1873 and established a very successful, though short-lived, canning operation there, producing twice as much as anyone else on the Fraser during the first few years. For the first half of this century Deas Island was home to several Greek gillnet fishermen and their families who built shacks along the banks of the island; and upland, a dairy farm was operated by Frank Fisher from 1919 to the 1940s.

No buildings remain of this period but you do get a sense of the island's past from its large open meadows ringed with tall cottonwood trees.

The island is now a Regional Park. Boat access is at the head of Deas Slough where there is a cleared sloping sandy beach for pulling out or hand launching small boats. Behind this beach is the park's information kiosk where a map of the island's dyke trails is displayed — the blackberries along the dykes are excellent during September. (A copy of this map is available by phoning Greater Vancouver Regional District Parks at 731-1155, local 132). There are picnic tables and outhouses near the information kiosk and also near the center of the island in one of Fisher's large open fields. The two sandy beaches on the river side of the island near the western end are popular picnicking and bar fishing spots and are accessible by boat. Plans for the park include a fishing pier on the river side of the island and an area for organized group camping.

11   Ladner Marsh and Islands

This 1500-acre marsh is very important for fish and wildlife. The trees and shrubs in the higher, drier areas, provide food (berries and seeds) and shelter for raptors, upland game birds, nesting songbirds and furbearers, while the seeds and foliage of the many marsh plants provide food and shelter for waterfowl and other birds, invertebrates (which are food for young salmon) and fish.

The picturesque and secluded channels through the marsh are excellent for shoal draft boating and offer good access for observing or photographing spring and summer marsh flowers as well as the large variety of birdlife. While gliding through this area, seeing and hearing nothing but natural sights and sounds, it is hard to believe that you are so close to the third largest urban area in Canada.

Canoe Passage provides a shortcut across Roberts Bank for those with local knowledge.

Ladner Marsh is owned by the federal and provincial governments and is operated as a wildlife management area. The Ladner Islands are reserved by an Order-in-Council to the B.C. Fish and Wildlife Branch, except for the four northeastern islands which are dyked, privately owned and farmed for private waterfowl hunting. In fact, hunting during the fall and winter is allowed throughout the whole marsh area, so caution should be exercised by pleasure boaters during this time.

The 'islands' are mainly below the high water and freshet river levels so if you plan to go ashore at lower water levels, rubber boats are a must. It is not the place for long walks through the grass, especially because the fragile marsh vegetation could be trampled, destroying valuable wildlife habitat.

The main (and deeper) route through the marsh is via Ladner and Sea reaches and leads to Ladner Harbour (#12), Port Guichon (#14) and Canoe Passage (#15). Ladner Reach, with a minimum depth of about 8 feet extends from Deas Slough to Canoe Passage. If you don't know the area and want to take this route in anything other than a shoal draft boat, use the DPW charts, as the main channel is not obvious from the hydrographic chart; it passes between Barber Island and the two smaller islands to the southeast (when approaching from the north there is a conspicuous red structure on the mainland to the southwest that will help you identify the correct channel to take). Sea Reach, with least depths of about 12 feet, extends from Reifel Island to Canoe Passage.

12   Ladner Harbour

Ladner Harbour, dredged to about 8 feet, is entered from the west, close to the mainland shoreline. It is mainly a fishboat harbour, although it also has the highest concentration of houseboats in the mainstem of the Fraser River. At the entrance to the harbour, at the southwestern tip of Ladner Marsh, there is Ladner Harbour Park, run by the municipality of Delta, with trails, picnic facilities and toilets. A commercial fishboat marina on the northern side of the harbour is opposite a private yacht marina for the residents of the adjacent apartment building. Both these modern facilities are, unfortunately, closed to visiting yachts. At the extreme head of the harbour is the Ladner Yacht Club (#13), 5011 River Road, Delta, 946-4056, which was the first marina to be built in Delta, in 1958. It is a private club, with a live-in caretaker, but they will accommodate a few overnight visitors with boats having as much as 7 foot draft. There are no facilities other than water and electrical plug-ins, but Ladner village is only a short walk away, with all the necessary amenities including a chandlery and a neighborhood pub.

Ladner's Landing was the name of the original farming community which grew up along the banks of the harbour in the 1870s. It was named after the Ladner brothers who first settled in the area in 1868. A government wharf was built at the mouth of the Cohilukthan Slough in 1873 and was the first stop for steamers from Victoria en route to New Westminster. Ferry service began in the 1880s between here and Richmond (first to London's Landing and then to Woodward's Landing in 1913) continuing until 1933, when Ladner's Landing was moved to the northern end of Ferry Road (west of Captain's Cove Marina).

As in Steveston, numerous canneries were built along the Ladner waterfront in the 1880s and 1890s. The earliest, that of the Delta Canning Company, built in 1878, was located on the eastern bank at the entrance to Cohilukthan Slough, where the old pilings on which the cannery stood are still visible as you travel up the channel to the yacht club. The fishing community which developed along the dyke built small narrow wooden houses on pilings or floats in the river (some of the abandoned ones can be seen on the northern side of the harbour). Most of these scow houses were later moved onto the dykes where commercial fishermen still live in them or use them for net storage.

14   Port Guichon

Further downstream, Port Guichon developed independently from Ladner, although there is little distinction now. The town was named after a pioneer farmer, Laurent Guichon, who settled here in 1881 and later built a hotel and landing to serve the local fishing and farming communities and "tap some of the river traffic". The town became (1903 - 1931) an

important railway terminus, connecting the mainland with Sidney on Vancouver Island.

15 Canoe Passage

Favour the Westham Island shoreline when entering Canoe Passage because of the shallows on the Port Guichon side. The swing bridge, built in 1909, will open on demand — use three short horn or whistle blasts or contact the bridge keeper by VHF channel 74 or at 946-2121. There is someone on duty 24 hours a day. Once through the bridge keep to the mainland side of the channel.

Passage across Roberts Bank from Canoe Passage is officially discouraged for anyone without good local knowledge. Consequently, there are no DPW sounding charts published of Canoe Passage. The tidal flats are nearly 4 miles wide here and the channel very shallow and winding. However, the channel is marked by privately installed dolphins and is shown on the recent hydrographic chart 3480, Active Pass to Burrard Inlet. If you are not familiar with the channel it would be best to follow someone with local knowledge or at least try it at mid-tide or better and on a rising tide.

16 Wes-Del Marina

Wes-Del Marina, 3473 River Road West, Delta, V4K 3N2, 946-4544, has a few visitors' berths for

Wes-Del Marina occupies the strategic site at the entrance to Canoe Passage.

boats up to 35 feet. Facilities include water, electicity, toilets and gas and diesel — open 0800 - 1700, Monday to Friday and 0800 - 1200 Saturday, closed Sundays. The marina also has an outboard shop, engine repairs and an aluminum boat building shop.

If you stay at the marina you have several options for side-trips: there is good access from here to the Ladner islands (see #11), to the Reifel Refuge (see #17) and to the marsh sloughs at Brunswick Point which offer good canoeing or kayaking. At Brunswick Point one of the earlier canneries in the Fraser estuary still stands. Some of the cannery workers' residences are still occupied although the actual cannery building is used for net storage. If you do visit Brunswick Point in a boat without a good motor, time your trip to take advantage of slack water or a flooding tide; the current can be substantial through here during freshet or spring tides. In addition, since you are right at the mouth of the river, any sudden squall or storm can quickly produce a choppy and dangerous sea, especially with a west or northwest wind.

17 Westham Island

Westham Island, first settled by farmers in the 1870s and later by cannery workers in the 1890s, is still mainly agricultural. The ubiquitous Harry Trim

The broad expanse of estuarine reaches offer protected sailing outside the main channels (photo: GVRD Parks)

Below, feathered visitors to Reifel Refuge attract sightseers year 'round.

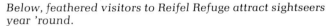

is said to have been the first farmer here, after earlier adventures on Texada Island and at Jericho (Ch. 3). The northern portion of the island together with Reifel Island are owned by the federal government through the Canadian Wildlife Service. Part of its holdings are leased to the British Columbia Waterfowl Society which operates the public area within the George C. Reifel Migratory Bird Sanctuary — better known as the Reifel Refuge. This is one of the most popular birdwatching areas in the lower mainland with trails, bird viewing towers, a nature interpretation house, washrooms and picnic area. The best time to visit the 'refuge' is between October and March when the migratory birds are wintering here. Over 230 bird species have been identified, including several rare species; the shy and beautifully coloured wood duck is rarely seen outside of the 'refuge'.

Access by boat is awkward because of the extensive tidal marsh and flats to the west of the island, so the closest you can get is to anchor temporarily in Ewen Slough at mid-tide or better. There are extensive shallows at the mouth of the slough but there is good depth inside and enough room for two or three shallow draft boats to swing. From the head of the slough (which is under lease to the Canadian Wildlife Service) walk south along the road to the sign indicating the entrance to the sanctuary and turn right. It is about a mile from the head of the slough to the ticket booth.

18 Tsawwassen Yacht Club

The only pleasure boating facility on the seaward edge of the delta is south of the B.C. Ferries Terminal. The Tsawwassen Yacht Club, P.O. Box 1028, Postal Station 'A', Delta, B.C., V4M 3T2, 943-7215 or 946-6765, is a private club with swinging moorings for its members and members of other clubs with reciprocal privileges. There is a club house, showers, toilets, kitchen, dinghy storage area and a summer (tidal) dock. The channel to the mooring basin has privately maintained markings, a least depth of 8 feet and at its narrowest is 50 to 75 feet wide.

The main caution necessary when entering this channel is to give approaching or departing ferries a wide berth. Access to the mooring channel is normally to the east of the small breakwater southeast of the ferry docks, although if there is no ferry in the vicinity you can go between the breakwater and the ferry causeway (the breakwater does give some protection from a southeaster).

The sandy south side of the ferry causeway is a popular swimming beach and is increasingly used for overnight camping, although this is officially discouraged. Birdwatching is also good here as is salmon and cutthroat trout fishing. Between May and July crabs can be caught by hand at low water, although they can be caught by boat all year round. There is a concrete boat launching ramp about halfway along the causeway on the south side, which can be used on a 5 foot or high tide, and at no charge.

For those who like to go ashore, a more detailed guide to the attractions of the estuary is the book *Explore the Fraser Estuary!* published by Environment Canada in 1980.

Ewen Slough, the closest anchorage for seaborne visitors to the bird sanctuary.

The long causeway to the ferry docks forms partial breakwater for Tsawwassen Yacht Club's mooring basin and channel.

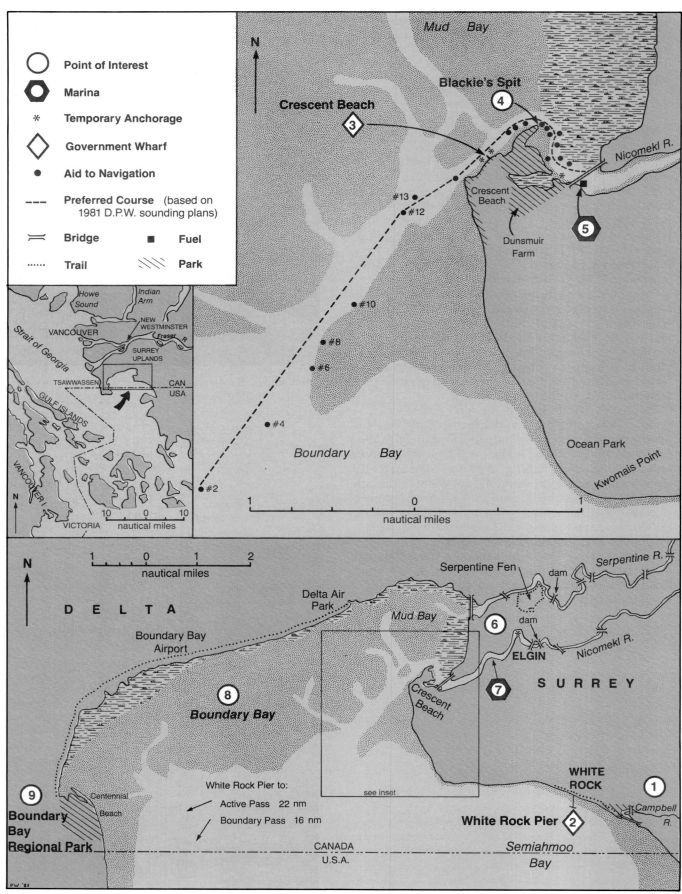

Point of Interest

⬡ **Marina**

✳ **Temporary Anchorage**

◇ **Government Wharf**

● **Aid to Navigation**

--- **Preferred Course** (based on 1981 D.P.W. sounding plans)

⫟ **Bridge**   ■ **Fuel**

...... **Trail**   ⫽⫽⫽ **Park**

N

Mud Bay

Blackie's Spit

④

Crescent Beach

③

Nicomekl R.

Crescent Beach

Dunsmuir Farm

⑤

#13 ●

#12 ●

#10 ●

#8 ●

#6 ●

#4 ●

#2 ●

Boundary Bay

Ocean Park

Kwomais Point

1
0
1
nautical miles

Howe Sound

Indian Arm

NEW WESTMINSTER

Fraser R.

VANCOUVER

SURREY UPLANDS

Strait of Georgia

TSAWWASSEN

CAN
USA

GULF ISLANDS

VANCOUVER I.

N

VICTORIA

10
0
10
nautical miles

N

1
0
1
2
nautical miles

D E L T A

Delta Air Park

Mud Bay

Serpentine Fen

Serpentine R.

dam

⑥

dam

Boundary Bay Airport

Nicomekl R.

✳

ELGIN

⑦

S U R R E Y

⑧

Boundary Bay

Crescent Beach

see inset

WHITE ROCK

①

White Rock Pier to:

← Active Pass   22 nm

↙ Boundary Pass   16 nm

White Rock Pier ◇ ②

Campbell R.

⑨

Boundary Bay Regional Park

Centennial Beach

CANADA
U.S.A.

Semiahmoo Bay

PW '83

CHAPTER SIX

Boundary Bay

White Rock, Crescent Beach

by Peggy Ward

If you were sailing in these waters a mere 8,000 years ago, just after the last ice age, you would have been able to travel north from Crescent Beach for about 12 miles before you hit land again — near New Westminster. Boundary Bay did not exist — there was just a wide open stretch of water between the higher land northeast of Mud Bay (Surrey uplands) and Tsawwassen (which was then an island, about 18 miles southwest of New Westminster). Since that time, large quantities (between 300 and 700 feet deep) of river-borne sand, silt and clay have filled in this gap and formed Boundary Bay. Boundary is therefore part of the Fraser estuary even though it is no longer being built up by it.

The Spaniards were the initial explorers to visit Boundary and Semiahmoo bays in 1791 and 1792. The first, Narvaez, probably only reached Kwomais Point at Ocean Park, since he left his map blank between here and Tsawwassen. The late Major Matthews, a well-known former Vancouver City Archivist, speculated that Narvaez may have gone further north, crossing the delta and reaching the Fraser — by boat! This would have been possible because during spring freshet and at the time of extreme high tides, much of the delta would normally be inundated if it were not for the extensive system of dykes. The following year, Galiano and Valdez explored the whole of Boundary Bay, but their disappointment at not finding a major waterway to the east seems to be reflected in the name they gave to the bay on their map — Ensenada del Engano — Deception (or False) Creek. The next Europeans in the area were Hudson's Bay Company employees, John Work and James McMillan, who were looking for a place to build a fort on the Fraser. In December 1824, they travelled north from the Columbia River overland to Puget Sound and then via Semiahmoo and Mud bays to the mouth of the Nicomekl. They proceeded up the river with some difficulty owing to the large amount of driftwood choking the channels, and then portaged to the Salmon River, which took them to the Fraser, near where they later (in 1827) built Fort Langley.

Boundary and Semiahmoo bays are more used by shoal draft boats and multi-hulls because of the shallow channels and extensive sand and mud flats. There is little commercial traffic so boating facilities are mainly recreational; there is a good size marina at Crescent Beach (see #5) and another small shallow one up the Nicomekl River (see #7); at the White Rock Pier (see #2) there are floats for transient moorage, Customs clearance and the White Rock Sailing Club.

Winds, Tides and Currents

Prevailing winds in Boundary Bay are mainly from the southeast and east (blowing over 50% of the time). Unlike the rest of the lower mainland, westerly winds are relatively unusual with onshore winds blowing most frequently from the south on summer afternoons.

CHART:
3450 — EAST POINT to SAND HEADS
(1:80,000)

Semiahmoo Bay shoreline, showing the White Rock pier, the mouth of Little Campbell River, and at the top, the Peace Arch.

which comes in very quickly because of the gentle slope of the flats. People have been stranded, sometimes with tragic consequences, on sand bars which are suddenly converted to tiny islands hundreds of yards from shore by the flooding tide.

1   Campbell River

Campbell River, also known as the Little Campbell River in order to distinguish it from the larger river on Vancouver Island, is a very shallow waterway, the mouth of which meanders through the Semiahmoo Indian Reserve. The area of the Reserve has been a permanent Indian settlement since before Europeans arrived. The river provides a quiet and protected respite from the open waters of Semiahmoo Bay and is navigable near high water by canoe, kayak and rowboat to about 200 yards upstream of the foot bridge. The access channel across the tidal flats can only be used above mid-tide and preferably on a rising tide.

At the entrance to the river, there are remnant pilings of the old Campbell River Sawmill which operated from 1913 to 1927. The mill company ran a large operation, employing several hundred men, until the local timber resources were depleted in the 1920's. On the west bank of the river mouth is a municipally operated park with playing field, washrooms, playground and tennis court.

As you pass under the foot bridge, nearly ½ mile upstream from the mouth, you are passing the junction of three historically important roads as well as the site of the base camp of the Boundary Survey Commission of 1857. The foot bridge is the beginning of the 1¾ mile beach trail that the surveyors built between their base camp and the border. The Semiahmoo Indian Trail led from here to the natives' summer fishing camps on the Nicomekl and then on to the Fraser River near the present site of the Patullo Bridge. In 1861, the government of the new colony of British Columbia widened this trail and encouraged its use as the main wagon road connecting the USA and the colonial capital at New Westinster, in order to control entry into the colony. The third road was built in 1858 eastward to Langley (Parsons, 1981).

Campbell River offers good sport fishing for coho, chum, steelhead and cutthroat trout and although it is the only river in the lower mainland with a chinook run, fishing here for that species is prohibited. At the mouth of the river, about a foot under the surface of the sand is found a burrowing species of shrimp which are dug up and used as bait by steelhead fishermen. The tree-lined lower reaches of the river are also good for seeing herons, raptors and waterfowl.

2   White Rock Pier

This 1500 foot long pier was originally built in 1914 to give foreign vessels access to the Customs facilities at White Rock which had been established as a Port of Entry for railroad traffic when the Great Northern

Both White Rock and Crescent Beach are Secondary Ports relative to Point Atkinson in the Tide and Current Tables; there is little difference between the time of the tide change but there is not as great a tidal range in the bays. Few studies have been done on water movement in Boundary Bay but those with local knowledge of the area estimate that under extreme conditions (large ebb tides in summer) currents can reach at least two knots in the tidal flat channels. Your best guide is to be aware that when the adjacent banks are dry, ebbing waters are confined to a relatively narrow channel, thereby increasing the current velocity. Current velocities are slightly less on the flood, decreasing as the water level rises and floods over the banks. The flooding tide is more concentrated on the eastern side of Boundary Bay and the ebb is more concentrated on the western side.

A hazard for the rower or the canoeist is the possibility of being blown out into the bay by a strong offshore wind although offshore winds are unusual, except in winter. For those who choose to walk out on the flats, it is advisable to watch for the flooding tide

Railway was built through here in 1909. The pier was renovated in the 1970s and now has two floats at its southern end behind a breakwater. The western float is used by the White Rock Sailing Club and commercial fishing vessels; the eastern float is reserved for transient moorage on its south side (between the breakwater and the float) and for fishing on its north side. There is little space for manoeuvring shoreward of the breakwater as it begins shoaling fairly close to the floats. If there is no space left at the transient float, contact the wharfinger (531-9766), living aboard at the western float, who may be able to arrange for an overnight tie-up. White Rock is still a Port of Entry — a phone call to 536-7671 will bring a Customs Officer to the wharf.

About ½ mile west of the pier there is a level railroad crossing which facilitates hand launching of small boats — leave your vehicle inland of the tracks, though, because many people get stuck in the soft sand.

On the beach 200 yards east of the pier is a large granite boulder (whitewashed in recent years, but now unfortunately covered by grafitti) after which the city was named. It was probably deposited by a glacier thousands of years ago, but the local Indian legend explaining its location is much more appealing:

A young Indian brave, in search of a new home for himself and his bride, threw this rock vowing that where it landed he would make his home. It landed on the beach in White Rock and this area became the permanent settlement for his descendants, the Semiahmoo Indian Band. (Parsons, 1981)

White Rock was established as a summer resort in the 1890s and still offers a seaside atmosphere with its fish and chip restaurants, museum, waterfront promenade and large sandy swimming beach. Two special events may be of interest to your crew. The well known Sand Castle Building Contest is held on the August Sunday with the lowest tides and begins 2 hours before low water, ending 2 hours after. The Sea Festival is held throughout the Dominion Day weekend and features a grand ball, pier exhibits, bandshell entertainment, sand castle building days for children, an adults and children's parade, fishing derby and chess tournament.

For the fisherman, there is smelt (fishery closed July 5-Aug 5) and cutthroat trout fishing in addition to crabbing which is popular here and in other parts of Boundary Bay. Crabs are found in the lower quarter of the intertidal zone and out to a low tide depth of about 10 feet. Sometimes they can be taken from tidal pools where they have been stranded by a falling tide, or they can be taken in traps all year long.

While en route to Crescent Beach, you will pass the Ocean Park foreshore which is the major crab fishing area in Boundary Bay; it also attracts various ducks,

There is little room for manoeuvring once inside the breakwater protecting the White Rock pier.

Well-marked channel around Blackie's Spit leads to Crescent Beach Marina at the mouth of the Nicomekl River.

geese and shorebirds and is one of the few places to see the spectacularly coloured harlequin duck. The name Ocean Park dates from 1910 when the area was chosen by the Ocean Park Syndicate — a group of prominent lower mainland Methodists — for recreational and educational purposes; a church camp was founded here.

3   Crescent Beach

The Hydrographic Chart which includes Boundary Bay, No. 3450, is quite small scale and not only lacks detail, but may not show any recent changes in the approach channel to Crescent Beach. The channel seaward of the Government Wharf is the worst bit; very little dredging is carried out here and there are a lot of groundings on shoal patches located between the markers. Daymarkers #2, 12 and 13 form a suitable lead-in range to help you avoid going aground in the area of #6, 8 and 10 markers. After passing #12, head for the numbered marker close to the point at Crescent Beach; the channel between these markers had a least depth of only 4 feet when surveyed by DPW in 1981. Once upstream of this daymarker you shouldn't have any trouble if you follow the aids to navigation.

Temporary moorage is possible for 2-3 boats at the Government Wharf which has 9 feet at low water. If the wharf is full, temporary anchorage is possible both upstream and downstream, on the south side of the channel. There are a few small stores and seasonal restaurants nearby. From here you can take a trip around to Blackie's Spit (see #4) or continue up the Nicomekl or Serpentine Rivers (see #6) or you can stretch your legs ashore and explore Crescent Beach. This is a popular swimming beach and municipal park, extending along the shore for nearly 1¼ miles.

Crescent Beach is important from an archeological point of view which the Municipality of Surrey hopes to highlight in the development of their planned interpretive center at Dunsmuir Farm (see #4). The Indians used this area as summer campgrounds as far back as 5,000 to 8,000 years ago. Much more recently, in the mid 1800s, a small settlement developed there as a base for fishing the Serpentine and Nicomekl Rivers, for crab trappers and oyster farmers, and soon became a popular resort area for campers and hunters as well. It began to boom when the railway came through here in 1909 and by 1914 it had a pier, hotel, 2 churches, a school and a shingle mill which provided much of the local employment. When logging declined in the 1920s, so did the population of Crescent Beach.

Today it is again a popular summer resort area and the surrounding waters are still good for fishing. The burrowing ghost shrimp is also found here in the flats off the southern part of Crescent Beach and cutthroat trout, crab, smelt and salmon are caught from small boats, from shore, and from the Government Wharf.

4   Blackie's Spit

The Blackie's Spit/Dunsmuir Farm area is being developed by Surrey as a 'nature park in harmony with its estuary environment'. The park will also allow for beach activities at the sandy spit and a nature/history learning center at the farm property.

Shoal draft boats can be beached almost anywhere around the spit, and temporary anchorage for deeper draft boats is possible on the south shore of the channel downstream of the railway trestle over the Nicomekl, just east of the marsh behind the spit. Because the channel is narrow, it would be best to put out two anchors or put an additional line around one of the dolphins. The marsh is a good place to spend a quiet evening after a day's boating listening to the birds and watching the sunset. During the day, watch for the harbour seals at the edge of the channels in Mud Bay and see the numerous ducks, geese and herons feeding or resting on the foreshore.

North of the marsh is a small dyked area on which the Crescent Oyster Company's shucking shacks, docking facilities and manager's residence were once located. Only a few pilings remain. Oyster farming began here in 1904 and continued until the late 1950s when B.C. Packers bought the business and moved operations to their facility across Mud Bay (Parsons, 1981). In 1960, shellfish harvesting was closed in Boundary Bay due to coliform bacterial pollution. Prior to this, Boundary Bay was the single most productive oyster bed in B.C., producing over 50% of all oysters cultured in the province. In Mud Bay and around the mouth of the Nicomekl there remains a population of Atlantic oysters, unique to the B.C. coast, which were imported by the Crescent Oyster Company.

At the entrance to Blackie's Spit is the Surrey Sailing Club, mailing address — 1758 127 A Street, Surrey, V4A 3S4, tel. 536-7894. This dinghy racing club has a dinghy compound, clubhouse and a gravel launching ramp which the public is welcome to use. They offer sailing lessons and have a mobile board sailing school in July.

5   Crescent Beach Marina

Access to the marina is via the northeastern draw of the railway swing bridge, which has an estimated

Below, Crescent Beach government wharf.

Boundary Bay is one of the most biologically productive sites on the coast.

clearance of about 9 feet on an average high tide. To have the bridge opened for you, call the marina at least one hour ahead of the required opening time and before 1530 hours.

Crescent Beach Marina, 12555 Crescent Road, Surrey, B.C., V4A 2V4, tel. 531-7551, is one of the larger marinas in the lower mainland. It has a Chevron gas float which is open seven days a week — summer hours are 0600 - 2000, Friday - Sunday and 0700 - 1900, Monday to Thursday; winter hours are 0900 - 1700. It can usually accommodate one or two visiting boats up to 30 feet and a 4 foot draft but it would be best to make prior arrangements if possible; smaller boats can be accommodated with no problem. Other faciities include a store, washrooms, chandlery and charts, repairs, haulout facilities to 32 feet and a public lanching ramp. The Crescent Beach Yacht Club, 531-7669, leases space from the marina and is open on Saturdays and Sundays. They have a clubhouse and, in addition to various social functions, they participate in international sailboat racing. Reciprocal privileges with other yacht clubs are in the process of being arranged and they have recently succeeded in obtaining approval for telephone Customs clearance from the marina.

Shoreside property at Ward's Marina up the Nicomekl is used mainly for private boat construction.

6 Nicomekl-Serpentine Lowlands

The shallow and winding Serpentine and Nicomekl rivers are accessible to canoes, kayaks, and rowboats for about 3 miles upstream from Mud Bay to the floodgates at the King George Highway. By portaging the floodgates, it is possible to reach the town of Langley, several miles upstream on the Nicomekl. There is good fishing for coho, dolly varden, steelhead and cutthroat trout and good bird watching at the Serpentine Fen which is one of only two bird sanctuaries in the estuary. Located on the south bank of the Serpentine River between the freeway bridge and the dam at the King George Highway, it is run by the B.C. Fish and Wildlife Branch. The trail through the fen is open to the public between 0800-1800 hours. Watch for ducks, geese, shorebirds, songbirds, raptors and grebes.

There is a small and shallow marina about 1½ miles up the Nicomekl — Ward's Marina, 531-4680 which is used mainly for private boat construction. The Victorian style house adjacent to the marina was built about 1890 and is probably the oldest remaining structure in this area.

Temporary anchorage is possible upstream of the marina at the bend in the river, adjacent to the golf course (take your clubs ashore for a round of golf — it is open to the public). The river is unnaturally deep here because sand was 'borrowed' from it during the construction of the freeway. Access to the area is best at or near high water and by keeping to the middle of the channel. There is a posted speed limit of 4 knots.

Once an embayment of the sea, the surrounding lowlands are one of Surrey's most important agricultural areas. They were first farmed and settled in the 1860s and 1870s and some of the early farmhouses dating from the 1890s can still be seen near Mud Bay between the two rivers.

The town of Elgin developed on the south bank of the Nicomekl River downstream of the King George Highway to provide services for these farmers and for the loggers from nearby camps — the uplands south of the Nicomekl were extensively logged in the late 1800s. But what really gave the town impetus for development was its location on the Semiahmoo Trail (see #1). In 1886, Elgin became the Customs Port of Entry for road and river traffic pre-dating the White Rock Customs facility by 23 years. By the turn of the century it had all the necessary services such as a hotel, store, community hall, school, Post Office, wharf and Customs house.

7 Boundary Bay

Although Boundary Bay may seem flat and uninteresting to the untrained eye, it is actually teeming with life and is one of the most biologically productive areas in western Canada. Water access to Boundary Bay is limited to shoal draft boats but it makes a fascinating trip especially for those with an interest in ecology. Care should be taken however, to avoid

A quiet and deep anchorage on the Nicomekl.

being stranded on the flats by a falling tide. If you plan to make a day of it and take a picnic lunch, you can go ashore anywhere — there is a 12 mile stretch of public dyke paralleling the shore from Mud Bay west to the park at Centennial Beach (see #9). The Delta Air Park, near the eastern part of the dyke, is an interesting place to watch small airplanes do their 'touch and goes' and aerobatics (there is a coffee shop there too). The Boundary Bay Airport, a World War II aerodrome near the western part of the bay, will be reactivated for light aircraft use.

The intertidal area covers nearly 25 square miles and consists mostly of firm, clean sand which is popular year round for walking, horseback riding and bird watching. Extensive eelgrass beds near the low water line are spawning and rearing areas for herring and crab. Commercial crabbing has been going on in Boundary Bay since 1915 and at present supplies about 20% of the catch in B.C. Herring is second only to salmon in commercial value and is also a major source of protein for other fish and mammals. The wide variety of plant and animal life attracts numerous bird species, including thousands of ducks and geese (20,000 - 30,000 black brant stop over here in April during their northward migration), shorebirds, herons and in the backshore area, many kinds of eagles, hawks and owls (snowy owls are best seen around the foot of 64th and 72nd streets during their winter visit). The best viewing time is at high tide because it forces the birds to move around.

8   Boundary Bay Regional Park

One of the few large sandy swimming beaches in the lower mainland is found at the western side of Boundary Bay and while you're en route to the area remember fishing is relatively good here for salmon and cutthroat trout.

There are 360 acres adjacent to Centennial Beach which will be developed by the Greater Vancouver Regional District Parks Department, with beach and picnic facilities and wildlife interpretive areas. Facilities at present include tennis courts, picnic tables, water and washrooms. Plans call for reestablishing a salt water marsh ecosystem by removing an existing dyke and allowing intertidal flooding.

Slightly inland of the park is a very important archeological area known as the Beach Grove site. The remaining 3,000-year-old shell mounds and six house outlines are relics of a prosperous tribe of Indians who could afford to have permanent houses at their summer village here on Boundary Bay. One-third of the cultural deposits still remain.

99

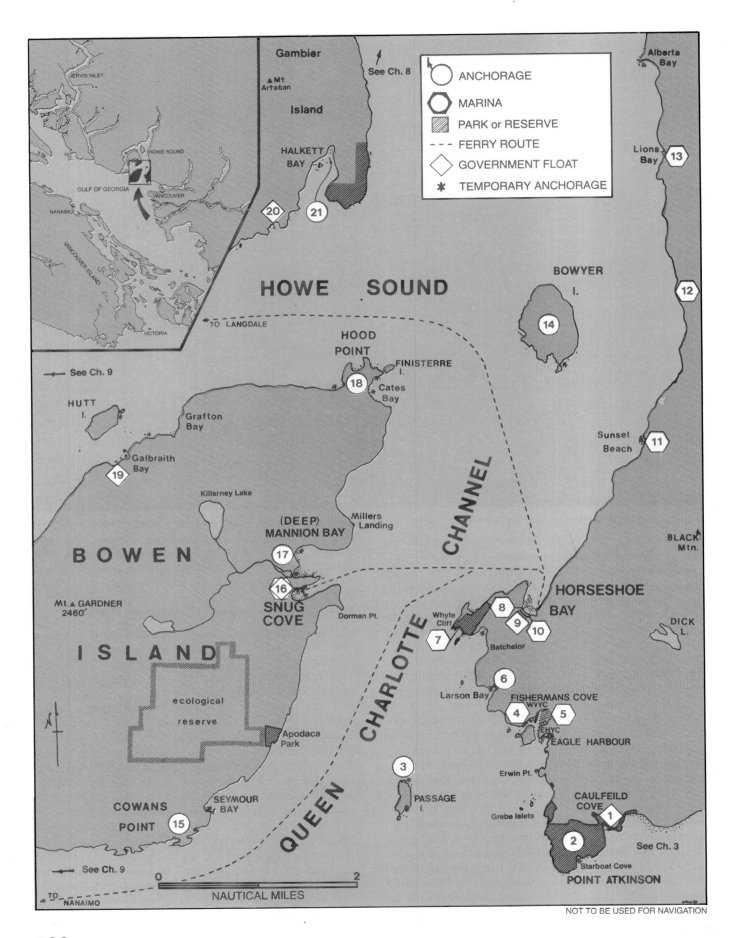

ANCHORAGE

MARINA

PARK or RESERVE

FERRY ROUTE

GOVERNMENT FLOAT

TEMPORARY ANCHORAGE

Gambier

Mt. Artaban

Island

HALKETT BAY

20

21

See Ch. 8

Alberta Bay

Lions Bay

13

BOWYER I.

12

14

HOWE SOUND

TO LANGDALE

HOOD POINT

FINISTERRE I.

18

Cates Bay

Sunset Beach

11

See Ch. 9

HUTT I.

Grafton Bay

Galbraith Bay

19

Killarney Lake

(DEEP) MANNION BAY

Millers Landing

CHANNEL

BLACK Mtn.

BOWEN

17

16

SNUG COVE

Dorman Pt.

Whyte Cliff

7

HORSESHOE BAY

8

9

10

DICK I.

Mt. GARDNER 2460'

ISLAND

ecological

reserve

6

Larson Bay

FISHERMANS COVE

WVYC

4

5

EHYC

EAGLE HARBOUR

Apodaca Park

Erwin Pt.

CAULFEILD COVE

3

PASSAGE I.

1

Grebe Islets

COWANS POINT

SEYMOUR BAY

15

Batchelor

QUEEN CHARLOTTE

2

Starboat Cove

See Ch. 3

POINT ATKINSON

See Ch. 9

0   2

NAUTICAL MILES

TO NANAIMO

NOT TO BE USED FOR NAVIGATION

JERVIS INLET

HOWE SOUND

GULF OF GEORGIA

VANCOUVER

NANAIMO

VANCOUVER ISLAND

VICTORIA

100

CHAPTER SEVEN

Queen Charlotte Channel

West Vancouver, Bowen Island, Halkett Bay

Howe Sound holds a special place in the memories of most Lower Mainland boating people, for it has always been a primary destination for day cruises and fishing, and its shorelines have provided a favourite camping ground for young people. Canoes, rented putt-putts, rowboats, and all types of backyard-built sailing dinghies have been used to explore the well-protected waters between the islands. The entrance to the Sound, Queen Charlotte Channel, is less than 10 miles from Vancouver Harbour and False Creek, and can be reached in an hour or so and explored in cursory fashion in a weekend.

It would take several months, however, to visit every nook and cranny, and there are some Lower Mainland boatowners who have spent a lifetime cruising its waters, never venturing beyond. The gradual change of wind, sky, weather, tide, marine life and shoreline development makes every stretch of water different, with continual surprises from day to day, season to season. For many, Howe Sound has provided the stimulus to fire the cruising imagination and to discover what lies further up the coast and across the oceans.

Howe Sound has been referred to as a typical B.C. "fjord inlet". In fact, while the upper third fits this description, the southern two-thirds, with its weaker surface currents and winds, and relatively shallower depths, less steep shorelines, sunnier skies and Gulf Island-like climate and vegetation, is more akin to the wide sounds at the mouths of certain other Mainland inlets — for example the Nelson-Hardy Island region of Jervis Inlet.

1   Caulfeild Cove

This delightful little cove is virtually the only protected anchorage in West Vancouver which is not completely surrounded by private homes. It is unusually peaceful and sheltered, since onshore winds from the southeast are rare in the summer months and there is no regular wash from passing B.C. ferries, unlike many of the other coves north of Point Atkinson.

Pilot Cove, just west of Caulfeild, could be used as a temporary anchorage but is more exposed to easterly winds as well as westerly swells which curl around Point Atkinson. Eight acres of waterfront parkland stretch around the north and west shores below Pilot House Road. A large anchor and stone monument honours Francis William Caulfeild who owned this area in 1899. He loved the wild life, flowers, rocks and beaches; and, laying out the village plan, ensured that all streets followed the natural slopes, no lot was square and each property had a view (Ainslie Manson, 1981).

A government float about 40 feet long is at the eastern entrance to Caulfeild Cove and small boats

---

CHARTS
3481 — Approaches to VANCOUVER
        HARBOUR (1:20,000) (covers Queen
        Charlotte Channel to Horseshoe Bay,
        Deep Bay, Bowen Island)
3311 — Strip Chart #2 — HOWE SOUND
        (1:40,000) (alternative to 3526, 3586)
3534 — Plans of Horseshoe Bay, Deep Bay and
        Snug Cove (1:8,000); Plan of
        Plan of Fishermans Cove (1:3,000)

Carefully manicured lawn caps breakwater protecting private float north of Lighthouse Park.

(canoes, kayaks or rowboats) could be beached and secured among the driftwood above the expected rise of tide while exploring Lighthouse Park which borders the western shore. Above the head of the cove there is a small open green or "common" with the little church of St. Francis-in-the-Wood hidden in the trees directly behind. The setting is so English that this might be the ficticious "Tiddlycove" made famous by Len Norris cartoons.

2 Lighthouse Park

Lighthouse Park is worth visiting because it is a virgin area which has never been logged and one can see here what the original forest with its associated plant and animal life must have been like. Despite its closeness to Vancouver this 185-acre park remains relatively undisturbed. There are more than eight miles of trails passing through cool damp valleys into deep woods, out along moss or grass covered clifftops

Familiar landmark to mariners since 1874 is Point Atkinson lighthouse. Behind it, 185-acre Lighthouse Park boasts virgin timber, with tallest Douglas Firs on lower mainland.

and down over barren, glacially smoothed granite rock faces to tidal pools and sea caves along the shore.

The tallest Douglas Fir trees remaining on the lower mainland rise to heights of over 200 feet and in the higher, wetter central part of the park, western hemlocks can be found. The close association of these two different tree types is unusual in such a small area but is indicative of the significant contrasts in topography, rainfall, temperature and plant associations found in the park. Starboat Cove does not provide as much protection from easterlies as Caulfeild Cove but in calm or westerly wind conditions is suitable as a temporary anchorage or as a place for beaching a small boat to explore the park or have a picnic on the rocks.

Point Atkinson was named after a "particular friend" by Captain George Vancouver on June 14, 1792. One of the first lighthouses in B.C. was constructed here in 1874. The point also serves as a major marine weather station and tidal reference point for the east-central portion of the Gulf of Georgia.

Winds

The winds recorded at Point Atkinson are not truly indicative of what winds may be blowing only a few miles away. In Burrard Inlet, for instance, the local topography funnels winds into an east-west trend. In the summer months, east and southeast winds in Burrard Inlet or the Gulf of Georgia are recorded as east or northeast winds at Point Atkinson (frequency about 55%) and blow mainly at night and early morning (81% at 6 a.m. dropping to 17% at 3 p.m.). The southeasterly appears to be deflected by the West Vancouver shoreline to register as a northeasterly at Point Atkinson.

In winter, easterlies (including northeasterlies and southeasterlies) blow about 65% of the time at Point Atkinson. The Howe Sound northerly or "Squamish" which can blow with considerable force (average 40 mph with gusts to 70 mph), can last 3 to 5 days with a frequency often over 30% in December and January, depending on the severity of the winter. "Squamish" winds seem to dissipate both in frequency and strength near Point Atkinson where they register as northwesterlies (15%). The "Squamish" type of wind is common in all major B.C. inlets and is similar to the "Mistral" in Southern France, and the "Bora" in Yugoslavia. (J. Emslie).

Westerly winds blow most frequently in the summer months (40% of the time) being strongest and most frequent in the afternoon as an onshore wind (72% at 3 p.m.). A westerly in Burrard Inlet may register as anything from northwest to southwest at Point Atkinson while at the same time it is blowing northwest in the Gulf of Georgia and from the south in Howe Sound.

Queen Charlotte Channel, to the north and west of Point Atkinson, is often an area of calms or confused but gusty winds. This is because it is the transition

area between the wind patterns which generally prevail in Burrard Inlet (east-west), the Gulf of Georgia (southeast-northwest) and Howe Sound (north-south).

The waters off Point Atkinson are notorious for tide rips and steep overfalls, being particularly boisterous when strong tides ebbing out of Howe Sound and Burrard Inlet meet, and are opposed by a strong westerly wind.

3 Passage Island

Passage Island, in the middle of Queen Charlotte Channel, was named by Captain Vancouver due to its position and aid as a leading mark (when lined up with Anvil Island to the north) in avoiding the dangerous shoals off the Fraser River. The island has not only proved useful as a navigational aid and bird nesting ground, but as a favourite fishing and diving area and more recently as a residential hideaway. The West Vancouver shoreline boasts some marvellous examples of west coast architecture and some of the more fantastic creations can be seen on Passage Island.

The efforts of some ingenious islanders to devise efficient raincatching roofs to augment sparse water supplies have had mixed results. Apparently the roofs tend to also catch offerings from some of the other one thousand residents on the island — Glaucous-winged seagulls.

Although Passage Island is private and there is very little foreshore to speak of, temporary anchorage is possible with protection from afternoon winds at the

Small boats anchor or moor off government float in cosy Caulfeild Cove, sheltered from all weather except a hard southeaster.

northeast end of the island or in calm weather, just off a small beach at the southeast end.

Captain Vancouver spent two days exploring Howe Sound. His journal notes:

Quitting Point Atkinson, and proceeding up the sound, we passed on the western shore some detached rocks, with some sunken ones amongst them, that extend about two miles, but are not so far from the shore as to impede the navigation of the sound; up which we made a rapid progress, by the assistance of a fresh southerly gale, attended with dark gloomy weather, that greatly added to the dreary prospect of the surrounding country. The low fertile shores we had been accustomed to see, though lately with some interruption, here no longer existed; their place was now occupied by the base of the stupendous snowy barrier, thinly wooded, and rising from the sea abruptly to the clouds; from whose frigid summit, the dissolving snow in foaming torrents rushed down the sides and chasms of its rugged surface, exhibiting altogether a sublime, though gloomy spectacle, which animated nature seemed to have deserted. Not a bird, nor living creature was to be seen, and the roaring of the falling cataracts in every direction precluded their being heard, had any been in the neighbourhood.

It is interesting to note that between Burrard Inlet and Jervis Inlet, 50 miles to the northwest, Vancouver named only the two relatively small islands (Passage and Anvil), the two entrance points (Atkinson and Gower) and Howe Sound itself. Vancouver named the Sound after Admiral, the Right Honourable Richard Scrope, Earl Howe. All other major place names within Howe Sound were conferred by Captain

Jampacked Fisherman's Cove has moorings for over 1200 boats. Eagle Harbour at right with Black Mtn. rising above the Upper Levels Highway.

Richards of H.M. Surveying ship *Plumper* in 1860 in association with the following incident in Howe's life which occurred two years after Vancouver had named the Sound. (See also Herbert L. McDonald, *Pacific Yachting*, Feb. 1982; and Oliver Warner, *The Glorious First of June*).

Eagle Harbour and miniature Parthenon can be seen in right foreground with Fisherman's Cove beyond narrow passage between Eagle Island and mainland.

The Glorious First of June

In 1776 Admiral Howe, as Commander-in-Chief off the American seaboard during the American Insurrection, had assisted his brother General William Howe in successful attacks on Long Island and Philadelphia. He also outmanoeuvred the French fleet which was attempting to assist the rebels, but could not bring them to battle. It was not until 1794 that Admiral Howe was able to close with a larger and heavier French fleet which was protecting a convoy of grain ships from America to France. The battle took place in the Atlantic Ocean, 350 miles northwest of Cape Finisterre; and the character of Howe, his officers and seamen were crucial to the final outcome.

Walbran in *B.C. Coast Names* notes that Howe's courage and taciturnity were almost proverbial, being described by Walpole as "undaunted as a rock and as silent." Because of his kind attentions to the condition of his sailors, Lord Howe became known as the "Sailors Friend", but because he was usually very glum-faced he also became known as "Black Dick". On the morning of the first of June a seaman is reported to have said "I think we shall have a fight today . . . Black Dick has been smiling." (Note Black Mt. and Dick Lake above Horseshoe Bay)

When the battle was over, the Royal Navy had captured seven line-of-battle ships including *L'America*, 74 guns, a naval ship built in the U.S. and presented to the newly republican France. Howe's flagship was the *Queen Charlotte*, 110 guns, after which Queen

Charlotte Channel between West Vancouver and Bowen Island is named.

North of Point Atkinson there are a number of small coves where temporary anchorage is possible and although the shoreline is quite developed there are a number of small waterfront parks. Klootchman Park (4.6 acres) is located on Indian Bluff. The Grebe Islets provide some protection from onshore southwesterly seas to a small cove north of Indian Bluff. A grass covered stone breakwater provides additional protection to a small basin with private floats. Two hundred yards north is tiny Gulf Beach Park. Temporary anchorage is possible in the lee of Erwin Point or near the small point at the entrance to Eagle Harbour. A conspicuous white miniature Parthenon on this point, was built by a lover of Grecian architecture as a memorial to his wife.

Eagle Harbour

Temporary anchorage for a very few small boats is also possible behind the private floats and moorings of the Eagle Harbour Yacht Club. There is a fine 200 foot sandy beach and a small park with picnic benches and drinking fountain at the head of the harbour. A line of red buoys stretched in front of the beach is intended to keep small boats from anchoring too close to the swimming area.

4 Fisherman's Cove

Fisherman's Cove is possibly one of the busiest pleasure craft havens on the coast with over 1,200 boats crammed into its water space. Although there are two entrances to the cove, one on either side of Eagle Island (see Plan on metric Chart 3534), the main entrance channel is to the west of the island. One should also stay west of a small islet and rocks connected to Eagle Island by cables about 12 feet above high water and by a rocky spit (covered at high water); and north of a light beacon in the centre of the channel which has a small drying rock extending to the south of it.

The Fisherman's Cove Marina operates a fuel dock at the entrance and Race Rock Yacht Services Ltd. provide dry storage, boat maintenance and repairs with a 40-ton capacity straddle crane for haulouts. Harbour Yacht Sales provide six floats for permanent moorage and brokerage. Incoming boats are requested to reduce their speed to less than 3 knots as higher speed wash can not only cause considerable damage to moored vessels and floats but the narrowness of the channel increases the risk of collision with boats manoeuvring away from the floats. The seventh float in from the entrance directly north of Eagle Island was formerly a federal government dock but is now used by the B.C. Corrections Service. The next four floats belong to the West Vancouver Yacht Club.

5 Thunderbird Marina

The head of Fisherman's Cove is occupied by Thunderbird Marina providing over 850 permanent berths (transient moorage when space available), fuel, boat repairs and maintenance (3½-ton hoist), marine supplies (Boathouse) and showers.

6 Larson Bay Park

This 2½-acre park is really an extension of the Gleneagles Golf and Country Club. It provides a nice beach, tennis courts, restrooms and in the summer — a swimming float. Temporary anchorage which is exposed to daytime onshore southwesterlies (not generally too strong except in spring or fall) is possible here.

The middle part of Batchelor Cove, in what is also known as Garrow Bay where underwater cables are charted as coming ashore, was once the site of a small marina operation. The head of Batchelor Cove is suitable for temporary anchorage and above the beach is the Rockwood Estate, controlled by UBC and a municipal park proposal.

7 Whytecliff Marina

Five rows of mooring buoys for up to 80 boats lie in Whyte Cove. There is a small store selling bait and tackle and a fuel dock in the north corner of the cove with facilities for emergency hull and engine repairs and boat rentals.

Whytecliff Park

Temporary anchorage for small boats is possible behind the marina moorings (enter close to Whyte Islet). Whyte Cove was formerly the terminus of the coast highway. What is now the marina dock served as the Union Steamship wharf for local passenger service to Bowen Island from 1924 to 1950. Thirty-nine acres of the Union Steamship property are now included in a municipal park which features a nice pebble beach, grass playing fields, tennis courts, restrooms, picnic tables and a refreshment stand. There are trails to a lookout seat atop Whytecliff Point, to Cliff Cove (along a narrow telegraph line from the

Whyte Cove in Whytecliff Park was a Union Steamship terminus until 1950. Temporary anchorage is possible behind marina moorings.

junction of Cliff and Arbutus Roads for a hundred yards to the beach), and along the top and side of the ridge between Whyte Island and Copper Cove.

In early summer, and occasionally at other times of the year, the waters here are cloudy and silt laden from the Fraser and Squamish River runoffs; but the crystal clear waters of the open Gulf of Georgia often penetrate up this side of Howe Sound making for excellent diving. An underwater reserve extends from Whyte Island around the point to Cliff Cove. Spearfishing and the removal of specimens is forbidden in this area.

Horseshoe Bay

Horseshoe Bay was known to the Indians as "Chahai" because of the "low sizzling noise" made by small fish along the shore in the evening. In the last few years this noise has been augmented by the hoots of B.C. Ferries, innumerable small boats and rail and road traffic echoing across from the lower slopes of Mt. Black which towers 4,000 feet above the eastern shore. Special care must be exercised when entering Horseshoe Bay to avoid the ferries. They should be given the right of way not only because they are bigger but because the harbour is so small with little room for manoeuvring. The western shore, known as Madrona Ridge is noted for its almost semi-tropical vegetation and has been suggested as a possible

One of the most popular fishing harbours, congested Horseshoe Bay is wide open to Squamish winds in winter. B.C. Ferries connect to Vancouver Island and Sunshine Coast.

ecological preserve for public use. Fine views are possible from the summit, 400 feet above Horseshoe Bay.

8   Sewell's Landing

Sewell's is located along the west shore of Horseshoe Bay and is protected to a degree from the "Squamish" wind by a large floating cement breakwater. A "Squamish" type wind of only moderate strength often blows into Horseshoe Bay on summer evenings for an hour or so starting around nine. In the winter months, before the breakwater was put in, it was not unusual for the marina floats, with boats still attached, to end up in the park above the beach after a particularly strong "Squamish". The Boat Centre offers fuel, moorage, engine and boat maintenance and repairs, elevator hoist for boats up to 26 feet, 5-ton capacity. Sewell's famous rental boats, and larger charter boats can be seen scattered around the Sound on most summer weekends. There is also a small chandlery here and The Keg restaurant on pilings over the water. Excellent fishing advice, bait and tackle are also available here (the Sewell's originated the annual salmon derby in 1938).

9   Horseshoe Bay Gov't Floats

There is over 500 feet of usually crowded float space provided along the south side of the government wharf south of Sewell's Marina. Floats on the northwest side of the wharf are used primarily by

various Howe Sound water taxi services. There is a park with children's playground behind the beach at the head of Horseshoe Bay and inland of the park, several cafes or restaurants (including Troll's — famous for seafood) and the Troller pub on Bay Street. Other community services here include grocery stores, post office, small shops, liquor store; and in the far corner of the bay, car ferry service to Nanaimo, Bowen Island, and Langdale on the Sunshine Coast.

10   Bay Boat Rentals

This facility is located in the middle of Horseshoe Bay and operates from May to October. Services provided include boat rentals, minor repairs, launching ramp, limited guest moorage, tackle and bait.

11   Sunset Marina

Two miles north of Horseshoe Bay at Sunset Beach is the Sunset Marina. Shelter from seas is provided by several large old barges. Over 150 small boats are accommodated at floats and dry boat storage is provided ashore. Berths for visiting boats up to 30 feet long are available; there is a launching ramp, fuel dock, facilities for repairing and hauling out boats up to 26 feet long (capacity 14 tons), small boat rentals and trailer camping facilities. A licensed dining room with outdoor patio, The Sundowner, is also located here.

12   Newman Creek Marina

A large conspicuous brown warehouse-like building provides dry boat storage at this marina. There is a launching ramp for private use.

Sunset Marina, two miles north of Horseshoe Bay, accommodates about 150 small boats, visiting boats up to 30 feet.

13   Lions Bay Marina

This facility also specializes in dry moorage although there is a small fuel dock and a launching ramp.

Brunswick Beach

Temporary anchorage is possible in Alberta Bay, a mile north of Lions Bay, where there is a very nice south facing beach providing opportunities for swimming or sunbathing. More protection from southerly seas is possible just north of the rock surrounded point where there is another small beach. This beach is the nucleus of the "Brunswick Beach" community, a camping haven since shortly after the turn of the century and now thriving so well that it holds itself firmly apart from more modern "upstart" developments to the south. (D. Stainsby).

Harvey Creek, which drains the slopes of mile-high Mt. Harvey and Mt. Brunswick (5,855 feet high), are named after Captain John Harvey of H.M.S. *Brunswick*, 74 guns. The duel between the *Brunswick* and the *Vengeur* during the battle of the "Glorious First of June" is one of the epics of the sailing navy, ranking with the attack by the *Redoubtable* on the *Victory* at Trafalgar and the duel between the *Shannon* and the *Chesapeake* in the Canadian-American War of 1812. Walbran notes:

> . . . in attempting to force an opening through the enemy's line, ahead of the *Vengeur*, the *Brunswick's* starboard anchor hooked in the *Vengeur's* forechains and dragged the *Vengeur* along with her. The master proposed to cut her free. "No," said Harvey, "as we have got her, we'll keep her."

Dry storage in "pigeon-hole parking", a small fuel dock, launching ramp and limited wet storage, are available at Lions Bay.

Conspicuous warehouse provides dry storage at Newman Creek Marina, which also has had a launching ramp and buoys for wet moorage in the summer.

The two ships were so close that the *Brunswick* could not open her lower deck gun ports and had to blast them off with her own fire. The two ships fought hand to hand, grappled together for several hours. A few French ships came to the aid of the *Vengeur* but received such heavy broadsides from the *Brunswick* that they retired. Walbran continues:

> Towards the close other British ships came to assist the *Brunswick*, and the *Ramillies*, commanded by Harvey's brother, Captain Henry Harvey, poured two tremendous broadsides into the unfortunate Frenchman. The grappling had been cut away and the *Vengeur*, dismasted and with water pouring in through her smashed side, showed British colours in token of surrender. Every effort was made to remove her men, but she sank with more than half her crew still on board. The *Brunswick*, severely damaged . . . lost more than 44 men killed and 114 wounded, (more than any other British ship in the battle). Captain Harvey was severely wounded, a splinter having struck him in the back and a round shot smashed his right elbow. He died . . . 30 June.

14 Bowyer Island

Bowyer Island is named after Admiral Sir George Bowyer, Bart. In the victory of the First of June he carried his flag in H.M.S. *Barfleur*, 98 guns, and like one of the five other admirals engaged in the battle

A string of logs forms a floating breakwater on west of Bowyer Island where residents can moor.

(Pasley), he lost a leg for which he received a pension of 1,000 pounds.

The southern portion of the island has several small coves which are either partially or fully exposed to southerly winds and seas but would offer some protection from the winter "Squamish". The cove just west of the southern point is filled with private moorings and floats for the island residents and guests. A string of logs forms a floating breakwater to protect a cove on the west side of the island. Private floats in this cove extend out toward a 5 foot drying rock.

Bowen Island

Despite its proximity to Vancouver, Bowen is still considered by many as an isolated hideaway, the summer cottage or weekend island with its own unique Gulf Island atmosphere of 20 or 30 years ago. The pace of life on Bowen is comfortably slow, the residents are sufficiently insular or eccentric to outsiders, and the surroundings are bucolic and relatively undisturbed. There are over 1000 people who live on the island permanently but this number increases to more than 3,000 in the summer months.

Alberta Bay at Brunswick beach provides temporary anchorage and fine beach. Brunswick Beach camping community is on beach to left of rock outcroppings.

The island was named by Captain Richards in 1860 after Rear Admiral James Bowen, who in 1794 was master of H.M.S. *Queen Charlotte,* Howe's flagship on the "Glorious First of June". For his valuable and exceptional services he was rapidly promoted over the next two years to post captain. It is a tradition of the service that Bowen took the ship so close to the stern of the French flagship — the *Montagne,* that the fly of the French ensign brushed the main and mizzen shrouds of the *Queen Charlotte* as she passed and poured her broadside into the French ship's starboard quarter. (Walbran).

15   Point Cowan

Point Cowan (or Cowan's Point as it is locally known) was settled at the beginning of this century by George Cowan, his family and friends. In the words of Irene Howard *(Bowen Island 1872-1972)* he:

> turned it into a "poetical commonwealth" (a Utopia, a New Atlantis) over which he and his wife ruled with enormous expense to themselves of effort and money, but with equally huge enjoyment in return. They were so beautiful these Bowen Island acres, and he, convivial and gregarious, wanted to share them with his friends . . . he was in no sense a developer. Point Cowan was . . . an exercise in creative planning . . . to get and preserve for the place a distinctive character . . . a "colonization scheme" . . . (it became) as self-sufficient as possible . . . with sheep, cows, hens, pheasants, vegetable and flower gardens and orchards, a regular gasoline launch commuter service to and from Vancouver every day . . . and a government dock in Seymour Bay . . . All sorts of boats anchored in the bay to shelter from storms . . . The community flourished.

Every small cove around the property was named at this time, from Fairweather (Winnipeg) Bay to Seymour Bay. The latter named after Alexander G. R. A. Seymour, a hermit who had preceded the Cowans, preempting 163 acres at Seymour Landing in 1890.

Unnamed cove on southern end of Bowyer Island is filled with mooring buoys and floats for island residents.

He was said to have been the tutor to the family of a relative of the Duke of Norfolk, fallen in love with a girl in the family, leading to great unhappiness for he could not aspire to marry her. He left England, sailed around Cape Horn, came to Bowen Island where he built a log cabin, planted fruit and nut trees, and lived alone with his dog. When the cabin was struck by lightning and burned down, he and the dog moved in with the chickens. Once a year he rowed across to Vancouver for a supply of books. He made a second yearly visit to drink afternoon tea with the Cowans, where he responded somewhat to the gentling influence of Mrs. Cowan. He eventually sold his property to the Cowans and moved away from the Island. (Howard)

Seymour Landing is the most protected bay at this end of the island but is exposed (like most of the others) to ferry wash. Despite the preponderance of easterly winds at Point Atkinson, the easterly and southeasterly is uncommon in the summer months on this side of Queen Charlotte Channel. Strong downchannel (Squamish) winds do, however, send seas into the bay, especially in winter.

There is a road from Seymour Landing which leads behind the Cowan Point properties past Josephine Lake to join the main road midway between Snug Cove and Bowen Bay. A few hundred yards up from the beach is a large cleared grassy field and an old orchard. The south end of Bowen Island tends to be sunnier and drier than the northern half of the island, there is a variety of vegetation, with less underbrush than in wetter areas, making for excellent hiking opportunities with views across the Gulf to Vancouver Island and east to the skyline of Vancouver. The wa-

Snug Cove and Mannion Bay, known to locals as Hotel Bay. Snug Cove site for new marina is almost totally landlocked, and well protected from all weather. Many boats anchor overnight in Hotel Bay on summer weekends, but it is wide open to southeasters.

ters off the south coast of Bowen Island are very popular for salmon fishing although strong westerly winds often result in a nasty chop.

Less than a mile up the coast from Seymour Landing is Apodaca Cove and Apodaca Provincial Park, 20 acres in size. The park was donated in 1954 by the late Major J. S. Matthews, Vancouver City Archivist, and named by him after the name given to Bowen Island by Don Jose Maria Narvaez who explored the southern Gulf of Georgia in 1791, one year before Captain Vancouver. In the early part of this century, Major Matthews was in a small boat which was stranded here late one summer evening. The major and his teenage son fought their way through the bush to reach assistance in Snug Cove late at night. When his son died accidentally at the age of 22, the major bought this property as a memorial.

Although well protected anchorage is not available in Apodaca Cove, small boats can be beached and hauled above the expected rise of tide and ferry wash. There is now a trail and road above the shoreline into Snug Cove. On the hill above this park there is a 960-acre ecological reserve which was proposed for scientific study by UBC's Department of Botany and established in 1973. The reserve is of special interest because the diorite, basalt and greenstone bedrock supports an open stand of second growth Douglas Fir

(established after a fire around 1920) to an elevation of 1,500 feet without good western hemlock development. The shallow soils and dry southeasterly aspect prevent hemlock growth where normally the hemlock would dominate in elevations above 500 feet along the south coast mountains.

A short distance north of Apodaca Park is an old copper mine which was operated from 1913 to 1921. A shaft about 150 yards long was excavated and many surface exploration pits are still in evidence.

16 Snug Cove

Snug Cove is an almost totally land-locked harbour that is well protected from most winds and seas. The only drawbacks are its small size, occasional crowding problems, and the periodic disturbance of docking ferries. Despite these drawbacks, it is at times idyllically peaceful. The government floats provide over 800 feet of moorage space but one must be prepared to tie alongside other boats on busy summer weekends.

Seven acres of foreshore at the head of Snug Cove and part of the old waterside promenade are protected by a recreational reserve but this inner part of Snug Cove is still used for the winter storage of many of the island's private floats.

Reconquista Marina

Immediately northeast of the government wharf there are floats providing year round moorage for about 40 boats with some limited space for transient

Major landmark in Howe Sound, Anvil Island, is dwarfed by snow-capped mountains ringing Sound.

overnight moorage. Fuel, bait and ice may also be available here, at the Snug Cove Marina or further inland at the gas station and the Bow Mart store which also includes a coffee bar. The old general store, originally the Union Steamships office, has been proposed as a heritage site. The Snug Cove General Store and a liquor store are located at the top of Government Road across from the gas station. There is a small crafts shop between the Bow Mart and General Store.

Snug Cove Marina

Snug Cove Marina with moorage space for over 100 boats is to be located in a dredged out basin behind the government floats.

In the first half of this century Snug Cove was also known as Wharf Cove and served as the terminus for the extremely popular Union Steamship excursions to the Island for company picnics, weekending cottagers, moonlight dance cruises later to be known as "booze cruises" and visitors to the holiday resort in Deep Bay. The peninsula which separates Snug Cove from Deep Bay was formerly the Union Steamships number one picnic ground, with dance pavilion, tea room and bandstand; but is now largely private, a portion being the site for the CNIB (Canadian National Institute for the Blind) Vacation Lodge.

A new 1235-acre provincial park and recreation area has been proposed by the Greater Vancouver Regional District for the Union Steamship Properties and certain Crown lands around Mt. Gardner and north of Killarney Lake. The Snug Cove area could be developed as a marine park with mooring buoys, picnic areas and a hiking trail to Doman Point.

17   Mannion Bay (Deep Bay)

Mannion Bay has been known over the years as Quo-la-Quom (Indian village), Hotel Bay, Cliftonville, Deep Bay, Deep Cove or just "Bowen Island". In Union Steamship days, the surrounding lands comprised a huge, 900-acre resort complex which stretched all the way from the south shore of Snug Cove to the north end of Deep Bay. A hotel was built, first known as the Terminal Hotel, then Mt. Strahan Lodge, then Bowen Inn with "incomparable" views of the Howe Sound mountains opposite. "Strahan" (or "stran") is the proper pronounciation of Mt. Strachan, 4,769 feet high, which is visible between Black Mountain and the Lions.

The Union Steamship resort area included six separate picnic grounds, pavilions, riding stables and woodland trails, hundreds of summer cottages, boat rentals, tennis courts, formal gardens, putting and bowling greens, a waterfront promenade which was lit up at night and a huge lagoon formed by the damming of Terminal Creek where it entered the sea.

Today, much of the northern part of the resort area has been subdivided and developed, but there are still several quiet trails and deserted lanes through the woods and around the lagoon where one can see many desolate, crumbling cottages sadly deteriorating in the damp woods. A trail follows Terminal Creek passing by Bridal Veil Falls, School Road, pastoral fields and farmsteads to the confluence of Killarney Creek and up to Killarney Lake, a mile inland. There is a road from Grafton Bay, which passes by the west shore of Killarney Lake and back to Snug Cove.

A mile or so up the road to Hood Point (just west of Millers Landing) one can find Branch #150 of the Royal Canadian Legion which had the honour of being the only Legion in Canada listing Lord Louis Mountbatten as a member. One of his former shipmates, a Bowen Island resident, invited Lord Louis to join and his application for membership was framed and hung on the wall.

Temporary anchorage is also possible in the ex-

A tombolo-like spit makes Finisterre Island a peninsula at low tide. Cates Bay pebble beach fronts well-established Hood Point community.

treme southwestern end of Deep Bay just off the spillway draining the Terminal Creek lagoon. Because this part of the bay dries only 3 feet it can be used by most small shallow keel or shoal draught boats as a summer evening or nightime anchorage when the tide is expected to remain high. Protection from easterly seas and ferry wash is afforded by natural and artificial stone and rock breakwaters which extend out from the Snug Cove peninsula. There is a beautiful sandy beach here, probably the best on Bowen Island. It is all that remains of the sandy beach which once encircled the southern part of Deep Bay. Golden sand was imported from Scotland's east coast as ballast in the holds of the Union Steamship's *Lady Alexandra* and *Catala,* and dumped by barge on the foreshore, but through the years this sand has been washed out to sea. A string of logs which is partially beached at low tide separates boats from swimmers.

The northern portion of Deep Bay is a reasonable summer time temporary anchorage although it is exposed to southeasterly seas and ferry wash. There are several private floats and moorings here and one of the better beaches on Bowen Island, known locally as "Pebbly Beach".

18   Hood Point

The bight north of Millers Landing could provide some shelter from southerly winds, but more protection is afforded in Cates Bay near Hood Point. The northeasternmost tip of Bowen Island (Finisterre Island) is probably named after the northwesternmost tip of Spain (Cape Finisterre), closest land to the site of the battle of "The Glorious First of June". Hood Point itself is named after Admiral Sir Alexander Hood, second-in-command to Lord Howe in this engagement. Hood's flagship, the *Royal George,* 110 guns, encountered a very hot fire, lost her fore and main topmasts and had 20 men killed and 72 wounded. (Walbran).

There are five place names on the chart between Cates Bay and Smugglers Cove, half a mile to the west. Topographic maps add an additional three place names, resulting in eight separate names — possibly more than for any other comparable area on the B.C. coast. Cates Bay is named after Captain John A. Cates, one of five brothers prominent in Vancouver's maritime history, who opened up Bowen Island as a resort in the early 1900s. At the north end of Cates Bay a stone breakwater to an offshore rock protects Safety Cove and a private float from easterly seas and ferry wash. A tombolo-like drying spit joins the prominent rocky Finisterre Island to Bowen. South of this spit is Poca Cove and north of it, next to Enchanta Bay, is Montevista Bay. Cates Bay and the two bays east of Hood Point, (Columbine Bay and Smugglers Cove) have many private floats and moorings. The entire Hood Point area is part of a well-established community with its own set of rules and regulations which have helped it to establish its own separate character and identity. All buildings must be approved by the community before construction; commercial enterprises, billboards and signs of any kind are banned and all camping is prohibited. Irene Howard notes:

> It is a model village and, like the utopians of other centuries, its people put little trust in the natural benevolence of man . . . In this respect at least they agree with that saintly and venerable Utopian, Thomas More: "And as nature bids us mutually to make our lives merry and delightful, so she also bids us again and again not to destroy or diminish other people's pleasure in seeking our own".

Smugglers Cove, Grafton Bay and Galbraith Bay are all somewhat exposed to daytime westerly winds or seas which tend to enter Howe Sound via Barfleur Passage to the west of Bowen Island. Temporary anchorage in calm conditions is possible in a few nooks or behind small rocks or islets attached to the Bowen Island shore inside Hutt Island. Hutt Island is named after Captain John Hutt, H.M.S. *Queen,* 98 guns, flagship of Rear Admiral Gardner. In the battle of the "Glorious First of June" the *Queen* was almost totally disabled, and drifted away from the bulk of the fleet, having to independently fight off eleven French ships. Her casualties were second only to those of the *Brunswick.* Captain Hutt was wounded, lost a limb

Summer homes ring Montevista Bay west of Hood Pt.

One of the last undeveloped anchorages in Howe Sound is Halkett Bay, which may become a marine park. Two dangerous rocks, visible just beneath the surface in the centre of this low-tide photo, are charted as one rock.

and died 30 days later on the same day as Captain Harvey of the *Brunswick*. Both Hutt and Harvey were buried together and remembered by the same monument in Westminster Abbey. Walbran notes:

> ... to complete the coincidence, before leaving England these officers had driven down together in the same post-chaise to join their respective ships.

The remains of a wharf structure can be found on the tombolo spit which joins the tiny Flower Island to the eastern end of Hutt Island. This eastern end of Hutt Island was blasted out several years ago and a rough road snakes up the barren cliffside. It is possible to moor temporarily between dolphins (grouped pilings) about 50 feet offshore.

Grafton Bay is named after early Bowen Island homesteaders but by a curious coincidence, the home of General William Howe, where Admiral Codrington (a chronicler of Lord Howe's life and naval battles) first met Lord Howe (when Codrington was a junior officer) was in Grafton Street, London.

19 Mount Gardner Park

A small government float is located in Galbraith Bay, the most sheltered nook from summer winds on the west side of Bowen Island. The float provides about 150 feet of temporary moorage and is used mainly for the storage of local residents' dinghies. This bay is quite cool in the heat of summer, shaded by the 2,500 foot high bulk of Mount Gardner directly behind. In winter, this bay is cool as well as rough due to an open exposure to "Squamish" winds.

Several hiking trails from all sides of the island lead to the top of Mt. Gardner which is named after the Rear-Admiral who trained his men to fire broadsides at a phenomenal rate — a "subject of astonishment throughout the fleet." In 1786 Gardner had served as lieutenant to Captain George Vancouver in Jamaica. (H. L. McDonald).

Mount Gardner Park Lodge operated here as a summer resort from 1919 to 1954. Previous to this there had been much mining speculation which did not excite the local residents as do such developments nowadays. Irene Howard notes:

> "American capitalists" in 1906 bought the Bonanza group of lead-silver-gold claims on the west side of Mount Gardner and employed a small work crew on what was said would certainly be "one of the great mines of the Howe Sound region". "The values have been deemed so large that it was considered best to say little concerning them . . .." Even less has been said about them since.

Gambier Island

20 Fircom

A small government float with less than 150 feet of moorage space is located directly south of Mount Artaban on Gambier Island. This float provides access to a United Church camp known as Fircom after the First United Church of Vancouver which established a Community House and campgrounds here in 1923.

21 Halkett Bay

This bay is named after the naval family of Halkett of which Sir Peter Halkett, Bart. was in the service at the time of Lord Howe's victory, 1794. (Walbran). The bay offers well protected anchorage and as the last significant, undeveloped anchorage left in Howe Sound has been suggested as a possible marine park. Halkett Point at the eastern entrance comprises a 108-acre recreational reserve with potential for camping and viewing the surrounding scenery. There is an old homestead on flat pastoral land at the head of the bay. The bay is often used for the storage of log booms to which it is possible to tie alongside. One must be prepared to move off when the booms are moved and take care not to tie where the boom might shift into shallow water or over any of the dangerous rocks in the centre and along the west shore of Halkett Bay.

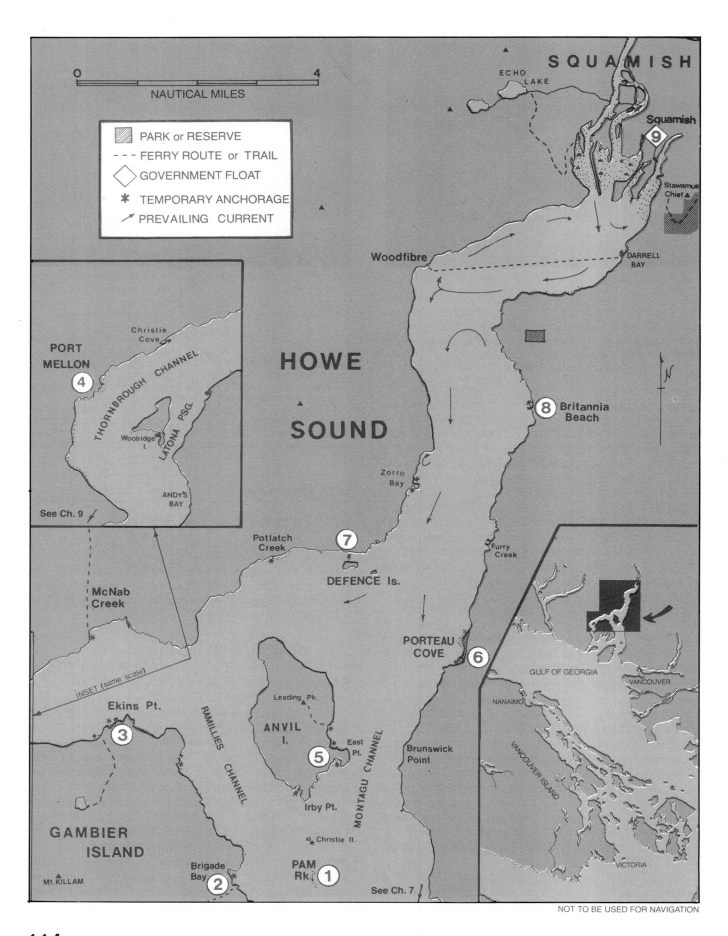

0 NAUTICAL MILES 4

PARK or RESERVE
FERRY ROUTE or TRAIL
GOVERNMENT FLOAT
TEMPORARY ANCHORAGE
PREVAILING CURRENT

SQUAMISH

ECHO LAKE

Squamish ⑨

Stawamus Chief ▲

Woodfibre

DARRELL BAY

HOWE

SOUND

PORT MELLON ④

Christie Cove

THORNBROUGH CHANNEL

LATONA PSG.

Woolridge I.

ANDY'S BAY

See Ch. 9

Britannia Beach ⑧

Zorro Bay

Potlatch Creek ⑦

DEFENCE Is.

Furry Creek

McNab Creek

INSET (same scale)

Ekins Pt. ③

RAMILLIES CHANNEL

Leading Pk. ▲

ANVIL I.

⑤ East Pt.

MONTAGU CHANNEL

PORTEAU COVE ⑥

GULF OF GEORGIA

VANCOUVER

NANAIMO

VANCOUVER ISLAND

Brunswick Point

Irby Pt.

GAMBIER ISLAND

Mt. KILLAM ▲

Brigade Bay ②

Christie It.

PAM Rk. ①

See Ch. 7

VICTORIA

NOT TO BE USED FOR NAVIGATION

114

CHAPTER EIGHT

Northern Howe Sound

Northern Gambier Island, Anvil Island, Britannia, Squamish

Northern Howe Sound is seldom visited by cruising yachtsmen, even when the weather is good and southerly winds are pushing the pulp mill smoke away and deep blue skies highlight the snowy peaks of Garibaldi and the Tantalus Range. On summer weekends when a thousand boats may be plying the waters south of Gambier one may be hard pressed to find more than 20 boats north of Anvil Island. For those yachtsmen who value uncongested waterways, beautiful scenery and good sailing winds, northern Howe Sound has much to offer. Alternatively, boats looking for calm waters with little wind will usually find them in Thornbrough Channel, northwest of Gambier Island.

Winds

Although winds in southern Howe Sound are often light, winds north of Montagu Channel tend to be brisk due to the narrowing of the Sound. During the summer months the land/sea breeze caused by the differential heating and cooling of the land and water surfaces has a marked influence on wind speed and direction. This land-sea breeze is also known as the "diurnal" or twice daily wind. As the interior heats up during the day, updrafts suck in air from the Gulf of Georgia.

Near Squamish, gusty south and southwest winds commonly reach velocities of 25 mph, with gusts to 35 or in extreme cases 50 mph. This onshore wind is phenomenally regular, occurring over 90% of the days between noon and 6 p.m. in the month of June —

a higher frequency of occurrence than for any other station on the B.C. coast. After sunset, velocities drop off, and wind direction often reverses to a light northerly around midnight which continues until about 9 a.m. (50% to 60% frequency).

In the winter months, large masses of cold arctic air spread from high pressure areas in the interior toward the coast, seeking the path of least resistance. The Cheakamus and Squamish valleys to the north of Howe Sound provide one such path. Wind velocities in northern Howe Sound commonly reach 35 to 40 mph, with gusts from 50 to 70 mph. Such northerly or "Squamish" winds often persist for three to five days and may be triggered by the passage of a low pressure centre down the B.C. coast. Strong southerly inflow winds are also common in winter when SE gales are blowing in the Gulf of Georgia. Such southerly winds, while not as persistent as the cold northeasterly "Squamish", tend to occur more frequently and sometimes dramatically. In the winter of 1972 the wind changed from light northerly to south 55 mph within three to four hours, with gusts to 94 mph! (*The Squamish River Estuary*, Environment Canada, 1975).

Another wind common to steep shorelines along the B.C. coast is the downslope, or "katabatic" wind

CHARTS
3311 — Strip Chart #2 — HOWE SOUND
    (1:40,000) (alternative to 3526, 3586)
3534 — Plan of Squamish (1:10,000)

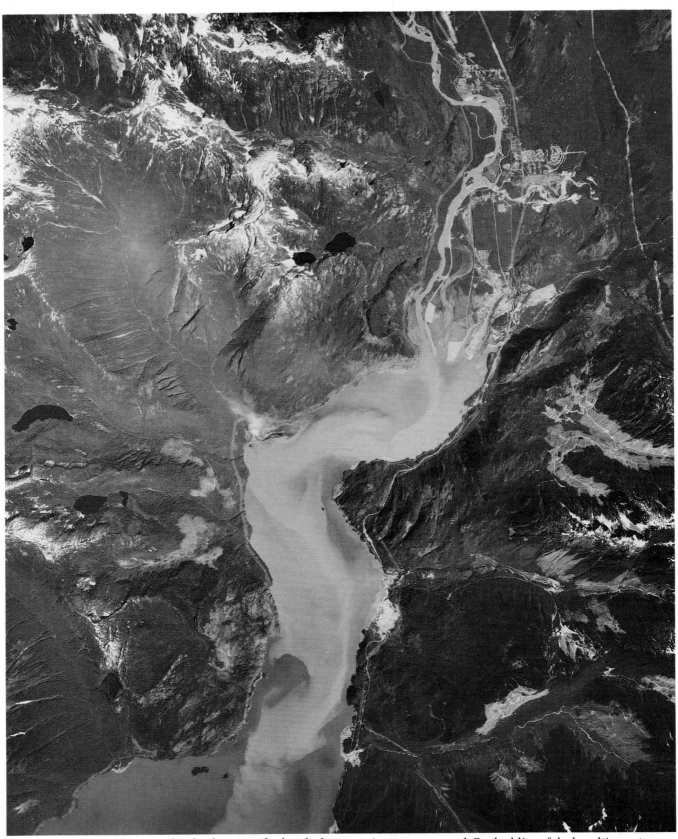

Currents and backeddies are clearly shown at the head of Howe Sound in this federal government high altitude photo taken August 6, 1972. Silty main flow of the Squamish River is deflected from one side of Howe Sound to the other as it moves seaward. Backeddies of dark, saltier water can be seen off Zorro Bay, and dark pulpmill effluent from Woodfibre is being carried north toward the head of the Sound by another backeddy.

(also known as the "williwaw") which most often develops overnight, particularly on clear, calm summer nights in the steep narrow ravines along each side of the Sound. (J. Emslie). This wind affects the waters immediately adjacent to the mouth of many streams, and since suitable depths for anchorage are often only found at such locations, one should be prepared with a well grounded anchor or stout line ashore.

1 Pam Rocks

A temporary wind recording station at Pam Rocks indicates that winds in this part of Howe Sound blow up (from the S and SE) the Sound only about 30 to 40% of the time in the summer months and hardly at all in the winter (less than 15%). In winter, northerly winds blow about 70% to 80% of the time.

There are over 13 individual drying rocks and tiny islets extending north and south of Pam Rock for about half a mile. A few of the larger rocks and Christie Islet, a mile to the north, serve as an important breeding colony for over 700 pairs of seabirds. The Glaucous-winged gull is most numerous (600 pairs) with Pigeon Guillemots and Pelagic Cormorants concentrating on Christie Islet and Double-crested Cormorants found only on Pam Rocks.

2 Brigade Bay

A mile to the west of Pam Rock, on Gambier Island, is Brigade Bay — named in 1945 because of its use by the Vancouver Boys' Brigade as a summer camp. Temporary anchorage is possible in the southernmost part of the bay inside a one foot high islet or, with

Silt from Squamish river runoff can be seen off Brigade Bay shoreline.

more protection from northerly winds, in the northern part of the Bay.

Although all of the anchorages around the north shore of Gambier are somewhat gloomy because of their lack of southern exposure, this bay is not without its own quiet charm. When the Sound is socked in with low-overcast and drizzle (a not infrequent occurrence) one can hear strange hoots and see long thin wisps of smoke extending laterally just above the eastern shore of Howe Sound as the Royal Hudson excursion steam train runs north to Squamish and back again every day in the summer.

The land here was originally preempted in 1891. A log cabin was built and an orchard started. In 1907 Mr. G. W. Wiegand built a garden, an artificial lake and raised canaries, pheasants and Belgian horses. His special hobby was growing lilies-of-the-valley and violets. There are trails from the abandoned homestead across the isthmus to Camp Artaban at the head of Port Graves. An old logging road leading from Brigade Bay up the north face of Mount Artaban provides magnificent views of Mount Garibaldi.

There are several tiny nooks in the northern Gambier shoreline in which small boats can find shelter or temporary anchorage. Many of these nooks are quite deep, requiring the use of a line or two ashore to prevent swinging into the shoreline. Care should be taken in Douglas Bay to avoid shallows which extend some distance out from the mouth of Gambier Creek.

Ramillies Channel, between Anvil and Gambier Islands is named after H.M.S. *Ramillies*, 74 guns,

Members of Gulf Yacht Club rafted up in mist-enshrouded Latona Passage.

Captain Henry Harvey, who came to his brother's assistance in the battle of the "Glorious First of June" (see note under (13) Lions Bay, Chapter Seven).

3   Ekins Point

The northern point of Gambier Island is named after Sir Charles Ekins, captain of H.M.S. *Defence* from 1806 to 1811. There is a narrow, one-chain (66

Daybreak Point separates two small bays just northwest of Irby Point at the south end of Anvil Island.

feet) wide provincial recreation reserve which extends for half a mile on either side of Ekins Point. This reserve provides access above the foreshore for picnicking, upland camping and hiking opportunities.

Floats in the second bay southwest of Ekins Point serve as an outstation for the Thunderbird Yacht Club. The old government floats at Camp Latona provide access to the Roman Catholic summer camp in the third bay south of Ekins Point. There is a boomed off swimming area to the north of this float. An old logging trail from Ekins Point climbs south for a mile and a half to Gambier Lake, hidden behind an encircling ring of hills at an elevation of 1,200 feet. This lake is obscured by a compass rose on Charts 3577 and 3586 but is shown on metric Chart 3526. Frieda Van der Ree suggests this hike as an invigorating, hour-long climb in her book *Exploring the Coast by Boat*, 1979.

Ekins Point and Thornbrough Channel are particularly notable for the general lack of wind. While it can be blowing quite strongly in other parts of Howe Sound, this area often experiences little, if any wind. Thornbrough Channel also seems to avoid the worst of the winter "Squamish" despite its northeast orientation. On one occasion while it was blowing over 60 mph from the north, east of Anvil Island, the wind in Thornbrough Channel was 5 mph from the east. On other occasions however the "Squamish" has blown Port Mellon pulp mill smoke over the hills and down onto the Sunshine Coast north of Roberts Creek.

A temporary wind recording station at the north end of Woolridge Island indicates a fairly even distribution of winds in summer and winter (40 to 50% from the N to E; 50 to 60% from the SE to SW). Both sides of Woolridge Island, Latona Passage and Thornbrough Channel are heavily used for the booming and storage of logs.

4 Port Mellon

Port Mellon is the oldest pulp mill operating in British Columbia. It was built in 1908, began production in 1910 and was named after Captain H. A. Mellon who had founded the B.C. Wood, Pulp and Paper Company in Vancouver in 1886. The mill is located on the south bank of the delta of the Rainy River and as the *Small Craft Guide* (Volume 2) notes: "there is a considerable amount of rain."

Seaside Park, across the delta, was started as a resort with a lodge, picnic grounds and regular steamship calls by Captain Cates prior to the construction of Port Mellon. There are floats here and just west of the main Port Mellon wharf for emergency use by small craft.

For many years, log booms blocked off access to a delightful small anchorage in Christie Cove, just south of Stolterfoht Creek. Although strong winds are uncommon in summer, the northeast exposure makes winter anchorage somewhat tenuous.

McNab Creek has long been used by fishermen, hikers and loggers. Logging roads from the west end of the McNab Creek bight extend over a low pass to Salmon Inlet, 10 miles to the northwest. The McNab Creek estuary delta is quite muddy but the creek itself is popular for fishing and camping. There is a small dredged out boat basin just east of the creek mouth at the east end of McNab bight.

5 Anvil Island

As Captain Vancouver approached this island in 1792, he noted:

> . . .The sun shining at this time for a few minutes afforded an opportunity of ascertaining the latitude of the east point of an island which, from the shape of the mountain that composes it, obtained the name of ANVIL ISLAND. . .

Anvil Island was referred to as So-Sah-Latch (meaning "lots of mats" (tents)) by the Squamish Indians because of its use as a halfway campsite between the head and the mouth of Howe Sound.

Leading Peak is the "leading mark" noted earlier (Chapter Seven) by Vancouver and is 2,500 feet high, accessible by a hiking trail from a small cove at the mouth of a creek draining into Montagu Channel. Montagu Channel is named after H.M.S. *Montagu* and her captain, James Montagu, who was killed in the action of the "Glorious First of June." The north and south points of Anvil Island (Domett and Irby) are also named after officers who took part in this battle.

Temporary anchorage is possible on either side of the "east point" noted by Vancouver which is also shaped something like an anvil. Protection from afternoon southerly winds is afforded off the north facing beach while the south facing beach (Fern Bay) is preferred at night or when a "Squamish" type wind is expected. Small boats might also find some degree of protection behind several drying rocks and islets between "east point" and Irby Point, dependent on local wind and tide conditions.

Pungent odor of Port Mellon pulp mill is familiar to cruising yachtsmen.

Christie Cove is a cosy little anchorage for a few boats, but northern exposure makes it dangerous in winter.

Small boat basin has been dredged out just east of McNab Creek.

Eastern shore of Anvil Island has miles of deserted pebble beaches.

This area was first settled in 1891 by T. J. Keeling. A large brick making factory, the Columbia Clay Co., operated 200 yeards west of Irby Point around the turn of the century (F. Temple Keeling)

Daybreak Point is operated as a Bible camp by the Plymouth Brethren and was so named because of the

One of the most protected anchorages in northern Howe Sound is Porteau Cove, part of a 14-acre provincial park.

views from here of morning sunrises over the mountains, changing Howe Sound gradually from darkness to light. Temporary anchorage (reasonably protected from most night-time winds) is possible in either of the two small bays on either side of Daybreak Point.

6 Porteau Cove Provincial Park

In 1981 Porteau Cove Provincial Park was established on 11 acres of land belonging to B.C. Rail near the old settlement and steamer stop of Glen Eden. A summer resort with lodge, cottages, tennis courts and a boat basin operated here from the 1930s to the 1950s. The park includes about half a mile of sea frontage, mostly shallow gravel beach, extending north of the small nook at the southern end of Porteau Cove. This small nook dries out almost completely at low tide but has long served as one of the most protected anchorages in northern Howe Sound. The deepest water is available close to the small wooded rocky peninsula which protects the nook from northerly winds and seas. Brunswick Point provides reasonable protection from up-inlet winds but southerly seas have a tendency to curl in here.

Development planned for the park includes floats and mooring buoys in the southern nook, trails, limited camping facilities and picnic area. An old concrete walkway (1924) encloses a shallow basin tidal lagoon at the north end of Porteau Cove. At the northern end of the park, near an old breakwater and wharf ruins, a launching ramp and scuba diving stage area will be built. The subtidal community here includes octopus, rockfish, anemones and sponges. To increase colonization, the wrecks *Cape Spuce*, M.V. *Fort Langley*, *H & L* and concrete and tire reefs have been sunk here. Boaters desiring to stretch their legs may wish to climb up to the Howe Sound Crest Trail which follows the ridge top down to Cypress Provincial Park behind West Vancouver. An easier land route will be provided by the reopening of the Royal Hudson passenger station above the cove.

Upper Howe Sound

Porteau Cove marks the eastern end of a shallow (30 fathom) sill which crosses Howe Sound to the Defence Islands and opposite shore and marks the transition line between the real "Sound" to the south and the real "Inlet" of upper Howe Sound to the north. The deepest part of Howe Sound is only 2 miles to the north of Glen Eden. This deep (159 fathom) was probably the result of intense downward scouring by a glacier as it passed through the narrow inlet walls 10,000 years ago. As the glacier passed into the much wider southern part of Howe Sound it was able to broaden out and drop the ground-up materials it was carrying under it as an "outwash deposit", much as a river does when it flows out from a narrow channel onto a wide shallow delta. Alternatively, this sill could have been formed as a terminal moraine —

material pushed up in front of an advancing glacier, which then retreated leaving the moraine to mark its furthest advance. (Mathews, et al, 1966).

North of Glen Eden the wind gradually increases in strength to a marked degree and surface currents, which in the southern sound are quite weak, increase to rates of 1 to 2 knots (generally *out* of the Sound — see chart). This prevailing current varies in strength with the volume of fresh water inflow into the Sound at Squamish; and the surface waters take on a distinctly "milky", opaque appearance, caused by glacial rock "flour" — fine silt in suspension. The silty coloured water does not necessarily indicate where the outflowing current is strongest as winds have a considerable influence on net surface current movement (see: *Oceanography of the British Columbia Coast,* by Richard E. Thomson for a concise and easily understood description of these phenomena).

Prolonged winds from the south can often reverse the surface current and increase and advance the height and time of high tide at Squamish. Prolonged northerly winds can increase the strength of the outflowing current and depress and delay the time of high tide at Squamish. The roughest, largest seas (maximum 4 to 5 feet) in upper Howe Sound are generally caused when a fresh southerly wind blows against a strong outflowing current. Seas generated by a "Squamish" while short and steep are less rough closer to the head of the Sound because of the limited fetch. Boats travelling in upper Howe Sound can avoid the roughest water by either keeping in the lee

Merry Dance *and* Tumbo *spend a quiet morning in Christie Cove.*

of projecting points or away from those areas where a fresh wind will be blowing against a surface current (see chart).

7 Defence Islands

These islands are named after H.M.S. *Defence,* 74 guns, Captain James Gambier. In the battle of the "Glorious First of June", the *Defence* was the first ship to pass through the French line. Walbran notes:

> The vessel had a most active share in the battle, during which she was totally dismasted, and had eighteen killed and thirty-nine wounded . . . At the Nile (1798) she . . . captured the *Franklin,* 80 guns and at Trafalgar (1805) she captured the *San Ildefonso,* 74 guns . . . on the 23 December, 1811, she met a most tragic fate . . . driven on shore on the coast of Jutland, in a fearful northwest gale, when out of 600 men on the *Defence* all but five perished.

Temporary anchorage is possible behind the largest Defence Island in depths of 4 to 6 fathoms but one should ensure one's anchor is well grounded if staying overnight or leaving the boat unattended even for a short while. There are often very strong non-tidal currents along this shore which can reverse when a back eddy develops. The Squamish Yacht Club is planning to set up a security station in this relatively isolated part of Howe Sound to assist yachtsmen who may be stranded by bad weather. Temporary anchorage is also possible behind a tiny 4-foot high islet where there are depths of at least 4 feet below a zero tide. There is a fairly strong easterly flowing current

Floats of Britannia Beach Boat Club are protected by old wharf. B.C. Museum of Mining is now on site of Britannia mine, once largest copper mine in Commonwealth.

and poor holding ground here (Stathers). More secure temporary anchorage is possible off the Potlatch Creek delta. There is a private wharf and floats at the west end of this delta which provide access to a summer camp operated by the Boys and Girls Club of Vancouver.

Less than 2 miles to the north of the Defence Islands there is a small peninsula joined to the mainland by a narrow isthmus with beaches on either side. This area is known locally as "Five Coves" or "Zorro Bay". Temporary anchorage is possible on either side of the isthmus with good protection from southerly or northerly seas. There is a 4-foot drying rock south of the isthmus which, when covered, is unmarked by kelp and obscured by the opaque waters. The remains of a wharf extend out from the north facing side of the isthmus.

8 Britannia

Britannia is the site of what was once the largest copper mine in the Commonwealth. It was originally prospected in 1888 and staked in 1897 by trapper Oliver Furry, who left his name on the creek south of here. The Britannia mine was opened in 1899 and over the next 75 years it survived catastrophic landslides, floods (37 died in the 1921 flood), fires and depressed copper markets to become the oldest continuously working copper mine in B.C. The B.C. Museum of Mining opened here after the mine closed and features an underground train ride, demonstrations of historical and present day mining techniques with rocker boxes, slushers, muckers and hoists in action, and a tour through the conspicuous concentrator building which climbs the hill face south of the old townsite. A huge gravel pit operation has bared the hillside south of Britannia. It is possible that

Britannia could be rejuvenated in the future. The flat area left by the gravel operation and deep water offshore provide some potential for port-industrial development.

Floats which provide moorage for members of the Britannia Beach Boat Club are located south of Britannia Creek. The floats are protected from southerly seas by the old wharf structure, but are open to the occasional winter northwesterly which blows across Howe Sound from the valley behind Woodfibre. There is a locked gate above the floats which makes access to shore difficult. The town takes its name from the creek and range of mountains south of here which was named after H.M.S. *Britannia*, 100 guns. (Walbran).

An old wreck is found in one of the few sandy (silt covered) coves in Howe Sound south of Murrin Provincial Park. This park is located half a mile inland and surrounds Browning Lake.

There is a ferry landing at Woodfibre since most of the pulp mill workers do not live here anymore but cross over daily from just south of Darrell Bay (or from Britannia). Darrell Bay is shallow, filled with log booms and open to up-inlet winds and seas. There is a private campground above here with both trailer and tenting sites, showers, laundromat, restaurant and a small grocery. A small park is located at the base of 700-foot high Shannon Falls. North of here is the Stawamus Chief, the largest granite monolith in Canada and second highest (to Ayers Rock, Australia) in the Commonwealth. Climbers from all over the world come here to test themselves on the sheer rock face but for those who want an easy climb to the top (2,138 feet above sea level) there is a trail around the back end. Magnificent views of Garibaldi, the Tantalus Range, the Squamish valley and Howe Sound are obtained. A 450-acre provincial recreation reserve covers this mountain.

9 Squamish

"Squamish" is the Indian name for "birthplace of the winds," and as previously noted, this area is subject to very strong winds and summer afternoon southerly (onshore) winds.

Captain Vancouver on reaching the head of Howe Sound noted:

> ... all our expectations vanished, in finding it to terminate in a round bason, [sic] encompassed on every side by the dreary country already described. (Chapter Seven).
> ... In this dreary and comfortless region, it was no inconsiderable piece of good fortune to find a little cove in which we could take shelter, and a small spot of level land on which we could erect our tent; as we had scarcely finished our examination when the wind became excessively boisterous from the southward, attended with heavy squalls and torrents of rain, which continuing until noon the following day, Friday the 15th, (June, 1792), occasioned a very unpleasant detention. But for this circumstance we might too hastily have concluded that this part of the gulf was uninhabited. In the morning we were visited by near forty of the natives, on whose approach, from the very material alteration that had now taken place in the face of the country, we expected to find

Sailing in Howe Sound, Mount Wrottelsey in background.
(The Jib Set)

Two miles north of Defence Islands is a small isthmus with beaches on either side, known to locals as "Five Coves" or "Zorro Bay".

some difference in their general character. This conjecture was however premature, as they varied in no respect whatever, but in possessing a more ardent desire for commercial transactions; into the spirit of which they entered with infinitely more avidity than any of our former acquaintances, not only in bartering amongst themselves the different valuables they had obtained from us, but when that trade became slack, in exchanging those articles again with our people; in which traffic they always took care to gain some advantage, and would frequently exult on the occasion. Some fish, their garments, spears, bows and arrows, to which these people wisely added their copper ornaments, comprized their general stock in trade. Iron, in all its forms, they judiciously preferred to any other article we had to offer.

The first settlers who arrived in the Squamish area in 1888 found platforms built high in spruce trees on the delta which had been used by the local Indians as lookout posts to watch for raiding Yaculta Indians. These settlers attempted to grow crops on the rich argicultural land of the delta but experienced great difficulty in adjusting to the periodic flooding, continual erosion and shifting of the various river distributaries.

Serious flooding has occurred in Squamish in 1908, 1921, 1937, 1940, 1949 and 1980 and the town itself was usually inundated with nearly 5 feet of water about once every 16 years. In the 1921 flood, the Mamquam River which formerly entered Howe

Sound to the east of the town of Squamish, changed its course to empty into the Squamish River, three miles upstream. The worst flooding often occurs after heavy rainfalls in October and not during the spring runoff or "freshet". The spring freshet often extends into August as the Squamish watershed is fed by many glaciers with maximum melting in midsummer.

Mamquam means "smelly water" and to live up to its name the old river channel (now known as "Mamquam Blind Channel") is becoming increasingly industrialized. Entrance to the government boat basin is made to the east of the FMC Chemicals wharf along a bearing of 034° (True). There are two leading beacons which serve as range marks to assist in passage up the dredged channel which is lined with log booms (Chart 3586). The leading beacons are not shown on metric Chart 3526 (1980 edition) and the passage beyond the range marks appears more shallow on this chart and on the plan from metric Chart 3534 than it actually is. There is reported to be at least 6 feet of water below chart datum as far as the government floats. (J. Stathers, 1982).

The Squamish government floats provide over 1,000 feet of berthage space and are located about a thousand feet beyond (NNW of) the leading beacons at the south end of the town of Squamish. The Squamish Yacht Club maintains floats and a launching ramp immediately south of the government floats.

Squamish government floats provide about a thousand feet of berthage space in Mamquam Channel.

The town of Squamish has a population of about 10,000; several hotels, restaurants and other medium sized town facilities. There are parks close to the railway station and in 1982 the Harbour Ferries *Britannia* was to commence passenger service from Vancouver to the Squamish government dock in conjunction with the Royal Hudson steam train schedule.

Chart 3586 indicates that the only navigable water at the head of Howe Sound is Mamquam Channel, the rest of the estuary is shown as drying out completely. Metric Charts 3526 and 3534 show navigable (but shallow) water west of the new port developments. In 1860, Richard Mayne reported that the "Squamisht" river was navigable by canoe for 20 miles. He had come down the river during the spring runoff after hiking overland from Jervis Inlet. In 1972 a training dyke was built on the east bank of the lower three miles of the main stem Squamish River. This dyke, which was built to prevent erosion, has confined the normal runoff to the west side of the estuary and deepened what is now the major distributary of the Squamish.

Although the mouth of the estuary is extremely hazardous for small boats when there is an onshore wind blowing (against the outflowing current) in calm conditions it is possible to explore up the river in a suitable (stable, shoal draught) boat and into the various estuarine channels and sloughs.

The estuary is alive with a variety of bird and animal life at various times of the year. There are ducks, geese and trumpeter swans; numerous waterbirds including cormorants, murres, pigeon guillemots,

Dredged channel up the Mamquam Channel to the government floats is lined with log booms. Mt. Garibaldi on horizon is an extinct volcano rising to 8787 feet above sea level.

gulls, grebes, coots, loons, oystercatchers and murrelets along with at least thirteen species of shorebirds including both blue and green herons. Eagles and other raptors (hawks) are so abundant as to seem commonplace (Environment Canada, 1975). The population of bald eagles is said to be one of the largest in North America. During the spawning season as many as 1500 eagles congregate on the lower river to feed on dead and dying salmon and as many as 70 single eagles have been observed from one location. Other notable wildlife include the ruffed grouse, harbour seals, coyotes, racoons, squirrels, muskrats, beaver, mink and deer.

There is a hiking trail which starts as a logging road from the west bank of the river and climbs up to Echo Lake and Alec Lake, 3,000 feet above sea level, nestled beneath Mt. Murchison and Mt. Lapworth. Canoes or other small boats can avoid the mouth of the estuary by launching upstream near the limit of tidal influence at the junction of the Squamish and the Mamquam and travelling downstream to the base of the trail where they can stash their boats above highwater line. Travelling back up against the current can be assisted by waiting for a flooding tide which will slow down or reverse the current in the lower part of the river. Trees along the old river channels were killed when the new training dyke prevented fresh water "flushing" of the channels and caused a salt water "wedge" to penetrate the delta area on high tides.

125

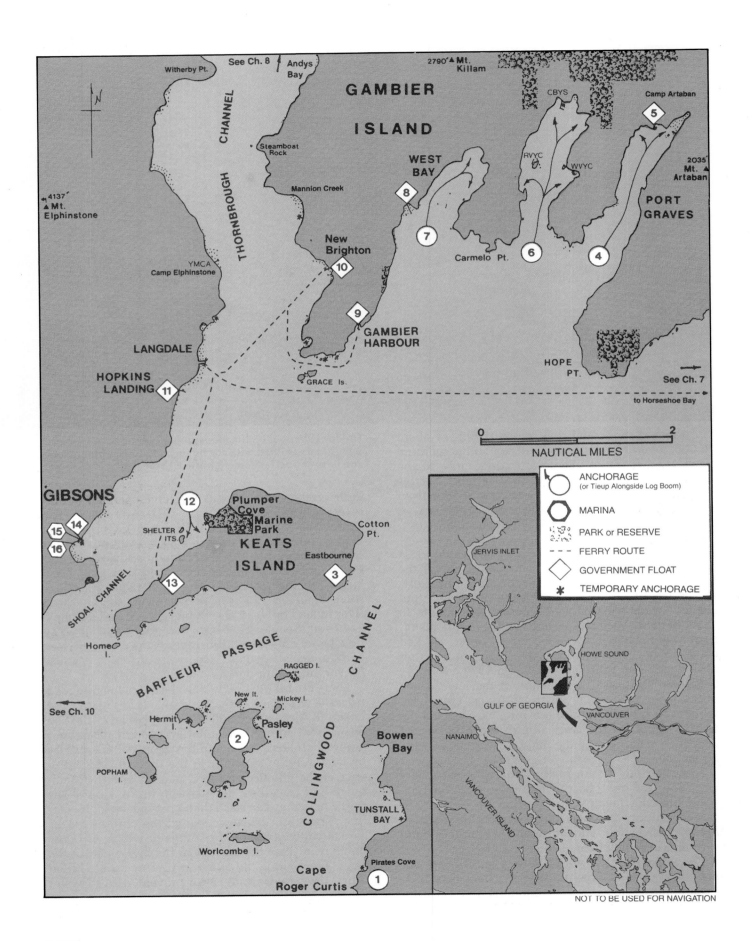

See Ch. 8

Witherby Pt.

Andys Bay

2790' ▲ Mt. Killam

CBYS

Camp Artaban

⑤

GAMBIER

ISLAND

Steamboat Rock

RVYC

WVYC

2035' Mt. ▲ Artaban

Mannion Creek

WEST BAY

⑧

PORT GRAVES

4137' ▲ Mt. Elphinstone

⑦

Carmelo Pt.

⑥

④

New Brighton

⑩

YMCA Camp Elphinstone

THORNBROUGH CHANNEL

⑨

GAMBIER HARBOUR

LANGDALE

HOPE PT.

HOPKINS LANDING

⑪

GRACE Is.

See Ch. 7

to Horseshoe Bay

0 ———— 2

NAUTICAL MILES

GIBSONS

⑫

Plumper Cove Marine Park

Cotton Pt.

14

SHELTER ITS

KEATS ISLAND

Eastbourne

15

③

16

13

SHOAL CHANNEL

ANCHORAGE (or Tieup Alongside Log Boom)

MARINA

PARK or RESERVE

FERRY ROUTE

GOVERNMENT FLOAT

TEMPORARY ANCHORAGE

JERVIS INLET

HOWE SOUND

Home I.

BARFLEUR PASSAGE

RAGGED I.

COLLINGWOOD CHANNEL

New It.

Mickey I.

GULF OF GEORGIA

VANCOUVER

See Ch. 10

Hermit I.

Pasley I.

②

Bowen Bay

NANAIMO

POPHAM I.

TUNSTALL BAY

Worlcombe I.

VANCOUVER ISLAND

Cape Roger Curtis

Pirates Cove

①

NOT TO BE USED FOR NAVIGATION

126

CHAPTER NINE

Southwestern Howe Sound

Western Bowen Island, Gambier and Keats Islands, Gibsons

This area of islands and islets, long inlets, heavily wooded coves, wide pebble beaches, scattered cottage settlements and spectacular scenery is probably the most popular cruising region on the B.C. coast. Only a few hours from Vancouver, its protected waters are teeming with boats during the five to six months of the major cruising season.

Gibsons Landing, the largest community, is also an important sport fishing centre, with Salmon Rock, at the entrance to "Gibsons Gap" (Shoal Channel) one of the most productive areas on the lower coast for springs and coho. The picturesque town is home base for the CBC's perennial "Beachcombers" series, which makes good use of the long strings of log booms which line much of the shoreline northeast of Gibsons. According to the B.C. Forest Service, Howe Sound is the largest log booming ground in the world.

Despite its popularity, this area has only one substantial marine park, at Plumper's Cove, and its floats and mooring buoys are jam-packed on a summer weekend. The two major Vancouver yacht clubs, Royal Van and West Van, have put in major private float installations in Center Bay in recent years, and the log booms of Gambier Island provide highly valued temporary moorage tie-up for visiting boats.

Winds

Winds in southern Howe Sound are largely local, rather than being the result of the large scale patterns prevailing in the Strait of Georgia. Bowen Island and Mt. Elphinstone present a considerable barrier to prevailing winds so that wind speeds here are much lighter than in the northern portion of the Sound. Winds can come from any direction in this area and there is no well-established diurnal pattern as at Point Atkinson or Squamish.

A temporary wind recording station established at Worlcombe Island in 1972 indicated a very irregular distribution of winds for the summer months with S.E., S.W. or N.W. winds each blowing approximately 15% of the time (for each direction) and all other directions (N., N.E., E., S., W.) each having a frequency of about 10%. It is only in the winter months that a definite pattern emerges with winds from the N.E. quadrant blowing collectively more than 60% of the time. (J. Emslie).

1   Cape Roger Curtis

The westernmost extremity of Bowen Island, like most of the other major points, islands, and waterways, is named after a prominent naval figure of the "Glorious First of June", 1794. Admiral Sir Roger Curtis was flag captain (captain of the fleet) aboard

CHARTS
3311 — Strip Chart #2 — HOWE SOUND
          (1:40,000) (alternative to 3526, 3586)
3577 — For coastline west of Gower Point
          (1:77,300)
3534 — Plan of Gibsons, Plumper Cove and
          Shoal Channel (1:12,000) (supercedes
          3508)

Lord Howe's flagship, the *Queen Charlotte*. Walbran notes that after the battle:

> he was sent home with Howe's despatches; and the King on visiting the *Queen Charlotte* at Spithead threw over his neck a massive gold chain, desiring him to keep it in his family as a lasting proof of royal regard and friendship.

The rocky foreshore around Cape Roger Curtis is gently to moderately sloping and provides interesting opportunities for hiking and for observation of intertidal life. Some of the few tidal pools around Bowen's coastline can be found here. The two small but shallow bays just north of the Cape could provide temporary anchorage depending on the tide and local wind conditions. It is unlikely that this area experiences particularly strong or prolonged onshore winds except in the spring or fall. The southernmost bay which is very shallow (2 feet of water at chart datum) is known locally as Pirates Cove. A trail leads from a nice beach here to Tunstall Bay.

Although all the bays on the west side of Bowen Island are open to west or southwest winds blowing in from the open Gulf (summer frequency at Worlcombe I. of 25%) it is likely that such winds are purely local. The presence of many mooring buoys and private floats in Tunstall and Bowen Bays indicates that heavy seas from the southwest are uncommon. These bays are also the most protected on Bowen Island from the winter "Squamish".

Tunstall Bay

Explosives Creek, flowing into Tunstall Bay, commemorates the existence of a dynamite and powder

Tiny cove north of Cape Roger Curtis has pleasant beach, trail to Tunstall Bay, but shallows to two feet.

plant which operated here from 1909 until the First World War when it was moved to James Island just north of Victoria. Making explosives was a dangerous business in those days and in the first two years of operation 12 men were killed in four separate explosions. The last blast was so strong it was felt in Nanaimo, 25 miles across the Gulf. (Howard).

Because of the fine gravel beach and southwest exposure, the bay has long been popular for camping and picnics. Camp Gates, for Vancouver Sun paper carriers operated here in the 1950s, but like Bowen Bay and King Edward Bay to the north, the upland has been subdivided and is now moderately settled. Bowen Bay is more protected from westerly seas and was once the base for a small commercial marina operation. Private moorings now fill much of the bay.

2 Pasley Island

The Pasley group of islands between Collingwood Channel and Barfleur Passage are of particular interest to small boat explorers as they offer a miniature "Gulf Island"- or even "Barkley Sound"-like archipelago without the open ocean exposures. There are many small coves, nooks and crannies; only a few of which are exposed to seas or swells from the open Gulf of Georgia. There are, however, numerous (at least 21) drying rocks and reefs between the islands, some of which are particularly dangerous. The islands are all private and exploration ashore is usually discouraged. Most residents, however, do not mind the odd boat seeking a few hours of peaceful anchorage in a protected cove.

Worlcombe Island was named Swus-Pus-Tak-Kwin-Ace by the Indians and like most of the others of the Pasley group was used as a base for whaling and seal hunting operations around the turn of the century. More recent residents have relied on wind generators to provide their own electricity — a more secure and reliable source than mainland hydro sources subject to occasional brownouts from winter storms. There is a small stone breakwater protected haven near the eastern end of the northern shoreline.

Pasley Island was named after Admiral Sir Thomas Pasley who carried his flag as a Rear Admiral in H.M.S. *Bellerophon*, 74 guns, Captain Hope (note southernmost tip of Gambier Island) at the battle of the "Glorious First of June". Walbran says that Pasley "bore a very distinguished part in the battle" and lost a leg for which he was granted a pension of 1,000 pounds. Collingwood Channel and Barfleur Passage are named after Vice Admiral Lord Collingwood who, as Captain Cuthbert Collingwood of H.M.S. *Barfleur*, had an important share in the battle of the First of June. Eleven years later he served as the second in command to Lord Nelson at the battle of Trafalgar for which he inherited immortal fame. (Walbran).

There are several small bays around Pasley Island which are suitable for temporary anchorage depending on wind direction. At the south end one can find reasonable protection from westerlies and there is a small nook inside the southeast tip which provides some shelter from light southeasterlies. The main anchorage, where most of the island residents keep their boats on mooring buoys, is at the northeast end of the island. Another possible anchorage is on the lee side of New Islet which is connected to the northern shore of Pasley by a tombolo spit which dries about mid-tide. There are a number of dangerous rocks just east of this spit, A very similar type of anchorage can be found a quarter of a mile to the west where another tombolo spit (drying about 10 feet) joins a small islet to Hermit Island.

Mickey Island is named after Malcolm McBean (Mickey) Bell-Irving who was killed in the First World War. As a child, he and his sister had spent summers exploring these islands. Hermit Island was named by them after a very tall Norwegian who lived there alone in a small driftwood cabin, wore nothing but sealskin furs and lived on fish and sealmeat. His cabin was surrounded by the skulls of all the seals he had caught and his abrupt manner discouraged visitors but he was friendly to those who did not seek anything from him.

Temporary shelter is also possible between the rocks and islets off the east end of Ragged Island or behind a stone breakwater off the south end of Popham Island. It is possible that Popham Island and Home Island, a mile to the north, are named after Rear

Mooring buoys off the summer community of Tunstall bay belong to local residents.

Admiral Sir Home Riggs Popham, author of *Coast Signals* (1803) (J. S. Matthews)

Keats Island

The east shore of Keats Island does not offer particularly good anchorage although shelter for small boats is avaialable in a few small coves or behind offshore rocks or islets. Keats Island can be distinguished as being virtually the only major feature in Howe Sound named after an officer of the Royal Navy who did not take part in the battle of the "Glorious First of June". Walbran notes that the island was named "after Admiral Sir Richard Goodwin Keats,

Summer cottages line Bowen's rugged west shore. A few coves like this one are seldom used as anchorages, but are moderately well protected from most summer winds.

Pasley's abundance of nooks and crannies are fun to explore, but at least 21 drying rocks and reefs make it hazardous.

Big enough for only two or three boats is picturesque temporary anchorage at east end of Ragged Island in Pasley group.

K.B., a distunguished officer . . . second to none in gallantry, genius or talent."

In 1801 Captain Keats in the 74 gun ship *Superb*, as one of the squadron of Rear Admiral Sir James Saumarez, Bart., made an attack, near Cape Trafalgar, on a combined French and Spanish fleet, the result of which is without parallel in naval history. The circumstances of this gallant attack are as follows:—

While the British fleet were refitting at Gibraltar, after the repulse at Algeciras, the French fleet of four sail of the line was joined at the latter Spanish port on the 9th of July by five Spanish line-of-battle ships, the combined fleet sailing for the westward at noon of the 12th. The British fleet, consisting of five line-of-battle ships and a frigate of 32 guns, though far from ready, with the exception of the *Superb* and the frigate, immediately prepared to follow and by 7 o'clock were off Cabrita point and under full sail after the enemy. "A fresh easterly wind was blowing and as night came on the enemy were lost sight of, when at 9 o'clock Saumarez hailing the *Superb* directed Keats, whose ship was in splendid order not having been in the engagement at Algeciras, to try and overtake the enemy and delay them by attacking their sternmost ships. Keats with the greatest enthusiasm most readily obeyed, set every stitch of canvas that would draw and going between 11 and 12 knots was soon out of sight of his companions. Shortly after 11 o'clock the *Superb* ranged abreast of a strange sail, looming large in the darkness, known afterwards to be the *Real Carlos*, 112 guns; Keats, without any hesitation, poured his port broadside into what he knew must be an enemy, following it with a second and third, and then passed on to another sail ahead which he attacked and captured. Many of the shot from the broadsides fired at the *Real Carlos* struck another towering sail about a quarter of a mile on the other side of her, known afterwards to be the *Hermenegildo*, 112 guns, the crew of which ship in the surprise of the attack were all in confusion, and assuming in the darkness that the *Real Carlos* was a British ship and that the shot came from her, immediately opened fire on her. On board the *Real Carlos* the surprise and confusion were equally as great, and thinking they were between two enemies fired wildly on both sides; the *Hermenegildo* furiously continued her attack on the *Real Carlos* and the latter hotly replying, the result was that the two Spanish three-deckers destroyed each other, both taking fire and blowing up. In the meantime the remainder of the British fleet came up, and passing the two burning ships, completed the victory by driving the remaining vessels, left after the attack of the *Superb*, in headlong flight into Cadiz. It is recorded that the two Spanish vessels destroyed were crowded with officers and men, the former scions of the most noble houses in Spain. Nearly 2,400 lives were lost through the disaster, it being one of the most tragical events in naval history." (Biography of Keats, and Brenton's Naval History.)

Keats in the *Superb* was with Nelson off Toulon in 1803, and the latter had such a high appreciation of Keats and his ship, as to state in a letter to Hugh Elloitt, 11 July, 1803, "I esteem his person alone as equal to one French 74, and the *Superb* and her captain to two 74-gun ships."

For a period after 1813, Keats served as Governor of Newfoundland.

3 Eastbourne

There is a small, 100 foot government float here providing access to the community at the east end of Keats Island. There are magnificent views north to snowcapped, 8,800 foot high Mt. Garibaldi (40 miles

Large population of cottage dwellers with private wharves and floats line Keats Island's west side.

to the north) flanked by Mt. Artaban, Gambier Island and Leading Peak, Anvil Island. Cotton Point is named after Admiral Sir Charles Cotton, Bart., who as Captain Cotton of H.M.S. *Majestic*, 74 guns, shared in Lord Howe's victory of the "Glorious First of June."

A mile west of Cotton Point there is a large farm, possibly the largest within Howe Sound, which serves as a conspicuous landmark.

Howe Sound is the largest log booming area in the world. Below is RivTow's boom assembly area in West Bay.

Outstation of West Vancouver Yacht Club in Centre Bay, with private floats on the right.

The wreck of the sailing ship Sir Thomas J. Lipton *dwarfs visitors to West Bay in 1962 photograph. (The Jib Set)*

Camp Artaban at the head of Long Bay has been operated by the Anglican Church since 1924.

Gambier Island

Gambier Island, the largest island within Howe Sound, is named after Admiral of the Fleet, James, Lord Gambier, who, in the battle of the "Glorious First of June" was captain of H.M.S. *Defence*, 74 guns, Walbran notes:

> Gambier's notions of religion and morality were much stricter than those in vogue at that time; the *Defence* was spoken of as "a praying ship," and it was freely questioned whether it was possible for her to be "a fighting ship" as well. The doubt, if it really existed, was set at rest by the gallant conduct of her captain and crew on the 1st of June, as they were the first to break through the enemy's line and hotly engage three French ships. The story is told that towards the close of the battle as the *Defence* was lying dismasted, Captain Pakenham, of the *Invincible*, passing within hail, called to Gambier in friendly banter: "I see you have been knocked about a good deal; never mind. Jimmy, whom the Lord loveth he chasteneth." Gambier's conduct had, however, attracted Lord Howe's notice, and he was one of those specially recommended for the gold medal.

Gambier Island is unique within the Strait of Georgia-Gulf Island region because it has the smallest population density of all the major islands. Despite its location less than 15 miles from Vancouver there are only 65 permanent residents on the island. This number swells to over 600 during the summer months. The determination of island residents to preserve their isolation and separate character makes them fiercely protective and wary of any incursions or unwanted developments.

The three finger-like bays at the south end of Gambier Island provide yachtsmen with possibly the finest and most readily accessible weekend cruising destinations available anywhere on the lower coast. The three bays are each bounded by moderately steep, rocky bluffs and knolls with virtually no development above the immediate shoreline. Under natural circumstances these bays might accommodate relatively few boats because (with the exception of Port Graves) the deep waters inhibit anchorage. The presence of log booms stored along the shoreline provide abundant opportunities for safe temporary or overnight moorage, thereby increasing the capacity of the bays enormously. As many as 400 boats have been observed tied to booms in these bays on a busy summer weekend. (James Alley, *Recreational Boating in Howe Sound*, Islands Trust, 1976).

In tying up alongside a log boom one should be prepared with "dogs" — eye hooks which can be hammered into the log and yanked out when leaving. "Dogs" are necessary where there are no chains or branch sticks to tie to. Fenders should be heavily weighted to protect the underside of the boat from pounding against the boom and the existence of any sinkers, logs hung up under the boom and branch sticks projecting under the boat should be ascertained. One should also be prepared to move off the boom in the event that a tugboat arrives to remove it. Otherwise one may wake the next morning to find oneself a few miles up the Fraser River.

4 Port Graves

Port Graves, also known as East Bay, Long Bay, Deep Bay(?) or Artaban Bay was named after Admiral Lord Thomas Graves who commanded the leading squadron in Lord Howe's fleet on the "Glorious First of June". His flagship was H.M.S. *Royal Sovereign*, 100 guns.

A small indentation just inside Gambier Point, the western entrance to Port Graves, is known locally as Daisy Bay — the site of a former government wharf. Although water depths within Port Graves are generally suitable for anchoring (average 4 to 6 fathoms around the head) the long history of logging and booming activity has left a bottom littered with sunken logs, cables and chains which have a tendency to snag anchors. Strong winter Gulf of Georgia S.E. gales have a tendency to be redirected by the local topography down into Port Graves as a gusty W.N.W. wind.

Grace Islands off the southwest tip of Gambier Island.

5 Camp Artaban

A tiny government float with space for only one or two boats is located inside the western end of the wharf at the head of Port Graves. Floats on the east side of the wharf belong to Camp Artaban, established in 1924 by the Anglican Church. The camp and mountain opposite are named after the "fourth wise man" who searched continually throughout his life for the new born King. His gifts (a sapphire, a ruby and a pearl) were given freely to help others and at the end of his life he seemed to have failed in his search. But his gifts were accepted and he did not fail according to *The Story of the Other Wise Man* by Henry Van Dyke.

With permission from Camp Artaban, one can hike from the head of the bay up to Lost Lake; across a low, pastoral isthmus where dairy cattle once grazed, to Brigade Bay; or up to the top of Mt. Artaban (2,035 feet high) where there are the remains of a forestry lookout tower and fantastic views. In the fall one can watch the struggle of spawning salmon swimming up the creek which drains into the head of Port Graves. The property east of Camp Artaban around this creek has been subdivided. It is hoped that any future development will not interfere with the beauty of this area.

Government wharf at Gambier Harbour is exposed to southerlies and ferry wash.

6 Centre Bay

Centre Bay serves not only as a very popular logboom-moorage area but also as a base for three yacht club outstations. A small cove on the east shore of the bay contains floats which are reserved for members of the West Vancouver Yacht Club. Guests must be approved by the executive. Behind Alexandra Island are the Royal Vancouver Yacht Club floats and at the head of the bay is the Centre Bay Outstation, members of which are mainly from the Burrard Yacht Club.

There is a large provincial recreational reserve just north of Centre Bay with no public marine access

Floats at New Brighton are used by passenger ferries from Langdale and water taxis from Gibsons.

other than a tiny corner at the head of the easternmost cove near the head of Centre Bay. Old trails and overgrown logging roads wind through the woods into the centre of the island and across to the adjoining bays. Most of these trails are through private land for which permission to cross should be obtained.

Carmelo Point, between Centre and West Bays commemorates the name given by Narvaez to Howe Sound in 1791 — Bocas del Carmelo.

7   West Bay

West Bay is not a favourite cruising destination for many because there is nothing of real importance here other than a great variety of log booms and strategically placed rocks which tend to slow down approaching boats. The bay is not completely without interest as it is noted to have reasonably warm swimming water, an old shipwreck (the four masted sailing ship *Sir Thomas J. Lipton*), beaches for beachcombing and waterfront nature trails. Several years ago, the Parks Branch recognized the very high potential of this bay as a possible future marine park. This interest by the Parks Branch so excited the local residents that they decided to designate this area for intensive subdivision development in their official community plan. The plan also recommended that all future

marine parks be located as far away from this end of Gambier Island as possible.

There is still a possibility however, that a waterfront wilderness type park with no upland development would be equally appreciated by both residents and mariners alike and permit the continued use of West Bay for log boom storage.

8   West Bay Gov't Float

A small float attached to the end of a long pier provides access to the shore here. The roads which lead south to the communities of New Brighton, Gambier Harbour and Avalon Bay are really country lanes and different from most other island and mainland roads in that there is so little traffic one can find grass growing in the tire ruts. The majority of the island's 65 permanent residents live on this southwesternmost peninsula of Gambier Island. The lack of car ferry access is viewed as a very positive benefit, preserving a feeling of splendid isolation and an independent mood somewhat similar to that found on Lasqueti Island — the only other major island on the

Most popular marine park close to Vancouver is at Plumper Cove. Protection is provided by Shelter Islets.

south coast without car ferry access. Any threat to this mood, whether real or imagined, is fought by the Gambier Islanders with ferocity. In so doing, the Islanders are also working to protect the scenic beauty and natural charm of Howe Sound — highly valued qualities for everyone who travels by boat in this area.

9 Gambier Harbour

The government float in Gambier Harbour (formerly Grace Harbour) has about 200 feet of moorage space. The floats are somewhat exposed to any southerly seas and to ferry wash. Gambier Island achieved a certain local fame during World War II as Headquarters of 119 Company, Pacific Coast Militia Rangers, better known as the Gambier Island Rangers. The Commanding Officer was Captain Francis Drage, veteran of the Imperial Army in World War I. Other officers included Lt. Joe Mitchell — boat builder and boom master in East Bay, Thomas Burns — the "doughty Irish author" who with his son Con trained wild pigeons to carry messages and made a highly accurate contour map of the island, Art Yule of Halkett Bay — veteran of the Boer War and a retired steel worker, W. S. Bradbury — road foreman and former Mountie, C. A. Lett — veteran, storekeeper and postmaster at Gambier Harbour (Vancouver *Province*, 1943). While these men guarded the home front many islanders served overseas and after the war a Memorial Hall was erected. The Gambier Island Branch of the Royal Canadian Legion is located just up the road from Gambier Harbour and maintains the tradition of

Dangerous rock 75 feet off the end of the government floats in Plumper Cove is seen here at 2 foot tide.

unswerving loyalty with "God Save the Queen" sung at midnight.

Gambier Harbour is also served by passenger ferry several times a day from Langdale, the B.C. Ferries terminal north of Gibsons.

While temporary anchorage is possible inside the Grace Islands it tends to become somewhat congested since it also serves as a thoroughfare for boats rounding this end of Gambier. Temporary anchorage with slightly more protection from the wash of passing boats is afforded in Avalon Bay, Thornbrough Bay and off the Mannion Creek delta. Temporary tie-up alongside log booms is possible in several of these bays and in Andy's Bay or across Thornbrough Channel on the mainland side.

10 New Brighton

New Brighton provides over 500 feet of government float moorage space. Some of the float space is kept open for the regular passenger ferry service from Langdale and water taxi service from Gibsons. The road from here leads north to a trail, a corduroy logging road and a major logging road between the two cone shaped mountains and thence by a slippery trail down to Gambier Lake. (See *Hiking Trails of the Sunshine Coast*, Harbour Publishing (1979)). The two mountains are named after two officers killed in action in World War II, Lt. David A. Killam, Royal Cana-

Gibsons has large government wharf, grocery, marine, fishing and liquor stores, making it central supply area for boats cruising west Howe Sound.

dian Navy and Flying Officer John R. Liddell, Royal Canadian Air Force, who as boys had spent their holidays at family summer homes on Gambier.

Mannion Creek is named after one of the first land-owners in Howe Sound, Joseph Mannion, who in

Floats at Keats Island opposite Gibsons Landing.

1883 preempted 142 acres here. A tiny but prominent islet just off the westernmost extremity of Gambier Island is known as Steamboat Rock. Since the waters around this rock have been used for many years as a burial place for dead seafarers and for the scattering of ashes, it has been designated as the "Mariner's Rest" memorial.

11 Hopkins Landing

There is a small government float at Hopkins Landing with space for about 3 or 4 boats located inside a wharfhead which is used for bulk oil distribution. Hopkins Landing is the only remaining public float access of other landings formerly located at Granthams and Williamsons which also served as steamer stops in the early part of this century. A small general store and post office is located at the head of the wharf. Just north of here is the B.C. Ferries Langdale Terminal (service to Horseshoe Bay), a Salvation Army summer camp, and opposite New Brighton — the Y.M.C.A. Camp Elphinstone. Camp Elphinstone has been operating since 1907, teaching young boys hiking, camping, canoeing and sailing skills. Long voyages are made in small boats throughout Howe Sound, Sechelt and Jervis Inlets. The camp is named after the 4,000-foot high mountain directly behind which was named after Captain J. Elphinstone who commanded H.M.S. *Glory,* 98 guns, on the "Glorious First of June". Elphinstone went to the assistance of Gambier and the *Defence* which was hotly engaged by three French vessels, thereby distracting the enemy's attention and diverting their shot.

12 Plumper Cove Marine Park

Plumper Cove is a very popular anchorage in the summer months as it is the closest provincial marine park to Vancouver. The cove is reasonably well protected from southwesterly seas by the Shelter Islets. Care should be taken to avoid a rocky patch, 2 feet below chart datum, located about 75 feet from the end of the marine park floats. These floats are intended for small boats which do not carry dinghies. A grassy picnic area with a few apple trees is all that remains open of what was once an extensive orchard. Old overgrown apple trees can be found still growing in the deep woods. Trails lead north from the picnic area to small camp sites and east through the woods to Lookout Mountain (795 feet) and Stony Hill (710 feet) which is referred to by Keats Islanders as "the highest peak". Lookout Mountain is also known as Carmichael Peak after an early pioneer who was also the unofficial mayor of Keats Island.

13 Keats Island Gov't Float

Despite the many "private" signs at the end of this wharf there is a very small public float attached to the inside of the wharf which provides about 100 feet of temporary moorage space. There are many other private floats attached to and adjacent to the government wharf. Space is also provided for the small passenger ferry from Langdale and a water taxi service from Gibsons. The Keats Island Baptist Camp was first established here after a 1925 purchase of land by the Keats Island Summer Home Company. Prior to this a farmer called William Read from Cheltenham, Gloucester, established his home here and tended gardens which produced enough vegetables for the entire island. He also operated a guest home called "Readhurst" which is now used as a hotel for guests of the Baptist Camp. Keats seems to have been very popular as a summer camp. Over the years camps were established by the Presbyterians, Anglicans, and United Church, but only the Baptists now remain.

In the spring of 1886 a retired Royal Navy Lieutenant, George Gibson was sailing his 18 foot schooner the *Swamp Angel* across the Gulf from Ladysmith to Vancouver when he was pushed off course by a southeast gale. Gibson and his two sons landed first at Keats Island then the next day crossed to the mainland shore where they established the community of Gibsons Landing.

14 Gibsons Landing

Gibsons Landing (or just "Gibsons") was established in the same year as Vancouver — 1886 — and while it has not grown quite as fast (present population, approximately 3,000) it is nevertheless a very lively community. A large government wharf and wood piling breakwater protect several finger floats providing over 2,300 feet of small craft moorage. Services provided include several grocery stores, liquor store (at the top of the hill where there is a large shopping centre) laundromat, restaurants, the "N.D.P. Bookstore" and the home base for one of the finest newspapers in British Columbia — *The Coast News.* Gibsons is also the home base for the popular T.V. series — "The Beachcombers", and "Molly's Reach" — where much of the indoor action takes place, is located at the head of the wharf. Unfortunately, this particular "cafe" is seldom open.

The All Sports Marine Building across the road from Molly's Reach provides fishing tackle, ice, bait, marine hardware, laundromat and showers. There is also a waterfront pub here known as "Gramma's Marine Inn" with a 200-foot float for guest moorage north of the Government floats in the summer months.

Less than a quarter of a mile west of the government wharf is the Elphinstone Pioneer Museum which features a fascinating range of exhibits including what is reputed to be the largest sea-shell and mollusc collection in Canada. There is also an excellent collection of photographs depicting the history of Howe Sound and the Sunshine Coast from the earliest days.

15 Smitty's Marina

Smitty's Marina is located inside the government floats. Services provided include fuel dock, engine repairs, moorage, hardware, rental boats, bait and tackle.

16 Hyak Marine Ltd.

Hyak Marine is located immediately southwest of the government floats. There is a fuel dock, marine ways, bait and tackle sales.

There are plans for a new 400-berth marina to be constructed south of the government floats after dredging of the tidal foreshore.

The central, shallow portion of Shoal Channel is known locally as "The Gap" and is very popular for fishing. Small boats anchor over the shallows between Home Island off the south tip of Keats Island and Gospel Rock or Steep Bluff on the mainland. Strong S.W. or N.E. ("Squamish") winds can raise 2 to 3 foot rollers in the Gap which tend to break when blowing over an opposing tidal stream. Home Island (Salmon Rock) is a one-acre recreational reserve.

There is a small shorefront picnic area known as Georgia Park located immediately west of Steep Bluff and a mile west of Gower Point is Chaster Creek Provincial Park with launching ramp, picnic areas, campsites and a pebble beach overlooking the Gulf of Georgia.

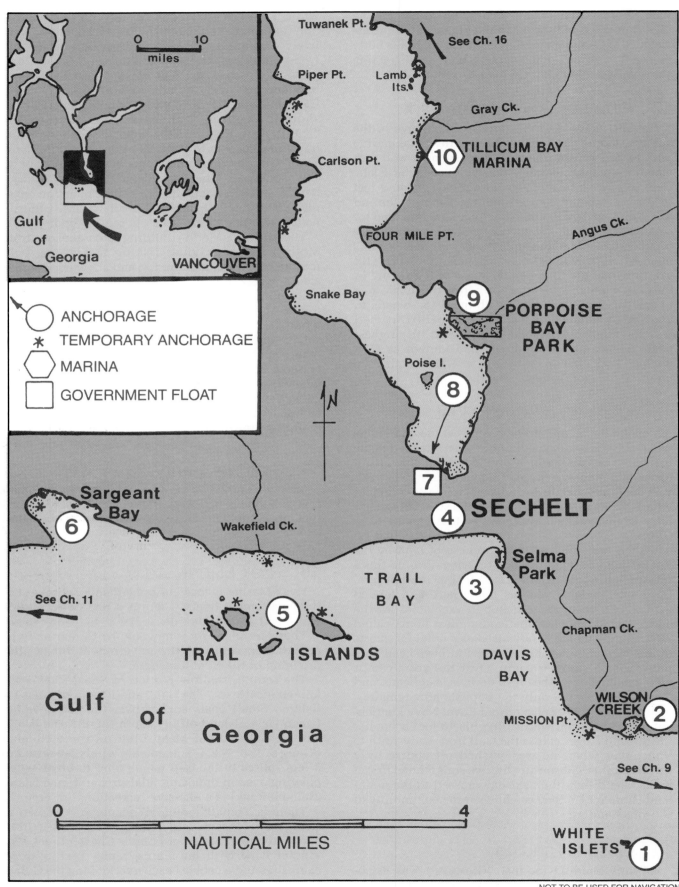

Tuwanek Pt.

See Ch. 16

Piper Pt.

Lamb Its.

Gray Ck.

TILLICUM BAY MARINA
⬡10

Carlson Pt.

Angus Ck.

FOUR MILE PT.

Snake Bay

⑨

PORPOISE BAY PARK

Poise I.

⑧

▢7

SECHELT

Sargeant Bay

⑥

Wakefield Ck.

④

Selma Park

③

TRAIL BAY

See Ch. 11

⑤

TRAIL ISLANDS

Chapman Ck.

DAVIS BAY

Gulf of Georgia

WILSON CREEK

②

MISSION Pt.

See Ch. 9

0   4

NAUTICAL MILES

WHITE ISLETS

①

Legend:

⬡ ANCHORAGE

✳ TEMPORARY ANCHORAGE

⬡ MARINA

▢ GOVERNMENT FLOAT

Gulf of Georgia

VANCOUVER

0   10
miles

NOT TO BE USED FOR NAVIGATION

138

CHAPTER TEN

Sechelt

Wilson Creek, Sargeant Bay, southern Sechelt Inlet

Stretching northwestward away from Vancouver and Howe Sound, the "Sunshine Coast" has been a magnet to yachtsmen for many years. The majority of visitors now arrive by car ferry while a lucky few, travelling north by small boat, have the opportunity to discover and experience the salubrious climate of this particular stretch of coast first hand. The term "Sunshine Coast" was possibly derived from Harry Roberts who described the Roberts Creek area as lying in the "Sunshine Belt". In the 1920s the Union Steamship Company applied the slogan "Sunshine and Sea-Charm along Holiday Shores on the Gulf Coast" to their passenger run along the northeastern shore of the Gulf of Georgia from Vancouver to Powell River. This coast does in fact receive up to 2,400 hours of sunshine annually, more than any other area on the west coast of Canada. The climate is so balmy that palm trees, eucalyptus, apricots and fig trees are reported to grow in this area.

While the stretch of coastline from Gibsons Landing in Howe Sound to Sechelt is fairly open and exposed, the waters off the coast are actively used by local residents with small boats for fishing, sailing, rowing or paddling and exploring. In the summer months parts of the coast are dotted with private moorings, despite the lack of protection from any onshore wind. The coastline here is relatively straight with lengthy stretches of sand or gravel beaches between rocky outcrops. Shallow depths up to half a mile offshore make even temporary anchorage treacherous or uncomfortable as any onshore wind or swell may result in breaking seas. For small (under 20 feet) boats of shallow draught there are a number of locations which offer some degree of protection or the opportunity for safe beaching.

Roberts Creek, halfway between Gibsons Landing and Sechelt (see Chapter 16 chart for location), was started by the Grandfather of Harry Roberts who built a cabin here in 1889. Several wharves have been built here for Union Steamship and local resident use but all have succumbed to the fury of winter southeast gales. The community is now distinguished from seaward by two large silver sausage-shaped propane tanks lying horizontally one behind the other on top of a stone breakwater which juts out almost 800 feet from the shore. Ruins at the end of the breakwater are all that remain of previous wharves.

Although the shallows off Roberts Creek are not particularly recommended as anchorage, temporary or otherwise, very small boats of shallow draught could find emergency shelter in the estuary of Roberts Creek west of the breakwater near high tide. There are other locations along this shore where there are isolated rock clusters up to a few hundred feet offshore

CHARTS
3311 — Strip Chart #3 — HOWE SOUND to
      PENDER HARBOUR (1:40,000)
3577 — SAND HEADS to BALLENAS (1:77,293)
3589 — JERVIS INLET and APPROACHES
      (1:76,384)
3535 — (supercedes 3510)

Most commonly used racing mark in the Strait of Georgia is White Islets, a mile south of Wilson Creek.

connected to the shore by sand or gravel spits which could offer a small amount of protection in their lee for very small boats.

Halfway between Roberts Creek and Wilson Creek, at the terminus of Flume Road in what is known

Sole anchorage between Gibsons and Welcome Pass along the Sunshine Coast is Selma Park at Sechelt. In the background is Sechelt Inlet.

locally as Elphinstone Bay, is a small 2½-acre provincial picnic site. This picnic site is identifiable from seaward as being the first non-developed wooded patch north of Roberts Creek. Those wishing to camp ashore should, after securing their boat above the pebbly beach, follow Beach Avenue ¼ mile to the west where Park Avenue runs north another ½ mile to the campground area of 96-acre Roberts Creek Provincial Park (where there are 25 campsites available).

1　White Islets

The White Islets, a mile south of Wilson Creek, are familiar to most Strait of Georgia racing sailors. On a hot day, the Islets first appear as a shimmering mirage surrounded by hundreds of hovering birds. The whiteness of the Islets is not solely due to the natural rock colour. Boats which pass too close are in danger of being splattered by birds defending their territory. Bird counts indicate the presence of over 435 Glaucous-winged gull nests and 45 Pelagic cormorant nests.

The waters off the Sunshine Coast may be relatively placid during the summer months but occasional storms or good weather westerlies can raise heavy seas because of the long fetches. Winter storms can be particularly spectacular. Fred Rogers (*Shipwrecks of British Columbia*) records that over 20 large vessels are known to have sunk in the stretch of water from

Gibsons to Trail Bay for one reason or another. On the evening of December 28, 1925, the Union Steamship *Cowichan* was sliced into by the bow of the steamship *Lady Cynthia* near White Islets in a thick fog. All the passengers and crew of the *Cowichan* calmly transferred to the *Lady Cynthia* by climbing over the forepeak railing. No one was lost or injured but the *Cowichan* sank in 60 fathoms within 11 minutes of the collision.

2 Wilson Creek

Wilson Creek estuary has been used for many years as a log storage area with protection afforded by a stone breakwater. The approaches to the estuary and the basin inside the breakwater dry out almost completely at low tide, except for a narrow channel leading into the estuary and a slough-like depression just north of the Wilson Creek outlet. At high tide, shoal draught boats could find temporary shelter behind the breakwater from westerly seas and at the head of the basin from southeasterlies. The Indians who own the land surrounding the Wilson Creek estuary have considered dredging the basin and constructing a small marina here.

The estuary delta of Chapman Creek, half a mile to the west of Wilson Creek, extends out from Mission Point for over 1,200 feet and is a hazard at high water.

Wilson Creek estuary is used for log storage, protected by a stone breakwater.

At low water, limited temporary anchorage to the lee of the sand and gravel delta is possible in calm or light wind conditions. Summer winds in this area, including the eastern end of Trail Bay (and what is known locally as Davis Bay), tend to be directly onshore or from the southwest, bending around to become the onshore wind which blows over the village

Old pilings, pebble beaches mark Wilson Creek estuary.

Looking north over Sechelt, with Sechelt Inlet in the background. Porpoise Bay floats and beach are visible at head of inlet.

of Sechelt and up Sechelt Inlet. West of Sechelt, afternoon onshore winds often seem to counteract any prevailing westerly to blow into Sargeant Bay.

The beautiful sand and gravel beach of Davis Bay extends north from Mission Point into Trail Bay and

Town of Sechelt, with Trail Islands in the background.

has long been popular with residents and visitors in small boats or travelling by car as this is one of the few places that the Sunshine Coast Highway comes down to the seaside. The Davis Bay Wharf offers no protection for small boats but is popular as a fishing platform or for dropping off passengers from larger boats.

3   Selma Park

Well protected anchorage is available behind a substantial stone breakwater at Selma Park. This area is named after the luxury yacht, *Selma*, originally owned by the Marquis of Anglesey, which cruised the Mediterranean with Edward VII and the actress Lily Langtree aboard as guests in the 1880s. The *Selma* came to British Columbia via the Horn and was converted for use as a passenger vessel on the run from Vancouver to Powell River in 1911. Land around Selma Park was bought by the All Red Line to serve as picnic grounds for holidaying steamship passengers and as an alternative access to the village of Sechelt.

4   Sechelt

For over 60 years the village of Sechelt was easily identifiable from seaward by mariners familiar with the prominent landmark of the Indian Church, *Our Lady of Lourdes*. It was visible from as far away as Vancouver Island when the setting sun was reflected off its steeples. In 1970 the church was destroyed by fire and shortly thereafter the Sechelt wharf which had been in disuse for many years also succumbed to fire. The first Sechelt wharf had been built in 1904 by Hubert Whitaker who also developed a hotel and resort. As many as three ships a day would call into Sechelt, bringing hundreds of holidayers and residents before the highway connected this part of the coast to the outside world.

The first white man to take up land on the Sunshine Coast was John Scales, who came to B.C. in 1859 as one of the detachment of Royal Engineers. Ten years later he applied for Crown grants covering the Sechelt isthmus from Trail Bay to Porpoise Bay. In the early 1890s, Scales sold his land to the Lieutenant Governor of B.C., Hugh Nelson.

The village of Sechelt is named after the local Indians who knew the area as "Chataleech" meaning "outside water" to describe the uniqueness of the narrow isthmus separating the head of Sechelt Inlet from the open waters of the Gulf. The Sechelt Indians have a reputation for diligence and industriousness.

They were instructed by the early missionaries in methods of digging ditches, dyking and draining the marshes near Porpoise Bay to plant and grow vegetables and berry plants on the rich land created. A popular myth relates how it occurred to them that a large ditch (or "canal") across the low and sandy isthmus could be easily dug and would ease the burden of portaging their canoes. The ditch was half completed when someone realized that tidal differences might result in swift currents similar to the Skookumchuck at the other end of Sechelt Inlet and rapid erosion of the sandy banks washing away the entire isthmus. Remnants of this uncompleted ditch can still be found behind the village of Sechelt. Helen Dawe, local Sechelt historian and a great debunker of popular myths, notes that this "ditch story" has through the years been expanded into a full scale canal development, still actively proposed by some Sechelt residents. A realization that canal development may be too expensive has led to plans for the development (1982) of the "longest boat ramp in the world" along Wharf Road across the isthmus. Boats

Trail Islands, with Sargeant Bay upper right. In the distance, Merry Island, Thormanby Island and Texada Island.

Sargeant Bay above and below is better known as Norwest Bay to oldtime mariners, and is open to southeasters. Extensive marsh and meadowland behind beach supports wide variety of bird and animal life.

will be stored at a dryland marina in the middle of the isthmus and a large trailer capable of carrying boats up to 40 feet in length will permit "portages" from the Strait of Georgia into Sechelt Inlet.

Sechelt itself is a small community (population of less than 1,000) but due to its central location on the lower Sunshine Coast it serves as a service centre for over 14,000 people who live between Gibsons and Pender Harbour. There are supermarkets, banks, laundromat, book stores, liquor store, pubs, hospital, pharmacy and resort motel facilities in the village. A new hotel, "The Driftwood Inn", is located on the Trail Bay waterfront.

Temporary anchorage is possible in favourable weather off the village front, but boats should not be left unattended or at least unwatched here for long as the wind has a reputation for changing direction and strength suddenly in this area.

5   Trail Islands

The Trail Islands do not offer particularly inviting anchorage as they are all private and rocky-shored with very little beach. Temporary shelter is possible behind them however, and if the wind is strong, this area is often used for the temporary storage of log booms to which it may be possible to tie alongside for a short while, with permission. The easternmost island offers the most protection in its lee from westerly winds and to a lesser degree, from southerly winds. There is also a very small park a few hundred feet north off the easternmost tip of this island. Temporary anchorage might also be possible between the two westernmost islands, south of the drying rocks in calm conditions.

In winter these islands serve as one of the largest sea lion colonies in the Strait of Georgia: as many as 75 sea lions have been observed sunning themselves on the rocks at one time.

Directly north of the Trail Islands, near the outlet of Wakefield Creek and an open grass field, is the Wakefield Inn. A logger's sports day which is planned to be an annual event was first held here in mid-August, 1979. Temporary anchorage just to the east of the Wakefield delta is possible, weather permitting, with the opportunity to sip some brew and enjoy the magnificent view from the Inn windows. Do not stay too long or you may have to watch your boat beach itself as the tide falls or the afternoon onshore wind arrives more rapidly than expected. Temporary anchorage is also possible in any of several small bights along the northern shore of Sargeant Bay with the most protection from the southeast afforded in a small nook north of a 10 foot islet.

6 Sargeant Bay

Formerly known as Norwest Bay, this deep bight is open to southeast winds although the Trail Islands offer some protection. Huge piles of driftwood on top of and behind a large gravel berm attest to the fury of winter storms. Oddly enough, strong northwest winds can also tend to funnel forcefully into the bay. In calm conditions temporary anchorage would be possible off the wide and shallow sand and gravel beach at the head of the bay or in the tiny nooks behind a prominent rock headland which juts out into the northern section of the bay. Many people who come to enjoy the beach climb this rock for the magnificent views over the bay, beach and marsh behind the beach.

Care must be exercised if anchoring off the beach to avoid a drying rock less than 100 yards southwest of the prominent rock. The wide beach backed by extensive marsh and meadowland is unique as it is the largest such marsh area of its kind on the Sunshine Coast, providing habitat for a wide variety of bird and animal life. Local residents have proposed that 30 acres of land around Sargeant Bay be acquired as a

Man-made sandy beach, half a mile long, in front of Porpoise Bay Provincial Park, is one of most popular camping sites on Sunshine Coast.

nature park, but the owner of the property has plans for a high density condominium, housing and marina project for the area.

7 Porpoise Bay Floats

The government floats (1,200 feet of moorage) at the head of Porpoise Bay are actively used by local residents who live throughout Sechelt, Narrows and Salmon Inlets or outside the Skookumchuck in Jervis Inlet, as the most convenient transfer point to the coast highway system or to the Tyee Airways float plane terminal immediately adjacent. The floats also provide convenient access to the town of Sechelt, the centre of which is located half a mile to the south.

These floats are not particularly recommended for anything other than temporary moorage because of the regular traffic of both boats and noisy float planes. Between the government floats and the Tyee Airways floats is a launching ramp serving as the main access point for small cartop or trailered boats traversing the "inside waterway" through Sechelt Inlet, Jervis Inlet and on up to Desolation Sound. With careful timing of

Government floats at Porpoise Bay have 1 200 feet of moorage, are used by local residents. Tyee Airways float planes use private floats, top. A new marina complex is planned.

slack water at the Skookumchuck and favourable wind conditions in northern Malaspina Strait, small boat operators can avoid the uncertainties of travel in the more open Strait of Georgia. Private floats are located here and at various points along the eastern shore of Porpoise Bay and on the western shore directly inside Poise Island. Some of these floats are located in dredged out basins, flanked by shoals or breakwaters providing year round protection.

The Royal Reach Resort, a new hotel and marina complex, is proposed for the area just east of the government floats. There are plans for a fuel dock, waterfront dining room, pub, diving centre and boat rental-charter service. The Sechelt marsh — a waterfowl refuge, is located at the head of Porpoise Bay, east of the new resort.

8 Porpoise Bay

Good anchorage is available throughout the headwaters of Sechelt Inlet where depths are suitable. Down Inlet winds (from the north) are not common in the summer and strong southeast winds have no fetch over which to build up a sea.

Care should be taken to avoid drying shoal patches which are considerably shallower than shown on the chart — particularly to the northwest of the govern-

Completely protected by rock breakwaters, Tillicum Bay Marina offers fuel, food, moorage, marine ways, hull and engine repairs.

ment floats (inside the 1½- and 1¼-fathom soundings) and south of Poise Island (between the 3- and 3½-fathom soundings).

9 Porpoise Bay Provincial Park

Temporary anchorage is possible close to a recently constructed sandy beach south of the mouth of Angus Creek. This beautiful, half-mile-long beach is the result of large amounts of sand being dumped on a previously unattractive foreshore in front of Porpoise Bay Provincial Park. The 150-acre park was established in 1971 and is one of the most popular parks on the Sunshine Coast with 89 campsites, picnic sites behind the beach and a nature interpretation programme. The waters of Porpoise Bay provide warmer swimming than one would expect due to the lower rate of tidal flushing at this end of the inlet and the absence of any substantial fresh water inflow. An area for swimming has been cordoned off by a buoyed line to prevent conflicts with boats. A short trail along Angus Creek provides a pleasant walk through open deciduous woodland near the estuary mouth into bankside coniferous forest and the opportunity to view spawning salmon in the fall. The park also serves as an excellent base for canoeists to explore the rest of Sechelt Inlet.

There are a number of small nooks and coves on both sides of Sechelt Inlet to the north of Porpoise Bay which can be used as temporary anchorages. In particular, between the huge gravel extraction operation north of Angus Creek and Four Mile Point (beware of drying rocks north of the 29 fathom sounding); and along the western shore in Snake Bay, opposite Four Mile Point and south of Piper Point where there is a 13-acre recreational reserve (See Chapter 8). Snake Bay derives its name from the local name — Oalthkym — site of a 9-acre Indian Reserve. Residential development along the eastern shore stretches as far north as the Lamb Islets but is mainly concentrated just to the north of Four Mile Point.

10 Tillicum Bay Marina

This small marina basin provides fuel, moorage, launching ramp, hull and engine repairs with a marine ways (capacity 10 tons), campsites and small grocery store. Boating people who want to stretch their legs can walk back to the East Porpoise Bay road (now known as "Sechelt Inlet Road") where there is a hiking trail alongside Gray Creek leading past two waterfalls. This hike is particularly interesting since Gray Creek is the last major unlogged creek on the Sunshine Coast. The old forest along its banks is draped with Spanish moss ("witches hair"). (see *Hiking Trails of the Sunshine Coast*, Harbour Publishing, 1979, for more details).

Temporary anchorage is possible along the eastern shore of Sechelt Inlet, north of a log booming area and inside Lamb Islets, but the shoreline here is quite densely developed. The quietest anchorage is located in a small cove to the north of Lamb Islets.

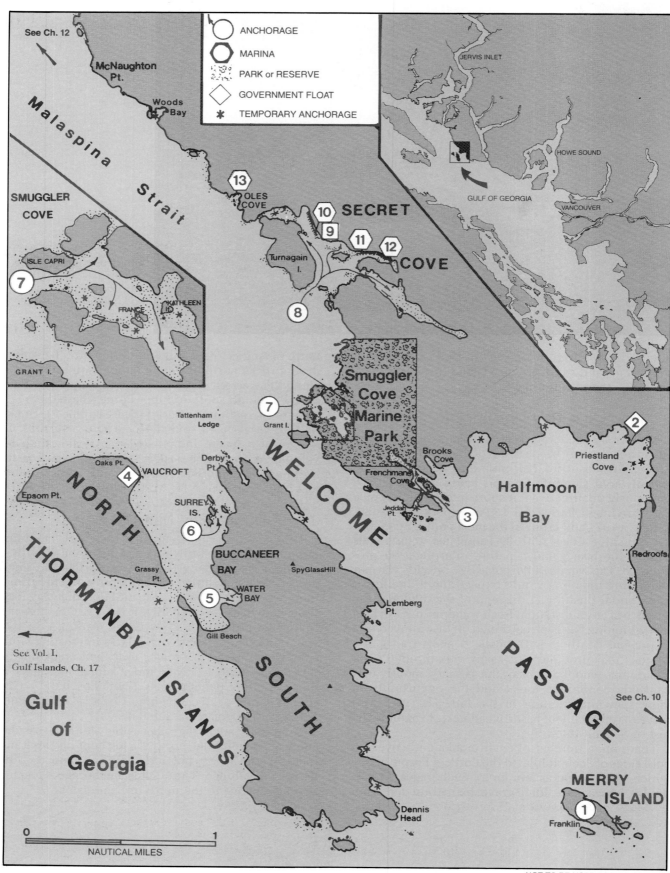

Legend

- ⬭ ANCHORAGE
- ⬡ MARINA
- ⬚ PARK or RESERVE
- ◇ GOVERNMENT FLOAT
- ✳ TEMPORARY ANCHORAGE

See Ch. 12

McNaughton Pt.

Woods Bay

Malaspina Strait

JERVIS INLET

HOWE SOUND

GULF OF GEORGIA

VANCOUVER

⑬ OLES COVE

⑩ ⑨ ⑪ ⑫ SECRET COVE

Turnagain I.

⑧

SMUGGLER COVE

ISLE CAPRI

⑦

FRANCE

KATHLEEN ID.

GRANT I.

Smuggler Cove Marine Park

Brooks Cove

Frenchmans Cove

⑦ Grant I.

Tattenham Ledge

Derby Pt.

Oaks Pt. VAUCROFT ④

Epsom Pt.

NORTH

SURREY IS.

⑥

Jeddah Pt.

③

② Priestland Cove

Halfmoon Bay

WELCOME

BUCCANEER BAY

SpyGlassHill

Grassy Pt.

THORMANBY ISLANDS

⑤ WATER BAY

Gill Beach

See Vol. I, Gulf Islands, Ch. 17

Gulf of Georgia

SOUTH

Lemberg Pt.

Redroofs

PASSAGE

See Ch. 10

Dennis Head

MERRY ISLAND

① Franklin I.

0 _____ 1
NAUTICAL MILES

NOT TO BE USED FOR NAVIGATION

CHAPTER ELEVEN

Welcome Passage

Buccaneer Bay, Smuggler Cove, Secret Cove

Welcome Passage really is a welcome sight for small boats beating or rolling up the open coast for over 30 miles from Vancouver or 20 miles across the open Gulf of Georgia from Nanaimo. The protection afforded by the Thormanby Islands may be somewhat illusory, however, since prevailing winds within the Passage often increase in strength and produce short, steep seas when blowing against the tidal stream. The tidal streams are strongest where the passage is narrowest, east of Merry Island (maximum 2 knots) and northeast of South Thormanby Island (maximum 3 knots). The seas however may be steepest and most confused off Lemberg Point and east of Merry Island where the bottom depths are irregular and where swells from the open Gulf often enter at an angle to the wind and tidal stream. An additional hazard particular to this area is the large number of deadheads and drifting logs. Reception Point light, located a mile east of Merry Island, should not be passed too closely as the drying gravel and boulder spit is continually changing location and at present extends some distance seaward, south of the light tower itself.

Winds

Wind speeds and directions have been recorded at the Merry Island Light station for many years and when averaged, yield useful information for yachtsmen wanting to know what type of winds they can expect in this area. In the summer months, winds tend to be strongest when blowing from the east in the morning between 0900 hours and noon (average 17 mph). Easterly winds actually blow least frequently at this time of the day (10%) but frequently at night (30%). Winds from the SE occur most frequently during the day (40%) reducing or backing east at night (20%). Because the southeast wind has such a diurnal variation, it cannot always be said to presage bad weather here but is more often, at least half the time, an 'onshore' or 'dry' southeasterly.

The westerly or northwesterly is a gentler wind, averaging 8 mph during the day and less than this at night. The westerly blows most frequently during the day (20% between 9 and 11 in July, and around 6 in the evening in August) reducing to less than 5% at night. The northwesterly blows most frequently at night (over 30%, reducing to less than 20% during the day.

When a westerly is blowing strongly in the Gulf of Georgia it is not unusual for the southern part of Malaspina Strait to be calm. This is because the southern half of Texada Island acts as a windbreak.

CHARTS
3311 — Strip Chart #3 — HOWE SOUND to PENDER HARBOUR (1:40,000)
3577 — SANDHEADS TO BALLENAS (North to Secret Cove) (1:77,300)
3590 — BALLENAS to CAPE LAZO (West of Halfmoon Bay) (1:77,000)
3598 — JERVIS INLET and APPROACHES (from McNaughton Point, north) (1:76,400)
3535 — Plan of WELCOME PASSAGE (includes west coast of South Thormanby Island) (1:25,000) - (supercedes 3509)

Merry Island light marks the southern entrance to Welcome Passage. Boats mooching for springs and coho mark one of the favorite fishing spots in the area.

The line between whitecaps and calm water is often abrupt, extending between Point Upwood on Texada Island and South Thormanby Island. Calms occur mainly at night (5-10%) and southwesterlies (the local onshore wind) rise to a frequency of 10% during the day.

In the winter months there is little diurnal variation with easterly and southeasterly winds blowing up to 60% of the time and northwesterlies 25% of the time.

1 Merry Island

The waters of Welcome Passage were being surveyed by Captain Richards aboard H.M.S. *Plumper* in 1860 when the 'welcome' news arrived from England of the winners in the Derby. Many geographic features in this area were named in the 1860 survey in association with this event (see Walbran). The owner of the winning horse, Thormanby, was a Mr. Merry, wealthy iron master. Descendents of Mr. Merry are now living in Vancouver.

In 1903 a lighthouse was erected here and the first lightkeeper, William T. Franklin, established himself on the island. Franklin tended the light for over 30 years, rescuing scores of shipwrecked sailors by rowboat, and building massive rock gardens which were said to be second only to the Butchart Gardens near Victoria in beauty and variety. Franklin Island is named after the first lightkeeper and is the second largest bird breeding sanctuary in the Gulf of Georgia

(Mitlenatch Island is first). Over 800 pairs of Glaucous-winged gulls and Pelagic cormorants have been observed nesting here in addition to 54 pairs of Double-crested cormorants.

In June, 1904, the Reverend John Antle, a Newfoundlander who loved the sea, made Merry Island his first stop out of Vancouver when he and his 9-year-old son sailed their 14 foot cutter *Laverock* over 200 miles up the B.C. coast to Alert Bay. The result of this holiday voyage was the founding of the Columbia Coast Mission which for many years provided vital medical and spiritual services to isolated coastal communities. It was in Halfmoon Bay that Antle first met Dr. W. A. B. Hutton who later became the first doctor of the Columbia Coast Mission. Antle, who has been called Canada's west coast Grenfell, sailed the 40 foot yawl *Reverie* from England to Vancouver in 1940 at the age of 75. (*The Columbia is Coming!*, Doris Anderson, 1982)

Temporary anchorage in calm weather conditions is possible just west or south of the light tower. The lagoon to the southwest of the light tower peninsula has been largely filled in. Divers interested in exploring sunken wrecks will find the remains of the 58-ton *Salvage Chief* and two 10-ton wrecks, *Linda-K* and *Carla-N* just north of the 2 foot drying reef south of Merry Island. Betty Pratt-Johnson (*141 Dives*) reports that the waters around Merry Island are noted for good visibility — the best she has experienced anywhere outside of the tropics. The *Salvage Chief* was wrecked on the reefs in February, 1925, in a southeast gale, while trying to rescue a drifting log boom.

150

Halfmoon Bay

The shores of Halfmoon Bay are surrounded by many homes and summer cottages with the densest settlement between the community of Redrooffs and the head of the bay. Many small boats are moored on buoys along the Redrooffs shoreline where there is a very nice sand and gravel beach. The Redrooffs Resort (Coopers Green) provides campsites and a launching ramp. Temporary anchorage is possible at a number of locations behind off-lying rocks or sandspits. A preferred temporary anchorage with fairly good protection from seas but moderately exposed to southwest winds is in Priestland Cove behind several tiny islets five to nine feet high. This anchorage area is hemmed in to the north and south by log booming and storage operations, mooring dolphins or piles and by local residents' private moorings.

Priestland Cove is named after the indomitable Clara Priestland, local postmistress, who rowed out regularly to passing Union Steamships to take off mail or to put a mailbag aboard. (H. Dawe).

2   Halfmoon Bay Gov't Float

This small float is located just inside the wharf head on the northern side and provides less than 200 feet of temporary moorage space, generally crowded. The B & J Store, providing groceries and fishing tackle, is located a few hundred yards inland and just beyond this is the coast highway.

The coves along the northern shoreline of Half-

Sand and pebble beach at Redrooffs in Halfmoon Bay is dotted with mooring buoys for residents.

Priestland Cove at head of Halfmoon Bay has government wharf, but 200 feet of moorage space is usually crowded. Grocery store is at head of wharf.

Frenchman's Cove provides one of the tightest anchorages on the coast.

moon Bay are more exposed to winds and seas from the south or east but do offer reasonable protection when westerlies are prevailing. Brooks Cove is encumbered by many rocks with an uncharted reef almost blocking off access to the innermost nook where temporary anchorage for one or two boats is possible (charted at 1.8 metres (1 fathom) on the new metric chart 3535).

3 Frenchman's Cove

Reasonably well protected anchorage is available hidden behind the islands in Frenchman's Cove but entrance might be hazardous in a strong southeast wind because of the narrowness of the passage. There are many uncharted rocks close to the shoreline of Frenchman's Cove; particularly south of the 9 foot high islet at the entrance, just west of the innermost islet and along the northeastern shore of the islands (favour the north shore if entering or leaving by the northern passage).

A provincial recreation reserve covers 175 acres of water and foreshore from Brooks Cove around to Welcome Passage and includes all the islands and islets within Frenchman's Cove and south of Jeddah Pont (but excludes the large island east of Jeddah Point which is private). Small boats prepared to dry out on the mud can find completely enclosed protection inside the long narrow inlet behind the islands in Frenchman's Cove. The land surrounding the inner portion of this drying inlet is included within the boundaries of Smuggler Cove Marine Park (7) but the shoreline around Frenchman's Cove is private and should be respected as such.

Temporary anchorage is possible immediately northeast of Jeddah Point with the offshore rocky islets providing good protection from seas but little protection from southeast winds. Care should be taken at low water to avoid an uncharted rock immediately south of the southwestern tip of the island, east of Jeddah Point.

South Thormanby Island

Across Welcome Pass on the northeastern side of South Thormanby Island there is a small cove which could provide temporary anchorage if a north wind or ebb tide is too strong to stem in Welcome Passage. There is an uncharted reef with outlying boulders drying about 3 feet located directly over the 1.4 metre (three-quarter fathom) sounding. At low tide one could anchor either inside or outside this reef.

When sailing north through Welcome Pass or attempting to enter Buccaneer Bay between Tattenham Ledge and Derby Point, one should be especially aware of one's position in relation to the drying rocks and reefs between the north end of South Thormanby Island and the Tattenham Ledge Buoy. Because the tidal stream sometimes flows *diagonally* across these reefs you may find yourself in the same predicament as the tug *C. P. Yorke,* which on the night of December 11, 1953, grounded on the rocks while attempting to seek shelter from a southeast gale. Five men died when the tug sank, but the captain and chief engineer were rescued. The drama of this story is recounted in the ballad "The Wreck of the C.P. Yorke" from Phil Thomas' book *Songs of British Columbia* (Hancock House, 1979).

There are a number of small, charming coves around the southern half of South Thormanby Island with varying degrees of protection from local onshore winds. None of the coves facing Welcome Passage would be suitable in moderate to strong southeast winds. An old farmstead with an orchard and large meadow is hidden behind the second cove north of Dennis Head. Logging roads from here lead past the farmstead and cross the island to Buccaneer Bay. In fact, the whole island is interlaced with logging roads connected to almost every cove around the island. The owners have been engaged over the years in gradual selective logging which has a far less devas-

tating effect than the clearcut logging prevalent in other coastal areas.

Boats crossing the Gulf of Georgia from Nanaimo often make their landfall on South Thormanby Island. From a distance the general appearance of this island is distinctly different from North Thormanby Island. Each island has a different type of geology characteristic of the two basic types found in the Gulf of Georgia. South Thormanby is composed of erosion-resistant volcanic rock, is sparsely forested (partly due to logging) with rolling rocky hills of varying heights. The shoreline is greatly indented with many coves and relatively deep water close offshore.

North Thormanby Island is composed of glacially deposited sands and gravels with steep cliffs facing the Gulf and a smooth, thickly forested profile rising to 500 feet. The shoreline is straight with extensive shallows and drying beaches up to 2000 feet offshore, caused by erosion of the unconsolidated sand and gravel cliffs.

A small peninsula connected to the middle of South Thormanby Island is identical in composition to North Thormanby Island and at one time might have been part of it. In 1792 Captain Vancouver iden-

South Thormanby Island has a few protected coves on the Welcome Passage side. Buccaneer Bay can be seen to the north, and Texada in the distance.

Buccaneer Bay, the most beautiful beach on the Sunshine coast.

Surrey Islands, with Vaucroft, upper left.

Sand patterns in the gap in Buccaneer Bay.

tified this peninsula as an island and Captain Pender in 1864 charted it as 'Sandy Islet'.

When southeast winds are piling up dark clouds around the mountains on the mainland shore, the Thormanby Islands are almost invariably bathed in sunshine. Very little rain falls here in the summer. Captain Vancouver also appears to have been more pleased with this 'sunshine coast' shoreline than he was with much of the rest of the B.C. coast. He records in his journal:

"At four o'clock on Saturday morning the 16th (June, 1792) we resumed our course to the northwestward, along the starboard or continental shore of the gulf of Georgia, which from point Gower takes a direction about WNW and affords a more pleasing appearance than the shores of Howe's sound. This part of the coast is of moderate height for some distance inland, and it frequently juts out into low sand projecting points (eg. Mission Point, Reception Point). The country in general produces forest trees in great abundance, of some variety and magnitude; the pine is the most common, and the woods are little encumbered with bushes or trees of inferior growth. We continued in this line about five leagues (15 miles) along the coast, passing some rocks and rocky islets

(White Islets and Trail Islands), until we arrived at the north point of an island (South Thormanby) about two leagues in circuit, with another (North Thormanby) about half that size to the westward of it, and a smaller island between them. From the north point of this island, which forms a channel (Welcome Passage) with the main about half a mile wide, and is situated in latitude 49° 28½', longitude 236° 31', the coast of the continent takes a direction for about eight miles N 30 W and is composed of a rugged rocky shore, with many detached rocks lying at a little distance."

Although few boats venture close to the western shoreline of the Thormanby Islands, this side offers more solitude and protection from easterly winds. Temporary anchorage is possible for small boats in a number of shallow coves on this side of South Thormanby Island but care must be exercised to avoid the boulder-studded drying shallows which extend between South and North Thormanby Islands (use chart 3535). The shoreline of North Thormanby Island of-

View south over Buccaneer Bay, Grassy Point, right, is 1-acre provincial park.

155

One of the most popular anchorages on the Sunshine Coast is Smuggler Cove Marine Park with 410 acres of upland and islands, and 40 acres of foreshore.

fers a very attractive sandy beach for wilderness-like hiking ashore but temporary anchorage should only be attempted close to shore in calm weather conditions, with a rising tide and close attention to the location of any nearby boulders. When rounding Epsom and Oaks Points it is wise to keep at least half a mile offshore as the shallows continually shift, changing depths from year to year, and may extend further seaward than indicated on the most recent charts.

Buccaneer Bay was named by the lucky surveyors aboard H.M.S. *Plumper* after the racehorse which came second in the 1860 Derby. Oaks Point is named after 'The Oaks', a race for 3-year-old fillies, run annually over 'The Derby' course at Epsom, Surrey in England (Walbran).

4   Vaucroft Gov't Float

This float provides less than 75 feet of temporary moorage space and seems to have been largely co-opted for the primary use of local summer residents and their guests. A sign on the float reads: 'This float is for the use of vessels actively engaged in loading and unloading only'. Vaucroft was at one time operated by the B.C. Telephone Company as a holiday camp for their operators. There is a small ½ acre public park behind the private mooring buoys just south of the Vaucroft government float.

Buccaneer Bay is very popular as a temporary anchorage with most boats anchoring close to the shallows between Grassy Point and the 'Sandy Islet' peninsula. North Thormanby Island offers reasonable

156

should be taken to ensure that any beach fires on crown foreshore do not endanger private property.

5   Water Bay

Boats which prefer to have more protection from any nightime northwester than is afforded in Buccaneer Bay, occasionally anchor in Water Bay. An offshore reef marked by a beacon provides fair protection from northerly seas. There is a private float in the bay providing moorage for local residents. A public telephone at the southeastern end of Gill Beach is accessible by road.

6   Surrey Islands

Good protection from northwest seas is available behind the Surrey Islands. Care should be taken to avoid an isolated drying rock in the centre of this anchorage and an uncharted rock below chart datum off the western shoreline of the southernmost island.

Temporary anchorage in southeast or calm conditions is available in any of three narrow nooks indenting Derby Point. The central inlet is probably the most sheltered with rocky reefs and islets at the entrance providing added protection from northwest seas.

Although temporary anchorage would appear to be possible behind Grant Island (some boats may actually anchor here assuming it to be Smuggler Cove); the tidal stream moves quite rapidly through here, scouring mud off the rockbottom and leaving poor holding ground. Near here there exists a tiny bowl-shaped spring in the rock known as Huhk-Ahls-Say-Ko, the 'Spring of the Gods' to the Sechelt Indians. The Sechelts, when paddling along the coast, would often stop at this sacred spring to refresh themselves. Today, a pretty cress grows in the clear, fresh water, and in summer wildflowers bloom around it (L. Peterson).

7   Smuggler Cove Marine Park

Smuggler Cove Marine Park is probably the most popular anchorage on the Sunshine Coast. Because it is well protected from all winds and seas, it tends to be quite crowded at times. The provincial marine park which surrounds the Cove includes 410 acres of upland and islands and 40 acres of foreshore and water. There are eight islets within the cove, seven of which are connected to the shore by drying reefs. The islets and reefs help to break up the cove into three separate anchorage areas. Two of the islets, France and Kathleen, have small cottages on them and 'private' signs around them. When the cove was transferred to the Parks Branch in 1971 an arrangement was made whereby the owners could continue to enjoy lifetime occupancy of their cottages if they so desired.

In addition to the three main anchorage areas there are five other semi-isolated nooks, three of which dry out to varying degrees. These nooks are particularly suited for small shoal draught boats, canoes or kayaks

protection from westerly or even northwesterly winds, and north winds are not too common in the summer months. However, any winds with a northerly component would tend to generate seas making this anchorage uncomfortable, particularly at night.

The passage between Grassy Point and 'Sandy Islet' dries at about 10 feet (the maximum tidal range here is 17 feet at springs) and when the tide floods in the water becomes sufficiently warmed for very pleasant swimming. Not only do water depths and drying heights change here from year to year due to constant erosion and deposition but also, apparently, the location of the high tide line. The gentleman who lives on 'Sandy Islet' has his hands full during the summer months, reminding visitors to the beach that they may be trespassing on what was once his property. Visitors to these islands should be aware that almost all the land above high tide is private and special care

Looking south over Smuggler Cove, showing the three separate anchorages.

and one can usually find small mossy flat patches above high tide for camping ashore. There are also 10 informal campsites south of the southernmost anchorage.

Chart 3535 (metric) shows Smuggler Cove at a scale

Entrance to Smuggler can be intimidating to first-time visitors. Rocks on both sides, just inside the entrance, can be clearly seen, and are dry at lower tides.

of 1:10,000 and several rocks which were not apparent on the earlier chart (3509). In particular, a shoal patch with 3 feet of water 150 feet off the south entrance point and two 3 foot drying rocks 100 feet off the north entrance point (Isle Capri). There is also a rock which dries 7 feet within the entrance located over the 2½ fathom sounding on Chart 3509 — keep to port when entering but watch for the 6 foot drying reef jutting out about 50 feet from Isle Capri directly opposite the 7 foot drying rock. The passage between the rock and the reef is less than 50 feet wide at chart datum. There is also a rocky patch 3 feet below chart datum in the middle of the central anchorage and the passage into the innermost anchorage is only 3 feet deep at chart datum — watch for the reef extending 150 ft. north of France Islet. In 1981 a standard beacon was placed at the end of this reef.

The tiny nook southwest of France Islet is awash at chart datum and would therefore be suitable as an almost totally enclosed temporary anchorage for one or two boats near high water or at neap tides for most boats. This also applies to the nook southeast of Kathleen Islet but there is a 5 foot drying rock in the centre of this nook. Temporary anchorage is possible

158

Looking north over Secret Cove; entrance on the left, Royal Van Y.C. outstation centre, government floats background.

Four marinas line the northeastern arm of Secret Cove.

Government floats and Secret Cove Marina dominate main section of Cove. Shallow basin in foreground is used only by small boats.

north or south of this rock with one to two feet of water at chart datum.

The cove owes its name to its reported use by Larry Kelly, the 'King of the Smugglers', a Royal Navy sea-

Entrance to Secret Cove is to the left of well-marked rock. Red can buoy has been replaced by starboard day beacon.

man who fought for the confederates in the U.S. civil war. After the completion of the Canadian Pacific Railway, many unemployed Chinese workers or 'navvies' sought to emigrate to the United States but were forbidden official entry. Larry Kelly, also known as 'Pirate' or 'Pig Iron', had found his way to this coast and attempted to assist the Chinese across the border

160

by boat for a fee of $100 each. Smuggler Cove was his hideout. As insurance against detection the Chinese apparently had to agree to being roped together, tied to a large hunk of pig iron which Kelly would throw overboard if these was a chance of his being apprehended by U.S. customs agents south of the border. In the 1920s this cove served as a storage area for liquor manufactured in a large still near Cook Bay on Texada Island. From here it was loaded onto large fast boats and smuggled across the border. During their prohibition years, many American yachtsmen enjoyed this cove, as they do now, and one would often hear the popular song:

'Four and twenty Yankees feeling rather dry,
Sailed into Canada to have a drink of rye,
When the rye was open they all began to sing,
God bless America, but God Save the King!'

Smuggler Cove is a delightful place to explore by dinghy in the evening with a rising tide carrying one into the innermost ends of the many nooks and crannies. Trails from Smuggler Cove wind through the quiet surrounding woods, south to Welcome Pass overlooking Grant Island, north to a rocky indented coastline with drying lagoons and tidal pools and east alongside a swampy meadow to the Brooks Cove Road. There has been pressure in the past to build roads into or through the park but any extension of road access could easily lead to demands for vehicle access right to the cove itself. The Parks Branch has wisely disallowed any developments which might encroach on the beauty of this unique marine park.

The shoreline of the park north of Smuggler Cove is treacherous to explore except on foot or by dinghy as there are many offshore rocks and reefs, some only recently discovered as shown on Chart 3535.

8   Secret Cove

Entrance into Secret Cove is possible close west of Jack Tolmie Island but is safer in the commonly-used channel west of the starboard day beacon atop a 12 foot drying rock patch southwest of Jack Tolmie Island. Anchorage within Secret Cove is available in a number of inlets with the most popular location being along the inside of Turnagain Island. Alternatively, there is space for a few boats behind a substantial drying reef just east of the government floats or in a long narrow inlet extending to the southeast. Boats which anchor alongside Turnagain Island should use anchor lights at night as there is a fair amount of traffic after dark. Temporary anchorage is also possible in a small shallow basin at the north end of Turnagain Island. This basin is isolated from the rest of Secret Cove by an 8 foot drying bar and is mainly used by local residents.

Turnagain Island is so called because when it was being surveyed in 1860, the commander of the 'jolly boat' attempting to circumnavigate it gave the order to his oarsmen 'turnagain' when he could not get through the very narrow passage which dries at about 12 feet at the northern end.

9   Secret Cove Gov't Floats

The floats here provide up to 700 feet of moorage space and are usually crowded. The Secret Cove store, part of the adjacent marina operation, is located directly above the floats. The coast highway passes above this side of the cove screened by trees only 200 feet from the shoreline.

10   Secret Cove Marina

This marina operation is the largest in Secret Cove and provides fuel, moorage, laundry, shower facilities and store.

11   Jolly Roger Marina

This facility provides moorage, showers, laundry, restaurant, pub and inn. Charterboats have also been available here.

The Smugglers Marina and Latitude 49 Marina, providing mainly year-round moorage, are located between the Jolly Roger Marina and Buccaneer Marina.

12   Buccaneer Marina

This marina (formerly known as Stones) provides year-round and transient moorage, dryland boat storage, launching ramp, fuel, marine ways (capacity 32 feet, 8 tons), boat repair facilities, ships chandlery and boat sales.

13   Lord Jim's Lodge

This resort provides accommodation, restaurant, heated pool, bar, games room, and a small float for guests and visiting boats. The float is located in Oles Cove behind a large drying rock patch which appears as two rocks close to high tide. There is less than a foot of water at the end of the float at low tide (chart datum).

Another delightfully small nook suitable for temporary anchorage is Woods Bay about half a mile south of McNaughton Point. The bay offers reasonably good protection from both southeast and northwest winds. The coast highway passes by less than a hundred feet from the head of the cove.

Temporary anchorages are also available in several small coves north of McNaughton Point. Many of these coves are used by local residents for moorage of their boats during the summer months.

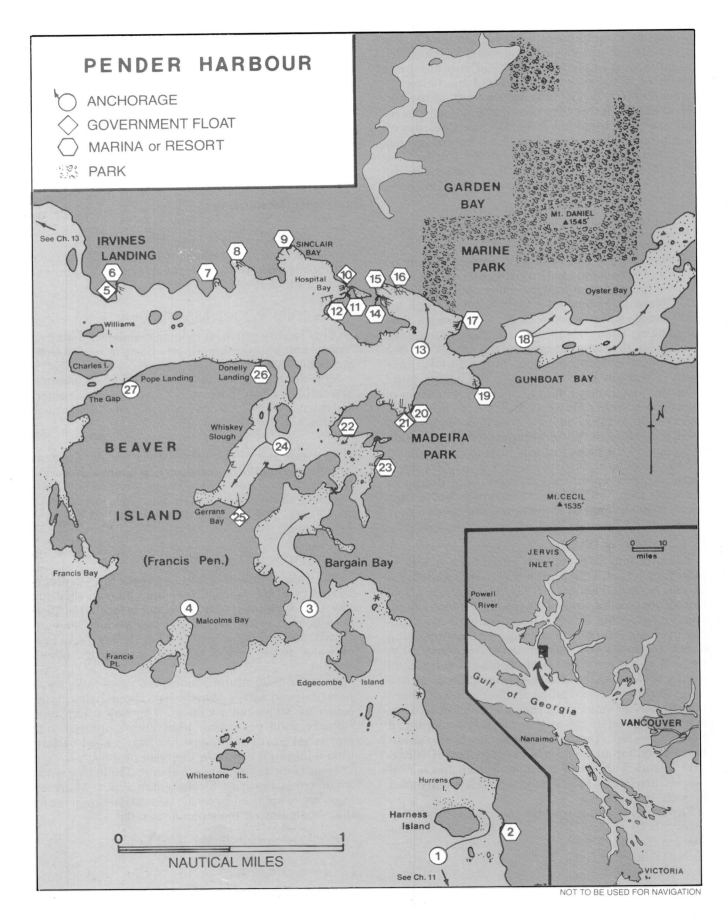

PENDER HARBOUR

- ⬡ ANCHORAGE
- ◇ GOVERNMENT FLOAT
- ⬡ MARINA or RESORT
- ▒ PARK

GARDEN BAY

Mt. DANIEL ▲1545'

MARINE PARK

Oyster Bay

See Ch. 13

IRVINES LANDING

SINCLAIR BAY

⑨

⑧

⑦

Hospital Bay

⑩ ⑮ ⑯

⑥
⑤

Williams I.

⑫ ⑪ ⑭

⑰

⑬

GUNBOAT BAY

⑱

Charles I.

Donelly Landing ㉖

⑲

Pope Landing

㉗ The Gap

Whiskey Slough

㉒ ㉑ ⑳

MADEIRA PARK

N

BEAVER

㉔

㉓

Mt. CECIL ▲1535'

ISLAND

Gerrans Bay ㉕

(Francis Pen.)

Bargain Bay

Francis Bay

JERVIS INLET

0   10
miles

Powell River

④ Malcolms Bay

③

Francis Pt.

Edgecombe Island

Gulf of Georgia

VANCOUVER

Nanaimo

Whitestone Its.

Hurrens I.

Harness Island

②

0   1

①

NAUTICAL MILES

See Ch. 11

VICTORIA

CHAPTER TWELVE

Pender Harbour

Sailing up Malaspina Strait it is easy to miss the entrance to Pender Harbour as it is somewhat obscured by small islands. Many of the early explorers bypassed it although Vancouver appears to have stopped for the night at Beaver Island (Francis Peninsula) as his journal of 16 June 1792 records:

'Along this rocky shore of the mainland we passed in quest of a resting place for the night, to no effect, until after dark; when we found shelter in a very dreary uncomfortable cove near the south point of an island, about a mile long, and about two miles to the south south east of a narrow opening leading to the northward'. (Agememnon Channel)

A year earlier, the Spanish explorer José Maria Narvez had sailed north up Malaspina Strait as far as Hardy Island and although he did not mention Pender Harbour in his journal, his chart shows two entrances which he named 'Bocas de Monino', leading east and north in the vicinity of where Pender Harbour and Agamemnon Channel are.

It was not until 1860 that the harbour was fully explored by Captain Richards and named by him after Daniel Pender, the navigating officer aboard H.M.S. *Plumper*. Seven years later Lieutenant Daniel Pender, RN, returned in command of the chartered survey vessel *Beaver* to resurvey some of the many rocks missed in the earlier survey. People are still discovering 'uncharted' rocks to this day. The metric chart of Pender Harbour (3535) provides excellent coverage but in the opinion of local residents is not much of an improvement on the earlier chart (3510) with soundings in the more familar fathoms. The first edition of the metric chart (1978) also appears to show many soundings 2 or 3 feet (.7 metres) shallower than they are shown on the older chart (3510).

1 Harness Island

The large scale chart of Pender Harbour also misses the southern half of a pleasant anchorage behind Harness Island. The small scale charts (3589 and 3590) do not show the southern approaches to this anchorage in enough detail for confident entrance. Shallow reefs extend between the 2 foot islet and the mainland making this passage difficult to negotiate for deep draught vessels and there are drying rocks between the 2 foot islet and the 10 foot islet. The safest passage is between the 10 foot islet and Harness Island, taking care to avoid a rock below chart datum (usually marked by kelp in summer) about 100 yards north of the 2 foot islet. The safest anchorage is in the lee of Harness Island depending on which way the wind is blowing. The islets and reefs to the south provide some protection from southerly seas. Harness Island is a provincial recreation reserve for the use, recreation and enjoyment of the public.

CHARTS

3311 — **Sheet #4 — PENDER HARBOUR to GRIEF POINT (1:40,000)**

3535 — **Large scale plan of PENDER HARBOUR (1:12,000) (3510)**

3590 — **BALLENAS ISLAND to CAPE LAZO (1:77,007)**

3589 — **JERVIS INLET and Approaches (south to McNaughton Point) (1:76,385)**

The major boating centre between Vancouver and Desolation Sound, Pender Harbour has almost two dozen marinas, marine stores, hotels, and repair facilities. It is one of the major salmon areas on the coast for sport fishermen.

Anchorage behind Harness Island, with Silver Sands Resort in foreground. Note rock underwater between drying reefs on left and Harness Island.

2   Silver Sands Resort

This resort provides mooring buoys for guests and a safe sandy beach for swimming. There are trailer and camper sites on the lawn, boat rentals, launching ramp, showers and laundromat. When leaving this anchorage it is advisable to favour the mainland shore once past the shallow delta of Haslam Creek as there is a reef which dries about 8 feet extending north of Hurren's Island.

3   Bargain Bay

Passage into Bargain Bay is possible to the west of Edgecombe Island or close to the mainland shore inside the locally known 'Seven Isles', as long as careful attention is paid to the exact location of the many rocks shown on chart 3535. Temporary anchorage is also possible at a number of locations close to shore in the lee of the islands, depending on the height of tide and strength of any onshore wind. There is fairly good protection inside Bargain Bay from all winds.

Captain Vancouver must have entered the southern part of Pender Harbour in 1792 because it is only possible to recognize that the Francis Peninsula is actually an island by navigating through Bargain Narrows (Canoe Pass). This very narrow passage is less than 20 feet wide at mid-tide and a 100 feet wide at high water under the bridge which has an overhead clearance of 13 feet. The passage is occasionally widened and deepened by a bulldozer but at present dries about 8 feet.

4   Malcolms Bay

It is possible that either this cove or Francis Bay to the north is the cove described by Vancouver as 'dreary and uncomfortable'. The cove dries out almost completely but could be used as a temporary anchorage overnight (when the tide is high) by shallow draught boats that can sit on the mud in the event of grounding. The deepest water is alongside a narrow reef to the east of the large island at the entrance to the cove. Residents would probably take exception to Vancouver's description. The cove is now in fact quite beautiful with pastoral farmland extending back from the head. The entrances to the cove would be uncomfortable, however, as would Francis Bay to the north of Francis Point, with southeast winds or southerly swells.

5   Irvines Landing

Entrance into Pender Harbour to the north or south of Williams Island is often accompanied by an abrupt wind shift, especially if it is blowing southeast (no matter how strong). The wind will quickly drop to nothing until one is past Williams Island and is

166

headed by a light easterly blowing out of the harbour.

Irvines Landing was once the major settlement in Pender Harbour with a hotel, saloon, store and post office. It was first established in the 1880s and grew to prominence because it was ideally situated to serve as the major steamer stop for the other waterfront settlements within the harbour. In his book *Whistle Up the Inlet*, Gerald Rushton notes that on the occasion of the first recorded Union Steamship excursion to Pender Harbour in July, 1891, the Vancouver *News-Advertiser* editorialized: 'Scarcely any place could be more naturally adapted for holidaying than this beautiful water which has the distinction of being the first land-locked harbour on the mainland north of Vancouver, deep enough for ocean vessels.'

When the steamer announced its arrival by whistle signal, people from around the harbour would drop what they were doing and row, paddle, sail or chug over to Irvines Landing to pick up their mail or supplies and to socialize. For many years there were no roads and all communication within Pender Harbour was by small boat, leading to its designation as the 'West Coast Venice'. Now that road highways link the Pender Harbour settlements; the predominantly logging, fishing and beachcombing communities have gradually adapted themselves to serving sports fishermen and recreational boating people, both tourists and people from the districts substantial summer and retirement home development.

No steamers stop in Irvines Landing now, but the government wharf remains with a small float attached and inside of this, the Irvines Landing Marina floats are located.

Malcolm Bay dries completely at low tide, but can be used as a temporary anchorage by shallow draught boats in good weather.

6   Irvines Landing Marina

This marina is ideally situated to service small to medium sized boats fishing near the harbour entrance and other boats which do not want to travel further into the harbour. Fuel, tackle, bait, ice, boat rentals, moorage, launching ramp, groceries and marine giftware are available as well as campsites, showers and washrooms. There is also a very nice licensed restaurant here specializing in local seafoods and family dining. A road from here passes beneath Pen-

View to northwest up Malaspina Strait from entrance to Pender Harbour. Irvines Landing is on the right. Government wharf, formerly terminal for Union Steamships, is to the left of Irvines Landing Marina.

Irvines Landing Marina can service small to medium sized boats. Licenced restaurant is among facilities here.

der Hill (5 minutes walk) and beside Hotel Lake a short distance to the north. A description of the view from Pender Hill and access into Sakinaw Lake is included in Chapter 13.

One of the unique idiosyncracies of Pender Harbour is the large number of local place names for almost every single bay and cove. These place names often change or are moved to an adjoining cove with the most popular coves having lived through four or five name changes. The many marinas and resorts also tend to change their names occasionally, with the result that any description or guide to the area is often out of date before it is published. Since there is a fair amount of competition among the marinas and resorts, some of them are continually improving quality and range of their services in efforts to attract more customers, while others occasionally lapse into obscurity.

7   Whittakers Garden Bay Resort

A prime example of misplaced names, this resort is not located in Garden Bay but in Errington Cove, formerly known as Battle Bay. Many of the resorts along the north shore of Pender Harbour take the name of the local post office — Garden Bay (now located in Hospital Bay). This resort provides cabins, rental boats, bait and moorage.

8   Duncan Cove Resort

Duncan Cove resort, like many of the resorts in Pender Harbour caters mainly to small boat sports fishermen and provides launching ramp, moorage (for boats up to 40 feet long), dry storage, rental boats, self-contained cottages, motel units and campsites. A marine pump-out station, laundromat and shower facilities, propane and ice are also available. One can hike from here to Hotel Lake (less than half a mile

north of Duncan Cove) and there is a tennis court one mile away.

9   Garden Bay Marine Services

Garden Bay Marine Services in conjunction with Pender Harbour Boat Works, Miller Marine Electronics and Haddock Boat Moving provide a wide range of facilities for boat and engine servicing and repairs. Covered winter storage, boat building and Sales, Engine sales (Mercury, Volvo Penta, Chrysler) are also available here. Despite its name, it is located in what is locally known as Sinclair Bay at the western end of Hospital Bay, within walking distance of the Garden Bay restaurants, stores and pub.

Sinclair Bay is named after the author and poet Bertrand Sinclair who owned a sailing fishboat and lived here for many years. Some of his novels such as *Poor Man's Rock* and *The Hidden Places* described life on the B.C. coast in the early part of this century. The Gibson's Landing historian, Lester Peterson, has noted that throughout Sinclair's work there is a "general disgust for the mere entrepreneur, the man who manipulates but does not actually produce goods or services. In the Sinclair philosophy, monetary gain must not be derived by means which destroy beauty or create waste, a creed which led Sinclair to oppose what he recognized, earlier than most, was senseless despoilation of natural resources." Although much of the dialogue in Sinclair's novels is now dated it is a shame that his books are so hard to find, even in local libraries. They give a fascinating perspective of the early development of the B.C. coast.

10   Garden Bay Gov't Floats

This facility provides almost 1,000 feet of moorage space and is convenient for transient yachtsmen wanting easy access to stores, marinas with boat supplies, and, within five minutes walk — a very pleasant pub in Garden Bay. Hospital Bay was named for St. Mary's Hospital, built by the Reverend John Antle of the Columbia Coast Mission in 1930, and a landmark within Pender Harbour that is easy to locate. The hospital building has now been converted into a hotel — The Sundowner Inn — which offers bed and breakfasts during the summer months. Accommodation ashore is also available at the Pender Harbour Autocourt within three minutes walk.

11   Taylor's Garden Bay Store

This store is accessible from the government floats by way of a bridge over the outflow channel of a small lagoon. The store provides a full selection of groceries including fresh meats and vegetables at reasonable prices, basic clothing, hardware, magazines and an exchange pocket book service. Several stores in Pender Harbour offer used pocket books for sale or exchange — a worthwhile service for cruising yachtsmen, especially when bad weather confines one to the boat. Taylor's store has one of the best used

book selections in the Harbour. Complete fuel supplies are provided at a float outside the store entrance and there is a post office at the back of the store building.

12   The Fisherman's Resort

This resort, located immediately ahead of Taylor's store, has a large amount of float space (shore power — 15 and 30 amps, water) and can accommodate almost any size of boat. The resort provides waterfront housekeeping cabins, campsites, showers, launching ramp, rental and charter boats, charts, ice, fishing and cruising information. The resort also includes a well-stocked fish tackle shop and is the only outlet in Garden Bay selling live bait. All the Garden Bay facilities (stores, reliable electronic repairs, restaurants, pub, Col. Flounders take out, etc.) are within two to five minutes walk and a ferry service is provided to the bus at Madeira Park for moorage guests.

13   Garden Bay Marine Park

This 163-acre provincial marine park was established in 1969. The beachfrontage on Garden Bay is quite small — less than 600 feet, but the park extends back up the hillside to include Mount Daniel and a small detached section at the head of Garden Bay Lake. The park provides an undeveloped forested shoreline in contrast to the rest of Garden Bay which has been almost fully developed with marine service facilities and waterfront homes. The most appropriate place to anchor in Garden Bay is off the park shoreline. Boats which choose to anchor off the marinas at the west end of the Bay stand a chance of being rammed by fast-moving boats which have a tendency to race around the Garden Peninsula enroute to the Garden Bay Hotel Pub float. Especially at night when there is no moon, and when one's anchor light is confused with the lights on shore.

An interesting and challenging hike can be made to

Old St. Mary's Hospital in Hospital Bay has been converted to Sunshine Inn, left. Fishermen's Resort and the Taylor's excellent Garden Bay store are in centre.

the top of Mount Daniel. The primary access is from the Garden Bay Road which passes around the west shore of Garden Bay Lake. About one quarter of a mile past the end of the Lake there is an old garbage dump road which forks into a logging road obscured by young alders and leading directly up the mountain. The western peak of the mountain provides a view of many lakes to the north; while the eastern peak, which is about 100 feet higher, provides a magnifi-

Morning sun turns water to silver in Whiskey Slough.

cent panorama of the whole of Pender Harbour from Irvines Landing around to Oyster Bay. This hike is described in detail in *Hiking Trails of the Sunshine Coast* published by Harbour Publishing, Madeira Park. To quote from this book:

'the eastern peak of Mount Daniel was for years the scene of puberty rites practiced by the Sechelt Indian maidens. At the time of puberty these girls were isolated to the mountain top for four months. During this time communication with the rest of the tribe was cut off, except for the daily visit of the older women bringing food.

While in isolation these girls used smooth stones to construct large circles twenty or thirty feet across. These circles, called 'Moon Rings', were symbolic of the moon. The Indians' beliefs were strongly involved with that planet's influence. Every evening at dusk a girl would begin her ritual with her Moon Ring, lifting each stone in turn and talking to it as though it were the moon. By dawn each stone would have had its turn and the ritual was finished. Evidence of these rings can still be seen on the mossy peak.

Mary Saul, a local Indian woman who participated in these rites as a girl, smiled at her recollections of conversion to Catholicism. For her the transition was easy, as telling a rosary was so similar to the Moon Ring ritual!

The young men of the tribe also had similar rituals which they performed in isolation on Mount Cecil (located directly across Gunboat Bay from Mount Daniel). Their constructions of stones were in the form of serpents, symbolic of fatherhood.'

14 Harbour Marina and Grocery

Located at the southwestern end of Garden Bay, this marina provides a convenient location with easy access to two dining rooms, a fish and chips shop, motel, inn, pub, post office and repair depots. Services provided at the marina include fuel, moorage, power, fresh water, ice, boat launching, showers and a laundromat in addition to groceries, charts, fishing tackle, hardware and dry goods at the store.

15 Garden Bay Hotel

The Garden Bay Hotel comprises a very pleasant waterfront pub and a small restaurant. There is a float in front of the Hotel for the use of patrons. Signs on the float read: 'Mooring — Slow or no Tie-up'. Good advice, but unfortunately seldom followed. There are no rooms for rent in this Hotel but for those seeking accommodation ashore it is only a short walk (watch your step) to the Sundowner Inn on Hospital Bay or to the Pender Harbour Autocourt.

16 Garden Bay Marina

This marina provides moorage and fuel. The easternmost float is reserved for members of the Thunderbird Yacht Club.

17 Penga Marina

Penga Marina, formerly Claytons, provides guest moorage and marine hardware, laundry and showers and facilities for boat maintenance and repairs with a marine ways capacity to 40 feet.

18 Gunboat Bay

Gunboat Bay was named by Daniel Pender for H.M. Gunboats *Grappler* and *Forward*, which were stationed on this coast between 1860 and 1869.

Entrance into Gunboat Bay is constrained by a narrow passage with less than 4 feet of water at low tide (chart datum) and a rock which dries about 2 feet. In addition, the tide rushes through here with considerable force at rates up to 3 knots, so it is advisable to enter close to high water. Excellent anchorage can be found in Gunboat Bay, behind the small islet directly east of Goat Islet, or at the entrance to Oyster Bay, a wide shallow arm which extends to the northeast and which dries out almost completely at low tide. There is a deepwater channel, navigable by dinghy or shoal draught boat, which threads its way through these tidal flats, past small islets and commercial oyster beds to the salt marshes at the head of the bay.

Despite the increasing shoreline development in Gunboat Harbour, this area is considerably more tranquil than the rest of Pender Harbour. This feeling of tranquil stillness is best experienced when entering the bay at the top of a spring flood tide and has been eloquently described by Captain Cates as quoted in 'Tides' from *Raincoast Chronicles* (Number 5):

"As the tide reaches its crest, the tension eases and peace seems to come to the shore of the inlet. In the summer this is usually in the evening and an old Indian friend of mine used to say, 'Take your white man's pleasures and give me a nice snaaquaylsh (dugout) and let me paddle far up the sloughs where the smell of the salt grass fills the air and I can see the flounders scooting away in the clear water and hear the birds in the trees along the shore singing their sleepy evening song. There is no peace like the peace of *Kwahaluis*, the full of the tide.'"

19 Headwater Marina

In a small cove at the southern entrance to Gunboat Bay is a small marina (formerly Trincomalee) which provides a launching ramp and long term moorage plus some transient moorage, campsites and showers. There is also a marine ways, capable of handling boats up to 48 feet in length, and facilities for non-mechanical boat repairs.

20 Madeira Marina

This marina is located in Welbourn Cove and provides moorage, rental boats, launching ramp, fishing supplies and marine hardware, engine parts and repairs, Campsites and housekeeping units are also provided.

21 Madeira Park Gov't Floats

The Madeira Park government floats provide 1600 feet of moorage space and access to shore. The main shopping centre serving the Pender Harbour area is located in the Madeira Park community about 300

H.M.S. Chatham and H.M.S. Discovery pass Pender Harbour with the two Spanish ships behind (Harold Wyllie).

yards inland from the government floats. If you plan to do some heavy shopping there are usually shopping carts at the end of the wharf which can be returned to the shopping centre and then wheeled back to the government floats with all your supplies. The shopping centre includes a large supermarket, Government liquor store, banks, pharmacy and hardware as well as several smaller stores.

Madeira Park is named after the Island of Madeira near Portugal, which was the birthplace of one of the founders of Pender Harbour, Joe Gonsalves. This community is also the home of Harbour Publishing which puts out *Raincoast Chronicles.*

22   Coho Marina Resort

Formerly known as Haddock's, this marina also provides convenient access to the Madeira Park shopping centre. Services at the marina include fuel, moorage, divers air, and diving charters for groups of ten or more, boat rentals, launching ramp and a marine repair-ways capable of hauling out boats to a maximum of 40 feet, housekeeping cabins and campsites with full facilities. Showers and laundry are also available and a store stocks fishing tackle and marine hardware.

23   Lowes Madeira Park Motel

This resort provides boat rentals and moorage, fishing tackle as well as housekeeping cabins and campsites. Access from the water via Gerrans Bay is by way of a rock shoal surrounded twisting channel with less than four feet of water below chart datum. This is a perfect harbour for small motor boats and dinghys but it is not at all convenient for deeper draught boats. There is a small lagoon to the south of here and to the west, the entrance to Canoe Pass leading to Bargain Narrows (3).

24   Whiskey Slough

Whiskey Slough, officially known as Gerrans Bay, derives its name from its early use as a favourite anchorage for gillnet fishermen who were primarily bachelors of Scottish extraction. Life was hard in the early days and any solace was welcome comfort. Most of these bachelors eventually married, became respectable and settled on the adjacent shore of Beaver Island in an area formerly referred to as 'Hardscratch'. Good anchorage is available at the head of the bay or behind Dusenbury or Calder Islands.

25   Gerrans Bay Gov't Floats

These government floats are primarily used by the local fishermen. If there is available space, the floats provide access to Beaver Island. There are no facilities or services for boats here and the upland is primarily residential.

26   Donelly Landing

This facility, formerly Ernie's Esso Marine, provides fuel for boats and is now known as Lloyd Hanson's Esso Marine. Immediately next door is Hassan's Store which has had a longstanding reputation as being one of the most thoroughly stocked stores in Pender Harbour. There is a small wharf and guest dock beneath the store where live bait is sold.

27   Pope Landing

Pope Landing was formerly the home of Murdock's Store and more recently the Indian Islands Marina. While there are no marine facilities in operation here now, there have been plans for reactivating the landing. A reef which dries about 17 feet protects the landing somewhat from any southerly swells entering through the Gap south of Charles Island, but moorage here is somewhat exposed to large boats which have not yet reduced speed as they enter the harbour.

171

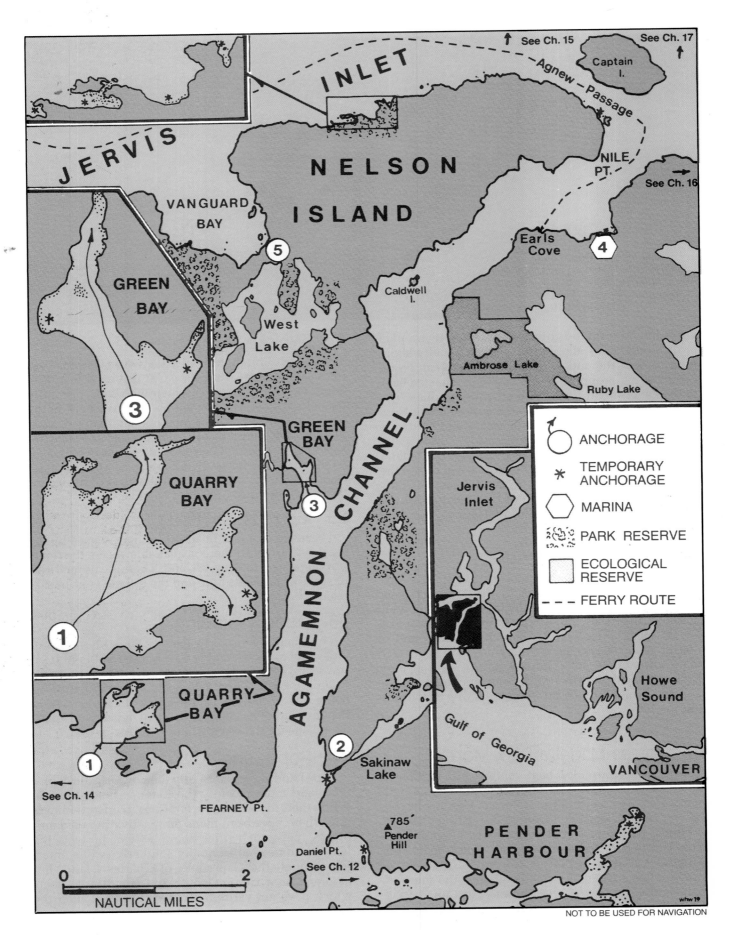

JERVIS INLET

See Ch. 15
See Ch. 17

Captain I.

Agnew - Passage

NELSON
ISLAND

VANGUARD
BAY

NILE
PT.

See Ch. 16

5

GREEN
BAY

Earls
Cove

4

Caldwell
I.

West
Lake

Ambrose Lake

Ruby Lake

3

GREEN
BAY

ANCHORAGE

TEMPORARY
ANCHORAGE

MARINA

PARK RESERVE

ECOLOGICAL
RESERVE

FERRY ROUTE

QUARRY
BAY

Jervis
Inlet

3

1

AGAMEMNON CHANNEL

Howe
Sound

Gulf of Georgia

QUARRY
BAY

2

VANCOUVER

1

Sakinaw
Lake

See Ch. 14

FEARNEY Pt.

785
Pender
Hill

PENDER
HARBOUR

Daniel Pt.
See Ch. 12

0   2

NAUTICAL MILES

whw 19

NOT TO BE USED FOR NAVIGATION

172

CHAPTER THIRTEEN

Agamemnon Channel

Eastern Nelson Island,
Quarry Bay to Vanguard Bay

Agamemnon Channel serves as the major passageway for boats from the south cruising beyond Pender Harbour to destinations up Jervis Inlet, Sechelt Inlet or into Hotham Sound. In the summer months, in stable weather, winds tend to blow up the channel during the day and down the channel at night. During unsettled weather, southeasterly winds in Malaspina Strait will become southerlies in the lower part of Agamemnon Channel but may peter out or become a gusty easterly or northeasterly in the upper part of the Channel.

The channel was named in 1860 by Captain Richards after H.M.S. *Agamemnon*, 64 guns, the first line-of-battle ship commanded by the great hero of the Royal Navy, "the immortal Nelson", after whom the adjacent island is named. The whole of the Jervis Inlet area, including Agamemnon Channel and Hotham Sound, is filled with names which honour the great battles, ships and men of the Nelson era from 1797 to 1805. Captain George Vancouver started it all in 1792 by naming the inlet after Admiral Sir John Jervis who, four years later, was to become Nelson's commander-in-chief. Captains Richards and Pender subsequently continued the tradition during their extensive hydrographic surveys in this area in the 1860s.

Nelson Island

Fearney bluff, 400 feet high, at the southern tip of Nelson Island, guards the western approach to Agamemnon Channel and is named after Lord Nelson's bargeman and follower, William Fearney. Walbran reports that at the battle of St. Vincent in 1797 in which Nelson first made his name by capturing the Spanish *San Josef*, 112 guns, from the deck of another Spanish ship he had just captured, the *San Nicolas*, 84 guns, Fearney received from Nelson the swords of the Spanish officers as they surrendered and coolly tucked them in a bundle under his arm as they were handed to him. This technique of boarding a large vessel from a small vessel by way of a medium-sized vessel came to be known as "Nelson's patent bridge for boarding first-raters".

To the west of Fearney Point there are several small coves along the southern shore of Nelson Island. Most of these are completely open to the south with barren, pinkish-hued granite headlands and large piles of driftwood above the high tideline indicating a dangerous exposure. The second (7 fathom) cove could probably provide some degree of shelter from southeast winds. The three small coves beyond this one could also provide temporary shelter in west or northwest winds. Tiny islets and drying rocks are found off the headlands between these coves and there are a few drying rocks within the coves (particularly the westernmost) which are not easily dis-

CHARTS
3311 — Sheet #4 — PENDER HARBOUR to
           GRIEF POINT (1:40,000)
3589 — JERVIS INLET and Approaches
           (1:76,385)

tinguishable on chart 3589, but shown clearly on the Strip Chart #4, 3311.

1 Quarry Bay

Quarry Bay has a wide entrance but its many nooks and arms are encumbered with drying rocks and reefs. The most popular anchorage is in a small cove south of the abandoned remains of the old granite quarry in the eastern end of the bay. Special care should be taken when entering this bay at low tide, to avoid a rock less than 6 feet below chart datum located less than 200 yards north of the southern shoreline. Another isolated rock, awash at chart datum, is located 50 feet north of the substantial drying reef which extends out from the southern shoreline toward the quarry face and which protects this anchorage from westerly swells entering the bay. Anchorage is not recommended in the northern part of this easternmost arm due to exposure to southwest seas and the danger of snagging an underwater B.C. Telephone cable which comes ashore here. The abandoned quarry is interesting to explore. In the early part of this century it was one of the largest granite quarries on the coast. Huge quantities of Nelson Island stone were used in the construction of buildings in Vancouver (University of British Columbia), Victoria and other localities down the Pacific coast. The quarry is no longer "conspicuous" as vegetation now shrouds the cuttings.

Anchorage is available in the shallow middle bay, but care must be taken if entering close to high water to avoid the several drying boulders and rock reefs which surround this bay. Temporary anchorage is possible in the western end of Quarry Bay behind two small islets or inside the westernmost nook. This part of Quarry Bay is somewhat exposed to swells from strong southeast winds.

Familiar light between Pender Harbour and Quarry Bay marks Nelson Rock.

Most popular anchorage in Quarry Bay is in this small cove south of the old granite quarry.

Pender Harbour

If one has been trapped inside Pender Harbour for a while by bad weather or other circumstances, it is a relatively easy hike to the top of Pender Hill (785 feet above sea level) from Irvines Landing (see Chapter Twelve). This hike has been described in the booklet, *Hiking Trails of the Sunshine Coast,* (Harbour Publishing, 1979):

> For the time it takes this may be the most rewarding little jaunt of them all. In the days when Pender Harbour served as a winter quarters for the entire Sechelt Indian nation and in fact boasted a larger population than it does today, this was the lookout preferred by sentries on the watch for parties of Yaculta or Haida war canoes, which might be expected to break into the clear around Cape Cockburn any moment of any day. Although only half as high as nearby Mount Daniel, Pender Hill affords a clearer and more comprehensive view of the Pender Harbour area in its relation to surrounding waters and it is much more quickly scaled. For the same reasons it makes

the best place for visitors to get an overview of the area's famous 'drowned landscape', (or to see what the weather is doing out in Malaspina Strait). You can sit for hours beside the bronze Geodesic Survey plate cemented into the top of the dome and watch trollers and plodding tugboats, luxury cruisers and streaking outboards come and go as the busiest harbour in the Sunshine Coast goes about its day.

Not the least of the attractions of Pender Hill is its terrain: on the east side is a cliff so breathtakingly sheer it seems you could take a modest leap and land in the cool green waters of Hotel Lake directly below (don't try it). The entire area on top is open, gently benched and carpeted with acres of cushiony moss. The west slope supports what must be the nearest thing you'll ever see to an 'arbutus forest' and the top is rich in the relatively rare 'hairy manzanita', a type of miniature bush arbutus with bright red bark. You will also find it a good place for wild herbs such as yarrow, juniper berry, kinnikinnik, and in season such flowering plants as wild violets, wild onion, tiger and chocolate lily give the area the appearance of a vast rock garden.

Temporary anchorage is possible behind Fisher Island in Lee Bay, directly beneath Pender Hill. There is

a 3.7 acre waterfront park at Daniel Point. Boats entering Agamemnon Channel from Pender Harbour should take special care near low tide to avoid a dangerous rock less than 6 feet below chart datum located 300 yards northwest of Daniel Point. Tidal currents in Agamemnon Channel flow at maximum rates of two knots.

2   Sakinaw Lake

Temporary anchorage is available near the mouth of a creek which drains Sakinaw Lake, located less than 1,000 feet inland. This anchorage is somewhat exposed to afternoon southwesterlies and the wash of boats powering up Agamemnon Channel. Small boats can be beached here and portaged into the lake over an old logging road with the permission of the Sechelt Indians who own the land. "Sakinaw" is from the Indian word "saughanaught" meaning salt water reaches the outlet. The surface of the lake is only 8 feet above sea level and the lower depths of the lake are salt, supporting oceanic growth, unusual in a "fresh water" lake.

Access by road is also possible from Irvine's Landing along Lee's Road. The closest islet to the lake outlet is a provincial park reserve with a cleared area in the centre for camping. Directly across the lake from the end of Lee's Road are sheer cliffs with Indian rock paintings which were executed as part of a yearly ritual by the local Sechelt Indians. Sakinaw Lake is rather sparsely populated and its winding indented shoreline with several islets and shelter from prevailing winds makes it an ideal canoeing area. There are several park reserves on the lake as there are throughout the Agamemnon Channel area. One of the larger reserves which fronts on Agamemnon Channel, directly across from Green Bay, surrounds Kokamo Lake and is accessible from either Agamemnon Channel or from Sakinaw Lake.

3 Green Bay

Just south of the entrance of Green Bay is the entrance to a shallow lagoon accessible at about half tide by shallow draught boat. At high tide it is possible for larger boats to enter into this lagoon although the entrance is extremely narrow. Small cabins at the entrance to this lagoon were once part of a small resort and had been moved here prior to World War II from the old Windsor Cannery inside Edgecombe Island south of Pender Harbour. (H. White).

Green Bay itself provides well protected anchorage either in the westernmost nook (5 fathoms) near a waterfall which is now largely obscured by vegetation, or close to the shallows (2 fathoms) near the northernmost part of the bay. Care should be exercised when entering this northern nook at high tide to bypass a substantial rock which dries 10 feet on the port side and rocks along the starboard (east) shore and near the head of the bay. Beachcombers and towboats often use Green Bay for assembling or storing their logs. In particular, a log dump is located in the westernmost nook and anchorage is often precluded by log booms. The logging road from the dump leads past a shallow marsh-surrounded lake of unique shape just ten minutes walk from Green Bay. At low tide the wreck of the fishboat *Marion T* can be seen beached between the log dump and the waterfall.

The outer easternmost nooks of Green Bay could also provide temporary anchorage but are more exposed to southerly winds and swell entering from Agamemnon Channel. The wreck of the tug *Viking Chief* was towed and left here after burning near Pender Harbour in December, 1959.

Ambrose Lake Ecological Reserve, comprising 564 acres, was established in 1971 to protect the virtually

Temporary anchorages at north end of Quarry Bay.

Above, Green Bay.

Lagoon south of Green Bay is accessible only at high water to shallow draught boats.

untouched shoreline surrounding Ambrose Lake as a unique example of coastal lake bog forest. The marsh meadow shoreline of peat deposits has prevented tree growth to a size which would have made logging economic. Access from Agamemnon Channel is difficult because of a steep shoreline and water too deep and exposed for safe anchorage. Shelter for very small boats is afforded behind an 18-foot high islet or near a creek beside an abandoned log dump to the south of the ecological reserve. This area is now protected by a provincial recreational reserve. An old moss-covered road from Earls Cove leads to the north end of Ambrose Lake where the stillness is only broken by the weird and lonely cry of loons vibrating over the lake. Earls Cove serves as the Sechelt Peninsula terminus for the ferry service link to Powell River via Saltery Bay on the other side of Jervis Inlet.

The shores of Agamemnon Channel from Green Bay north to Nile Point are often used for the booming and storage of log rafts. Caldwell Island (locally known as Alcatraz) seems to be joined to Nelson Island by the many log booms which almost fill this entire bight of Agamemnon Channel. The island was presumably named after the first commander of H.M.S. *Agamemnon*, Benjamin Caldwell.

4   Jervis Marina

The Jervis Marina resort is located in Agamemnon Bay just east of Earl's Cove. A cement launching ramp, moorage, washroom and showers are provided at this facility as well as campsites. The moorage area is partly protected by log booms.

Nile Point is named after the battle of the Nile

A tombolo spit north of Nile Point.

which took place during the evening and night of August 1, 1798. Twelve ships of the Royal Navy under Nelson destroyed or captured 13 larger French ships out of 17 at anchor in Aboukir Bay near the entrance to the River Nile. This decisive and overwhelming victory succeeded in completely severing Napoleon and his army in Egypt from Europe.

Just to the north of Nile Point is a small unnamed island linked to Nelson Island by a thin tombolo spit which is covered at high water. The most favourable temporary anchorage is on the north side of the spit behind a 6-foot high islet which is connected to the northern tip of the unnamed island. This 6-foot-high islet provides some protection from the wash of passing ferries and from seas generated by up-inlet winds in Jervis Inlet which may curl around through Agnew Passage. On the other side of Agnew Passage is Captain Island, named after the flagship of Commodore Nelson, H.M.S. *Captain*, 74 guns, at the battle of St. Vincent, February 14, 1797.

Along the northern shore of Nelson Island are many small nooks suitable for temporary anchorage depending on the state of the weather and tide and the size of your boat. The small scale chart (3589) of this area does not show the many rocks and reefs in enough detail to allow for confident exploration close to shore. This is a situation which appeals to those yachtsmen willing to risk an unexpected grounding or worse in their efforts to find an isolated, one-or-two-boat-sized anchorage that can be enjoyed in relative seclusion. There are at least 10 such small coves along this shore. Four of them are included in a provincial recreational reserve established to protect opportunities for swimming (in warmed up tidal pools),

upland camping and moorage for small boats in shallow sheltered bays. The cove which offers the most protection is guarded by a 15-foot drying rock and an islet joined to Nelson Island by rock-studded shallows. Most of the other coves are exposed by varying degrees to swells from up-inlet winds and the wash of passing boats and ferries.

5   Vanguard Bay

Vanguard Bay is named after H.M.S. *Vanguard*, Nelson's flagship at the Battle of the Nile. The bay itself is now filled with log sorting and booming grounds. Several years ago a marina with full services including fuel, store and laundry occupied the head of the bay. This marina operation was part of the Ocean Lake Estate development and was ideally situated to serve yachtsmen and West Lake cottage residents taking advantage of the beautiful scenery and recreational advantages of a warm, freshwater lake located less than 1,000 feet from salt water and only 36 feet above sea level. Nothing of the marina appears to have survived the onslaught of logging activities in the bay and the huge swath cut by a powerline across the isthmus between lake and sea.

Much of the West Lake shoreline and part of Vanguard Bay is protected by a provincial recreational reserve but the primary access from either Vanguard Bay or Agamemnon Channel is through private land. The main anchorages in Vanguard Bay, behind two islets along the eastern shore, are occasionally blocked by log booms. If access is possible, care must also be exercised to avoid drying rocks behind the islets.

Opposite: Forest steadily reclaims old excavations at Quarry Bay.

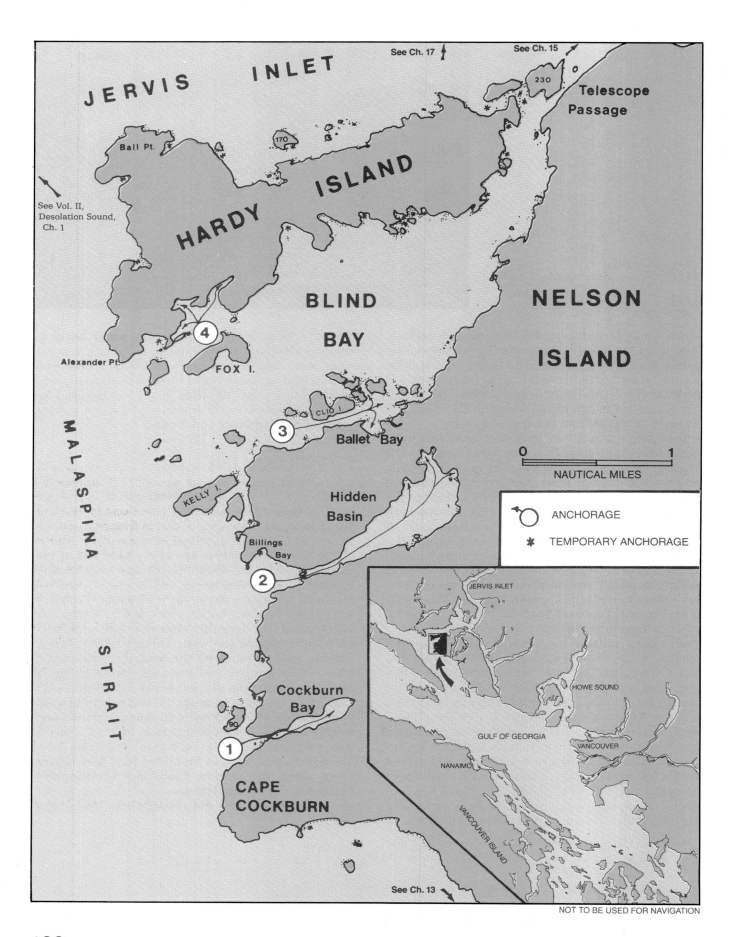

JERVIS INLET

See Ch. 17
See Ch. 15

230

Telescope
Passage

Ball Pt.

170

HARDY ISLAND

See Vol. II,
Desolation Sound,
Ch. 1

BLIND

BAY

NELSON

4

ISLAND

Alexander Pt.

FOX I.

CLIO I.

3

Ballet Bay

0   1
NAUTICAL MILES

KELLY I.

Hidden
Basin

ANCHORAGE

TEMPORARY ANCHORAGE

Billings
Bay

2

JERVIS INLET

HOWE SOUND

Cockburn
Bay

90

GULF OF GEORGIA

VANCOUVER

1

NANAIMO

CAPE
COCKBURN

VANCOUVER ISLAND

See Ch. 13

CHAPTER FOURTEEN

Nelson and Hardy Islands

Hidden Basin, Ballet Bay, Fox Island, Telescope Passage

Nelson and Hardy Islands are located in a strategic position for yachtsmen cruising the mainland side of the Gulf of Georgia. The islands are roughly halfway between Vancouver and the centre of the Discovery Islands archipelago north of Desolation Sound and halfway between Vancouver Island and Princess Louisa Inlet at the head of Jervis Inlet. These islands also offer the only opportunity for an abundant variety of isolated, relatively undeveloped and secure anchorages between Vancouver and Desolation Sound.

Cape Cockburn

The large bight east of Cape Cockburn is, by observation, completely open to the southeast. However, in stable weather or with winds from the northwest this shoreline is well worth exploration. There are several broad beaches here, with large, driftwood-covered gravel berms built up by wave action during winter storms. The most beautiful beach, about ¼ mile long, backed by tall, windswept trees and an extensive meadow, is to the northwest of two small islets. This beach and the meadow behind it are a 15-acre regional park. Temporary anchorage is possible off this beach behind a small rocky peninsula offering some protection from westerly swells which may curl around Cape Cockburn. Care should be taken to avoid the 4-foot drying rocks which extend out from the base of the peninsula for about 200 feet along the beach.

Directly behind the peninsula, is the site of Harry Roberts last home — "Sun Ray". Roberts was known to many as "Skipper Chack Chack" (Chinook for "bald eagle"). On the Malaspina Strait side of the peninsula lie the remains of Harry Roberts' last boat — the Chinese junk-shaped *Chack Chack III*. *Chack Chack III* was never launched; it was really a "dream boat" which Roberts referred to as a home, *not* a boat. Roberts, a man of prodigious talents and energy, died in 1979 after building many original boats and homes, both on land and water, for over 70 years. His family founded Roberts Creek and he himself was thoroughly familiar with much of the B.C. coast. He completed two books: *The Trail of Chack Chack* (1968) which chronicled his early life and coastal explorations, and *Natural Laws* (1969) which offered Roberts' own unique philosophy of life. In summary, he believed that "The Creator gives the ideas, Nature provides the materials and we must make the plan and become the instruments to produce the goods that provide our food and shelter. When two parts of anything are joined perfectly together our Creator gives us the nice feeling of Satisfaction. This Satisfaction is a taste of Heaven."

Roberts' philosophy also included several "Woes",

CHARTS
3311 — Sheet #4 — PENDER HARBOUR to
      GRIEF POINT (1:40,000)
3589 — JERVIS INLET and Approaches
      (1:76,385)

The late Harry Roberts, whose last boat, Chack Chack III, has been a Cape Cockburn landmark for many years. Picture was taken in 1973, six years before his death.

taught to him by his grandmother; among these were the following:

"Woe to the Father who fails to teach his son how to make the plan of the idea."

"Woe to the Mother who fails to teach her daughter how to change a house (or boat) into a home".

"Woe to him who leaves no space to be alone with Nature".

Cape Cockburn itself, the most prominent headland along the Sunshine Coast, is named after a great hero of the War of 1812, Admiral Sir George Cockburn, who had earlier served with Nelson and Jervis at the battle of Cape St. Vincent (1797). In 1814 he avenged the burning of York (Toronto) by sailing up the Chesapeake and marching overland to capture and burn the capitol buildings in Washington, D.C. This action assisted in terminating the American attacks

Harry Robert's home, south of Cape Cockburn, and a regional park site.

on Canada and resulted in a repainting of the smoke-damaged President's home to become the "White House". Apparently, another reason for the burning of Washington was Admiral Cockburn's intense dislike for the American pronounciation of his name. He always insisted on the original Scottish soft "ck" as in "Coburn", so passing sailors beware.

1   Cockburn Bay

Many boats are wary of entering Cockburn Bay because the approach channel appears treacherous and foul as indicated on Chart 3589 and 3311 #4. Entrance into the bay is possible for most boats near high water (there is less than a foot or so of water below chart datum at the narrows). Rocky shoals extend along the starboard (southern) shore between a 2-foot high islet and the narrowest part of the entrance. It is advisable to stay mid-channel until one is in the narrows and then favour the north (port) shore until a 6-foot drying rock pinnacle has been passed. Strip chart #4 (3311) indicates the presence of 3 rocks which dry 4.9, 0.9 and 2.1 metres within the narrows.

The inside of Cockburn Bay is well protected from all winds and seas. A road from the south shore extends around the Cape Cockburn peninsula to Harry Roberts' home and back across the peninsula to Cockburn Bay, bypassing a small pond a short way up from the bay. The two small lakes "Yolana" and "Zoe" next to Chackchack Lake, a mile to the east of Cockburn Bay, are named after Harry Roberts' daughters.

Temporary anchorage is possible in a number of nooks along the Nelson Island shore north of Cockburn Bay. In particular, there is a small nook protected from westerlies by a rocky shelf and offshore islets including a 90-foot high islet further to the southwest. Anchorage between this 90-foot islet and Nelson Island should not be attempted as there are underwater B.C. Tel cables here.

2   Hidden Basin

Hidden Basin is another delightful, totally protected anchorage which is seldom used because of its treacherous entrance. The Basin entrance should be negotiated only near local high water slack. There is some argument about when this actually occurs. My own experience and that of others (Graeme Matheson, PACIFIC YACHTING, February 1977) is that high water slack will occur anywhere from one to two hours after high water, Point Atkinson. A local resident however, maintains that one should "come in and out on the high slack at Point Atkinson — 10 feet of water will give 4 feet of water in the entrance". (H. T. Frederickson's letter to PACIFIC YACHTING, April 1977). This information is repeated in the Canadian Hydrographic Service *Small Craft Guide*, Volume 2. Delays in the arrival of slack water may be caused by extreme barometric pressure differences on the south coast or after periods of storm and high winds.

Cockburn Bay should be approached with caution because of foul entrance. At the narrowest part of the entrance (above) there is less than a foot of water below chart datum.

Maximum ebb makes Hidden Basin entrance impossible for most boats. Entrance can be negotiated at high slack, and once inside, there are some delightful anchorages. Passage is best made on the starboard side of the islet.

The entrance channel is blocked by a small islet with shoals charted as drying 3 feet north of the islet, and 2 feet south of the islet. In actual fact, the northern passage is completely encumbered by drying boulders, and the southern passage has boulders along the side of the passage which dry about 10 feet and boulders in the centre of the passage which dry about 5 feet (favour the starboard side of the southern entrance where there is a narrow channel).

Possible anchorages within Hidden Basin are located either side of a small islet connected by a drying spit to the south shore, in the easternmost end of the basin behind an uncharted isolated drying rock, in the northernmost nook less than ½ mile across a narrow isthmus from Ballet Bay, and in a shallow nook ¼ mile southwest of this latter anchorage. Hazards within the basin include the previously mentioned uncharted rock, another uncharted rock 200 feet from shore at the southern end of the head of the Basin, and shallows (2 feet of water below chart datum) near the 1½-fathom sounding east of the Basin entrance.

Leaving is easier than entering as one can await high water slack without worrying about committing oneself to the passage too early, with an opposing tidal stream keeping one away until the passage is safe.

Billings Bay

The northeast shore of Billings Bay should be given a wide berth when leaving Hidden Basin as there is an uncharted 8-foot drying rock located about 100 feet offshore. Billings Bay was once the location of a small government float and post office but only the float itself remained in 1979, with an aluminum trailer on it, the connection with the shore removed.

Entrance into Blind Bay is possible inside Kelly Island, which has an abandoned granite quarry on its south side; or inside the islet east of Kelly Island. This latter passage shallows to a depth of 4 feet below chart datum at its narrowest point but is otherwise deep and safe enough throughout as long as a central course is followed. There is a 6-foot drying rock just

Ballet Bay.

Ballet Bay is a favourite of many yachtsmen.

If Ballet bay itself (centre left) is crowded, many boats can anchor outside in the channel, and some find anchorages in the nooks and crannies of the islets opposite.

off the south entrance to a tiny drying nook at the south end of this channel where temporary anchorage might be possible. Many drying rocks can be found in the southern approaches to Blind Bay which is enough reason to obey the many "Slow Down" signs erected to protect several private floats and moorings along the shore.

3   Ballet Bay

Ballet Bay is a favourite anchorage for many, escaping from rough weather in Malaspina Strait or seeking an overnight haven before exploring up Jervis Inlet. The anchorage is also a favoured location for spending a few days exploring the 12 surrounding islets, tidal pools, lagoons and tiny passage-ways by dinghy. The most popular anchorage is within the 4-fathom cove (Ballet Bay proper) indenting Nelson Island. Care should be taken when entering this cove near high water to avoid several rocks at the entrance. In particular, there is a 10-foot drying rock about 100

ft. north of a large rock shelf off the western entrance point which is just covered at extreme high water (dries 17 feet). There is also a 9-foot drying rock patch extending out from the opposite entrance point.

When Ballet Bay itself is crowded, many boats anchor just outside in depths of 5 ot 6 fathoms. There is also a narrow shallow nook large enough for two or three boats between three islets about one third of a mile north of Ballet Bay. The shallow indentation east of Ballet Bay is blocked by drying rock shelves and is accessible only by dinghy at high water, revealing a hidden lagoon not shown completely on the chart (3589).

There are many drying rocks in this area. The most dangerous of these rocks have been marked by poles with cans on top by local residents. The main exit channel is marked as 6 fathoms on Chart 3589. There is a dangerous uncharted reef which extends out into this channel from the southeast corner of the adjoining islet. The extremity of this reef is marked by a pole and has now been charted (dries 3.4 metres) on the new Strip chart #4, 3311 (1982). There are also drying rocks north and west of the islet on the eastern side of the passage. Leading marks to assist passage between

186

Blind Bay and Ballet Bay have been erected on the islet connected to Nelson Island by a catwalk. An unmarked rock which would not be particularly dangerous except at extreme low water is located about 200 feet west of the western end of the catwalk islet.

4   Hardy Island

Hardy Island is named after Vice-Admiral Sir Thomas Masterman Hardy who was Lord Nelson's Captain in the *Victory* at the battle of Trafalgar, 1805. Hardy was one of Nelson's most trusted officers and closest friends. In 1796, Hardy served as a Lieutenant under Captain Cockburn on H.M.S *Minerve.* Walbran relates:

> . . . the *Minerve* (was) a large frigate lately captured from the French, and on board which Nelson hoisted his broad pennant when he went from Gibraltar to relieve Elba. On returning from this service to join Sir John Jervis off St. Vincent the frigate was chased in the Strait of Gibraltar by some Spanish line-of-battle ships, when the following incident occurred: A seaman accidentally fell overboard; Lieutenant Hardy, a friend and follower of Nelson, went after the man in a boat which was unable to rejoin the frigate owing to the current and the way on the vessel. With the words 'By God! I'll not lose Hardy, back the mizzentopsail,' Nelson had the *Minerve* brought to the wind and the boat picked up. The man was unfortunately lost. This bold proceeding so astonished the Dons that the leading line-of-battle ship also came to the wind, the others followed her example and the frigate, filling away again, escaped.

. . . At the Nile, Hardy commanded the *Mutine*, 16 gun brig, and, after the battle, was appointed by Nelson to the command of his flagship *Vanguard*, the captain of her, Berry, having been sent to Lord St. Vincent with the news of the victory.

During the War of 1812, Hardy was in command of a squadron blockading the New England coast. On June 25, 1813 Hardy and his flagship, *H.M.S. Ramillies*, narrowly escaped destruction. It appears that a vessel, ostensibly laden with fresh provisions, had been captured, the crew escaping on shore, when instead of having the tempting prize taken alongside the flagship, as was anticipated by the enemy, Commodore Hardy had her made fast to another American vessel. She blew up and nearly all on board perished. It was afterwards discovered that a clockwork mechanism had ignited the powder with which she was really laden. Hardy possibly had recollected a similar attempt being made on Admiral George Vandeput, 37 years previously during the American Rebellion of 1776. In this previous case the treacherous act was found out by a portion of the captured Americans being kept on board the prize, and in their terror they confessed that the vessel was laden with powder and would soon blow up.

Hardy ended his service as a governor of Greenwich

A quiet nook at Hardy Island.

hospital, devoted to the interests of the old sailors under his care.

> He had one characteristic improvement made in the regulations, which was the abolishment of the yellow coat with red sleeves which was worn as a punishment for being drunk on a Sunday, and which Hardy considered degrading to an old sailor and out of all proportion to the offence (Walbran).

Hardy Island has long served as a favourite anchorage and base for exploring the surrounding waters of Blind Bay and Jervis Inlet. It has been highly valued by cruising yachtsmen because of its relative isolation and almost complete lack of development, and because of the many opportunities for secluded anchorage provided by more than twenty individual coves. The most favoured anchorages are inside Fox Island at the southern end of Hardy. This portion of Hardy Island has also been considered as a potential marine park.

Two uncharted rocks can be seen on the starboard side of the eastern entrance to the main Hardy Island anchorage. Small island (centre right) was also uncharted in 1980.

Temporary anchorage is available in a cove just north of the unnamed island west of Fox Island. This cove is partly exposed to any swells from a southeast wind and there is an 8-foot drying rock just inside the thin peninsula along the eastern shore of the cove. A more secure but shallower anchorage is located on the other side of this peninsula. The innermost anchorage contains an old piling or mooring post (Dol) to which boats often loop a bow line around with a stern line ashore. This dolphin may have been part of a wharf structure when the island was actively settled in years gone by. There is an old trail (dotted line on Chart 3589) which crosses the island to a small cove facing the mouth of Jervis Inlet. The trail comes down to the cove through a deserted homestead with an extensive overgrown orchard and meadows. Overlooking the cove is a huge concrete swimming pool with a convenient stone barbecue fireplace nearby.

The tiny nook just east of 'Dol' cove is another delightful anchorage, big enough for only one or two

boats. This cove and the larger 9-fathom cove further east are similar in shape and character. The overhanging cliffs are steep and on quiet nights one seems to hear voices from somewhere echoing down through the fir and arbutus trees. The 9-fathom cove is 9 fathoms only at the entrance. The head of the cove is shallow (2 feet of water) but totally enclosed — a delightfully secluded anchorage.

There are old quarry workings on the steep rock face south of the 9-fathom cove and a substantial rocky islet extending out where it shouldn't be (between the 6½-fathom sounding and the rock with less than 6 feet of water over it as shown on Chart 3589). This islet is joined to Hardy Island by a rock spit and the rock with less than 6 feet of water over it is actually there — part of an extensive reef patch located about 100 feet to the southeast of the islet. This "phantom" islet has now been charted (6) metres on Strip Chart #4, 3311.

Log booms have long been stored in Blind Bay, frequently preventing access to the coves along the Hardy Island shore north of Fox Island. When access is possible, many of these coves offer good protection. The largest, immediately northeast of Fox Island, contains an uncharted rock located just south of the 4-fathom sounding (below 0.3 metres on 3311 Strip Chart #4). The next cove shallows near its head and is lined with drying rocks, but the third is deep enough for safe anchorage, taking care to avoid a 13-foot drying reef patch off the west entrance point.

Shallow draught boats can find secluded protection behind three tiny islets, the largest of which is noted as being 105 feet high on Chart 3589. The middle islet, 1 acre in size, is a provincial recreational reserve, virtually the only crown waterfront land in this entire area. Small limestone quarries were once worked on both sides of the approach to Telescope Passage where upper triassic rocks of the Karmutsen formation outcrop through the prevailing granitic rocks.

Telescope Passage

Blind Bay and Telescope Passage are named to commemorate the incident which enabled Nelson to win the battle of Copenhagen, 1801. At Copenhagen, Nelson was under the orders of Sir Hyde Parker, Commander-in-Chief, but Nelson had direct charge of the attacking fleet. Apparently, the commander in chief hoisted the signal of recall when things appeared to be going badly. Nelson put the telescope to his blind eye and therefore could not see "any signal". The battle continued and victory was won.

On a clear day it is possible to see the Freil Lake Falls through Telescope Passage, almost 10 miles away to the northeast in Hotham Sound. The Nelson Island shore of Telescope Passage should be favoured when negotiating the passage as there are rocks, stretching out to the middle of the passage from the

230-foot high island, which dry from 6 to 10 feet above chart datum.

Well protected anchorage is available to the southwest of the 230-foot island. The space available for anchoring is somewhat limited by shallow depths close to shore, reducing the opportunity for taking a line ashore except near high water. The passage west of the 230-foot island dries about 3 feet. Reasonably safe anchorage is also available in another shallow nook behind the island connected by drying rocks to the northern tip of Hardy Island.

The indented north shore of Hardy Island is well worth exploring with due attention to the many rocks and shoals. Temporary anchorage is possible in a number of locations: inside a small nook at the south end of a 170-foot high islet and behind a 15-foot drying spit which joins a small 110-foot islet to Hardy Island near Ball Point. There are also two small nooks suitable for anchorage on either side of Ball Point. The eastern nook is well protected from most summer winds but the western nook, which shallows from 48 fathoms at the entrance to 8 fathoms inside is moderately exposed to westerlies and swells from any southeaster. The two westernmost points of Hardy Island are named after Rear Admiral Sir Alexander John Ball and also after H.M.S. *Alexander,* 74 guns, of

One of the most popular stopovers for yachtsmen travelling from Vancouver to Desolation Sound is Hardy Island. Much of the timber has since been taken off the island.

which ship he was captain at the battle of the Nile. Walbran relates:

... Nelson and Ball formed a very close friendship, though the acquaintance did not open auspiciously. Nelson first heard of Ball as a young captain on half pay, economizing in France, during the peace of 1783, and describes him in a letter as a coxcomb for wearing epaulettes, which were not then a portion of naval uniform. And again when Captain Ball in the *Alexander* joined Nelson at Gibraltar previous to the battle of the Nile, and went on board the *Vanguard* to pay his respects, Nelson, it is said, greeted him with, 'What, are you come to have your bones broken?' Ball answered, 'He had no wish to have his bones broken unless his duty to his King and country required it, and then they should not be spared'. Not long after this, the *Vanguard* (with Nelson aboard) was dismasted in a heavy gale of wind, when the *Alexander* took her in tow, and though there was imminent danger of both vessels being lost, Captain Ball nobly perservered and brought his charge to a safe anchorage. Nelson immediately visited Ball, and warmly thanked him for his valuable services, remarking, as he had previously done some eighteen months before to Captain Collingwood at St. Vincent, 'A friend in need is a friend indeed'. Nelson never forgot this service, and a warm friendship was the result, which only ended with Nelson's life (at the battle of Trafalgar, 1805).

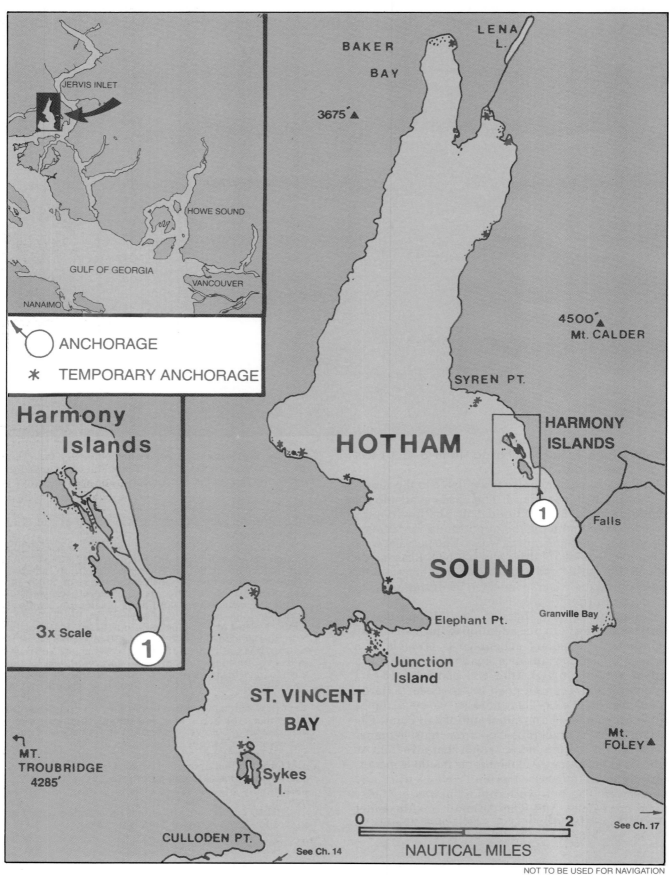

JERVIS INLET

HOWE SOUND

GULF OF GEORGIA

VANCOUVER

NANAIMO

⬆ ⭕ ANCHORAGE

✳ TEMPORARY ANCHORAGE

Harmony
Islands

3x Scale

①

BAKER
BAY

LENA
L.

3675 ▲

4500 ▲
Mt. CALDER

SYREN PT.

HOTHAM

HARMONY
ISLANDS

①

Falls

SOUND

Elephant Pt.

Granville Bay

Junction
Island

Mt.
FOLEY ▲

ST. VINCENT
BAY

Sykes
I.

MT.
TROUBRIDGE
4285'

0   2

See Ch. 17

CULLODEN PT.

See Ch. 14

NAUTICAL MILES

CHAPTER FIFTEEN

Hotham Sound

St. Vincent Bay, Harmony Islands

"Hotham Sound . . . has steep-to-shores and offers little or no anchorage". This quotation from the *Small Craft Guide* (Volume 2, Second Edition) is sufficiently discouraging to keep away all but the most curious yachtsmen.

The "steep-to-shores" understates the majestic scenery with tumbling falls of water down sheer rock cliffs and mountainsides walling in the Sound. The views are impressive from boats passing by in Jervis Inlet, but even more awesome within the Sound itself. Good anchorages are indeed scarce. There is only one really well protected but tiny anchorage in this area. Nevertheless, a number of factors make temporary anchorage for small boats possible in a number of tiny nooks despite the great depths offshore. Because of its orientation, Hotham Sound seldom experiences strong night time summer winds. The winds which blow down Jervis Inlet seldom penetrate over the narrow gap from Prince of Wales reach into Hotham Sound. The strong daytime westerly winds, or southeast gales in the Gulf, which tend to blow up Jervis Inlet usually dissipate into a light southerly in Hotham Sound. This general lack of wind also contributes to the warmer water temperatures here. Hotham Sound is second only to Pendrell Sound (just north of Desolation Sound) as an oyster breeding and spat (seed) collection area because of the warmer waters.

Hotham Sound, like other locations in the lower Jervis Inlet area, is filled with place names honouring the men, ships and incidents surrounding the exploits of the Royal Navy in the time of Lord Nelson and Earl St. Vincent (Sir John Jervis). St. Vincent Bay, the large bight at the western entrance, is named after the title given to Admiral Jervis after his victory over the Spanish fleet off Cape St. Vincent on St. Valentine's Day, 1797. Walbran notes that the title was suggested by King George III. Culloden Point, and Mount Troubridge directly behind it, are named after Captain Thomas Troubridge, commander of H.M.S. *Culloden*, 74 guns, the first ship to engage the Spaniards at Cape St. Vincent.

Sykes Island is named after John Sykes, an able seaman who for many years was an old faithful follower of Lord Nelson. He was present at the battle of Cape St. Vincent and saved Nelson's life in the bay of Cadiz. According to Walbran, Nelson's barge containing 12 men was attacked by a Spanish gunboat manned by 26. Sykes twice parried blows that were aimed at Nelson, and at last actually interposed his own head to receive a sabre-cut which he could not avert by any other means, from which he received a dangerous wound. Sykes also greatly distinguished himself at the battle of Trafalgar.

Temporary anchorage in depths of 5 fathoms is possible at the head of a deep indentation which penetrates the south end of Sykes Island. There is a small reef patch which dries about 12 feet attached to the inside of the eastern entrance point. Although it would appear that Culloden Point would give ample protection to this cove, a strong westerly tends to curl around the point and into the western part of St.

CHARTS
3589 — JERVIS INLET and Approaches
    (1:76,385)

Anchorages on both sides of Sykes Island offer protection from all but extreme winds.

Vincent Bay. In these conditions more protection would be afforded in small nooks on the other side of the island. Temporary anchorage is possible on either side of a detached 13 foot high rock pinnacle joined to Sykes Island by a 10 foot drying bar. Care should be taken to avoid rocks which are awash at chart datum immediately northeast of the 13 foot pinnacle.

Most of the western shore of St. Vincent Bay is taken up with log booms and logging camps. The north shore of the bay is actively used for collecting oyster spat, particularly the waters north of Junction Island. Although there is no direct reference in Walbran, it is possible that Junction Island is named after the incident whereby Nelson enabled Admiral Jervis to win the battle of Cape St. Vincent. Nelson made the daring manoeuvre of leading the last three ships in the British line out of the line of battle, thereby preventing the junction of the two separated portions of the Spanish fleet. This was a sudden and spontaneous act for which Nelson had no authority. After the battle

it was pointed out to Sir John, by Captain Robert Calder, his flag captain in the *Victory*, Sir John's flagship, that Nelson in turning out of the line had acted without orders. Sir John nobly replied to this innuendo, "I forgive him sir, and if you ever act in such a manner without orders, I'll forgive you too." (Walbran)

Temporary anchorage is possible, immediately north of the centre of Junction Island and away from the rafts which are used to collect oyster spat. Oyster leases cover the foreshore surrounding the reefs and shoals between Junction Island and the mainland. There is a hidden cove northwest of Junction Island which is guarded on both sides by rocks and drying shoals. Access into the cove is possible at all stages of the tide. The outer ends of the shoals are indicated by private markers. Private floats and oyster spat collection devices fill most of the cove which contains at least 10 feet of water below chart datum (appears to be foul ground on Chart 3589). A more isolated cove is located on the other side of the shoals north of Junction Island. This cove has average depths of 2 fathoms and is well protected from most summer winds despite its apparent openness to the southeast. There are

192

some rocks below chart datum along the western shore of the cove.

Elephant Point is probably named after H.M.S. *Elephant,* Nelson's flagship commanded by Captain Thomas Foley at the battle of Copenhagen, 1801. Captain Foley is honoured in the naming of the mountain opposite Elephant Point which guards the entrance to Hotham Sound. Foley also took part in the battle of St. Vincent as flag captain to Vice Admiral Thompson aboard H.M.S. *Britannia,* and in the Battle of the Nile, in command of H.M.S. *Goliath.*

Hotham Sound

There are at least four tiny nooks along the west shore of Hotham Sound where temporary anchorage would be possible. Some of these anchorages are conditional on the state of the tide. Despite deep waters offshore, a few small coves are bordered by shallow ground or drying lagoons accessible by small boat only near high water.

Hotham Sound is named after the Admiral who preceded Jervis in command of the Mediterranean fleet, William Hotham. He had distinguished himself 40 years previously while in command of H.M.S. *Syren,* 20 guns, (note point above Harmony Islands) when he had succeeded in capturing a large French privateer of 26 guns. Nelson, who served under him, did not have a high opinion of Hotham as an Admiral.

Walbran notes: "Hotham had succeeded to the chief command by the accident of Lord Hood's resignation. A good officer and a man of undaunted courage, he had done admirably in a subordinate rank, but he was wanting in energy, force of character and decision requisite in a commander in chief."

1 Harmony Islands

Walbran does not have a listing for the Harmony Islands, but, given the association of all other place names in this area, it is quite possible that these islands were named after the first ship known to have been captured by Nelson — the *Harmony,* a Cape Cod fishing schooner. In 1781, Nelson was the 22-year-old captain of H.M.S. *Albemarle,* 28 guns, assisting in the blockade of American ports. After capturing the *Harmony,* Nelson asked her master Nathaniel Carver, if he would pilot the *Albemarle* through the unfamiliar waters of Boston Bay. A recent book by Roy Hattersley *(Nelson),* described what happened:

"The English man-of-war (whose navigator could do no better than 'imagine we are getting into the gulf stream, by it getting very squally') was desperately in need of Carver's goodwill. It was provided in such generous measure that when the task was finished, Nelson addressed his captive with conscious and flamboyant courtesy: 'You have rendered us, Sir, a very useful service, and it is not the custom of English seamen to be

Steep mountains ring the head of Hotham Sound.

Kipling Cove between the three northernmost of the islands is the most popular anchorage in the Harmony Islands. Freil Lake Falls are in the foreground.

Sun-warmed basin near head of Hotham Sound.

ungrateful. In the name, therefore, and with the approbation of the Officers of this ship, I return your Schooner and with it this Certificate of your good conduct.' Nelson's gesture was both appreciated and reciprocated. Four months later, when the *Albemarle's* crew had gone eight weeks without fresh food, *Harmony* was sighted again. Sheep, fowl and fresh vegetables were unloaded on to the *Albemarle's* deck. Only after much argument would Carver accept payment."

The approach to the Harmony Islands takes one past the spectacular Freil Lake Falls which tumble 1400 feet down an almost sheer cliffside into Hotham Sound. In the spring or after a heavy rainfall the roar of these falls can be heard from the Harmony Islands anchorage, a mile to the north.

The Harmony Islands have long been considered as a potential marine park. The southern Harmony Island is crown land and the smallest northern island (one-acre is size) is crown land reserved for the recreation of the public. The preferred anchorage area is inside a small cove (known locally as Kipling Cove) between the three northernmost islands. Space is so limited that most boats tie a stern line to shore or tie alongside other boats to enable more boats to be accommodated. There is a rock in the middle of the entrance with about 3 feet of water over it at chart datum.

Reasonably well protected anchorage is also available between the Harmony Islands and the mainland and in the narrow but shallow (1 foot of water at chart datum) passage north of the southernmost island. Temporary anchorage is also available in Granville Bay, off a small beach north of the Harmony Islands and behind a group of rocky islets south of Syren Point. Mount Calder is named after Admiral Jervis' flag captain at the battle of Cape St. Vincent.

Anchorage at the head of Hotham Sound is possible in the northwest corner of Baker Bay or in the eastern arm. The eastern arm is more exposed however to any night time winds which may penetrate into Hotham Sound from Jervis Inlet. Such winds are unusual in the summer months, but when a particularly strong

Temporary anchorage off the west shore of Hotham Sound.

down-inlet wind is blowing in Jervis, it may gust through the narrow gap to the eastern head of Hotham Sound without warning. Lena Lake, half a mile from the sea is accessible by an old logging road. There is a hidden drying lagoon behind a small rocky islet which appears to be part of the shore just north of the headland separating the two bays at the head of Hotham Sound. The water in this lagoon becomes exceptionally warm because the rock face behind is heated by the sun during the day, transferring its heat to the waters during the nighttime high tide.

The steep, bare rock hills rising sheer from the west side of the Sound are the southern extension of the Parker Range of mountains. This range and the highest peak, Mount Diadem, 5,815 feet, are named after Vice-Admiral Sir William Parker, third in command at St. Vincent and after H.M.S. *Diadem*, 64 guns, a ship of the squadron under Jervis.

Cascading 1400 feet down sheer cliff, Freil Lake drains into Hotham Sound a mile south of Harmony Islands.

In the spring, the Harmony Islands are usually uncrowded and quiet.

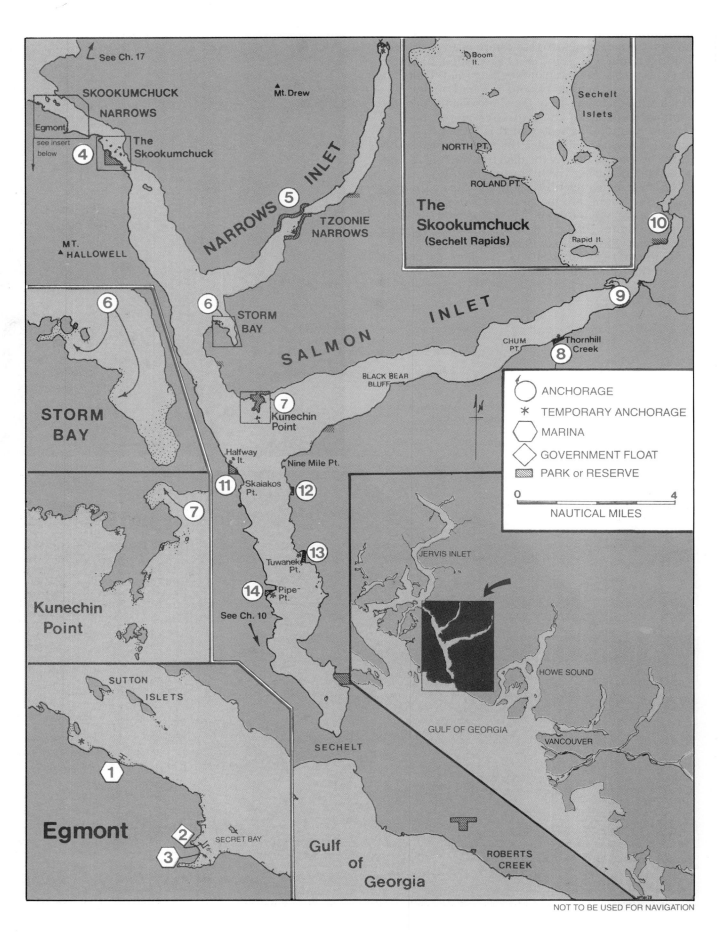

See Ch. 17

SKOOKUMCHUCK
NARROWS

Egmont
see insert
below

④

The
Skookumchuck

Mt. Drew

⑤

NARROWS INLET

TZOONIE
NARROWS

MT.
HALLOWELL

SALMON   INLET

⑥   ⑥   STORM
                       BAY

STORM
BAY

⑦
Kunechin
Point

BLACK BEAR
BLUFF

CHUM
PT.

Thornhill
Creek
⑧

⑨

⑩

The
Skookumchuck
(Sechelt Rapids)

Boom
It.

Sechelt
Islets

NORTH PT.

ROLAND PT.

Rapid It.

Halfway
It.

Nine Mile Pt.

⑪   Skaiakos
           Pt.   ⑫

⑦

Kunechin
Point

Tuwanek
Pt.   ⑬

⑭   Pipe-
     Pt.

See Ch. 10

SUTTON
ISLETS

①

Egmont

②   SECRET BAY
③

SECHELT

Gulf
of
Georgia

JERVIS INLET

HOWE SOUND

GULF OF GEORGIA

VANCOUVER

ROBERTS
CREEK

⭘   ANCHORAGE
✳   TEMPORARY ANCHORAGE
⬡   MARINA
◇   GOVERNMENT FLOAT
▨   PARK or RESERVE

0   4
NAUTICAL MILES

NOT TO BE USED FOR NAVIGATION

196

CHAPTER SIXTEEN

Sechelt Inlet

Egmont, The Skookumchuck, Narrows and Salmon Inlets

Sechelt Inlet is often bypassed by cruising yachts due to its detached location, hidden behind the Sechelt Peninsula, and to a well justified apprehension about the fearsome Skookumchuck, which guards the entrance. Boats which can be carried or launched from a trailer can avoid the Skookumchuck by entering the Inlet at Porpoise Bay. (see Chapter 10). Sechelt Inlet, together with its tributary arms, Salmon and Narrows Inlets, therefore tends to be a relatively placid, little travelled backwater where one will find fewer boats than in the open Gulf but abundant mountain scenery typical of B.C.'s fiord coastline.

Historically, this Inlet served as an important trading route of the Sechelt Indians and four of the points in the inlet are named after the four divisions of the Salish tribe — Tuwanek, Skaikos, Kunechin, Tsonai. More recently the Inlet and surrounding watersheds have seen intense logging activity. As this activity decreases, several coves previously obstructed by log booming or storage are becoming accessible to small boats. The provincial parks branch, recognizing the high potential of Sechelt Inlet for small boat recreaion, has established a unique marine park system comprising eight small sites located around the shoreline of the Inlet. These sites are intended primarily as locations where small boats can find some shelter or be beached relatively safely with some flat land for camping ashore. Their location does not make them particularly suitable as anchorages for larger craft; however, temporary anchorage is possible at most of them, depending on prevailing weather conditions. Many of the sites have been used in the

past for log booming and may be needed for this purpose again in the future.

Skookumchuck Narrows

The word Skookumchuck comes from the Indian for "strong or turbulent" (skookum) and for "salt water" (chuck). Tidal currents in the first 3-mile section of Skookumchuck Narrows proper (before one gets to the rapids themselves) run quite strongly at rates up to 4 knots, and in a direction quite different from what one might expect after local low or high water. The tidal stream will continue to flow in a westerly direction *out* of Sechelt Inlet for an hour or more (depending on the strength or range of the tide) after local low water (10 minutes after Point Atkinson). It will also continue to flow eastward *into* Sechelt Inlet for an hour or so after local high water. This is because Sechelt Rapids (the Skookumchuck itself) provides such a narrow constriction to the flow of waters. that the water levels on either side only become equal some time after high or low water outside has passed — anywhere from 1 hour and 45 minutes to 3 hours and 40 minutes *after* Point Atkinson.

This unexpected direction and strength of the tidal stream before one even gets close to the Skookumchuck Rapids may sometimes prove to be embarrassing. From Egmont I once watched a huge barge

CHARTS
3589 — JERVIS INLET and Approaches
(1:76,385)

Wise yachtsmen have a healthy respect for the Skookum-chuck, or Sechelt Rapids, one of the strongest and potentially most dangerous tidal passes on the coast. Top picture shows the rapids two hours before maximum flood, and the lower picture one hour before full flood. Boats in trouble can find very temporary safety in the backeddies behind Rapid Islet or Sechelt Islets, on the right.

The Skookumchuck (Sechelt Rapids) can be awesome at full spring tide, such as the ebb shown below.

Tidal pool marine life in the Skookumchuck is similar to that found in the surge zone of the open Pacific coast.

under tow by a small tug approaching the Skookumchuck about half an hour after high water Point Atkinson. The tug skipper must have been unfamilar with the local conditions and assumed he was approaching the rapids close to slack water. Suddenly, he realized what was happening and quickly turned around but it was almost too late. By the time the barge was also turned around, both tug and barge seemed to be slipping inexorably backwards into the rapids, caught by the relentless grip of the tidal stream. Slowly, very slowly, the barge and tug slowed, remained stationary and after several minutes gradually began to pull away from the rapids. Slack water did not arrive at the Skookumchuck for another two hours.

When the tidal stream is running strongly in Skookumchuck Narrows there is often a back eddy close to shore, west or north of Sutton Islets on the ebb and off Egmont on the flood. The Sutton Islets are named after Captain John Sutton who commanded H.M.S. *Egmont*, 74 guns, in the battle of Cape St. Vincent, February 14, 1797. (Walbran). The community of Egmont was originally located on the north shore of Skookumchuck Narrows but moved south across the Narrows when the coast highway was extended to the south shore.

1   Egmont Marina and Resort

This marina is located south of the Sutton Islets and provides a wide range of services including fuels,
moorage for boats up to 50 feet long, housekeeping cottages and waterfront campsites, shower and laundry facilities, launching ramp, boat rentals or charters, fishing tackle and bait, a small store and a cafe-restaurant.

2   Egmont Gov't Floats

The Egmont government floats are located in Secret Bay and provide over a thousand feet of berthage space. The tip of the easternmost float is reserved for float planes. There is a government launching ramp a few yards from the dock. The small community of Egmont has been used as the backdrop for a television series known as "Ritters Cove", based on the adventures of a float plane pilot.

3   Bathgate Egmont Enterprises

Skippers approaching Bathgate's fuel float without appreciating the significance of red buoys and port hand daymark beacons have occasionally gone aground less than 50 yards short of the float. It is an easy mistake for the unfamiliar to make; the buoy and the beacon are so placed that it might seem natural to go between them. What is particularly deceptive is that at mid-tide, the only part of the rocky reef that appears above water is to the starboard (west) of the

Skippers approaching Bathgate's fuel floats have occasionally tried to go between the white day beacon and the red buoy. Rocks between beacons dry at six feet.

day beacon suggesting that one should leave this beacon to starboard when in fact, the worst part of the reef lies hidden beneath the surface between the beacon and the buoy. Apparently sailboats with deep keels are the most frequent victims. There are no repair facilities nearby if damage is serious. Boats should approach the fuel float either by leaving the red buoy to starboard or leaving the beacon at least 30 feet to port (passing close to the Government float).

Bathgate's fuel float also provides moorage and there are showers and a laundromat, boat rentals, bait and tackle. A small but exceptionally well stocked store is located directly above the fuel floats.

4   Skookumchuck Narrows Provincial Park

If you happen to be in Egmont during spring tides you should not miss the opportunity to view the Skookumchuck (formally known as ''Sechelt Rapids''). This is one of the truly spectacular features of the British Columbia coast and anyone who views them over a spring tide cycle from slack to full ebb or flood cannot come away with anything other than an increased respect for the power of the sea.

The rapids are best viewed by hiking a 3-mile trail from Egmont to the park. The trail leaves the main Egmont road about ¼ mile west of the government floats and is marked by a Parks Branch sign and noticeboard. Direction and information signs and public toilets are located along the trail.

The noticeboard at the Egmont road gives the tidal predictions for Point Atkinson which, strangely enough, approximate the best time to view the rapids. To be absolutely sure one can calculate when the tide will be running at its fullest from Table 4, Volume 5 of the *Canadian Tide and Current Tables*. Slack water at the Skookumchuck will occur 1 hour, 45 minutes, plus 5 or 7 minutes for every foot of tidal rise or fall, after low or high water at Point Atkinson. Then add half the time difference between low and high water Point Atkinson for maximum flood or ebb and allow another hour for hiking along the trail. After making all these calculations you will probably find that the time one should be at the rapids (to view them at maximum flow) is very close to the actual time of low or high water, Point Atkinson.

The trail passes Brown Lake where one can often hear the roar of the rapids and almost feel the ground tremble as one approaches North Point. North Point is the best viewing point to watch an ebb tide. The flood tide is best observed from Roland Point another ½ mile to the southeast. In between these two points is a small bay into which the water surges in and out in a slow regular rhythm as the water level rises and falls 2 to 3 feet every 10 seconds or so. This phenomenon is similar to the surge one encounters on the open ocean coast even when it is flat calm.

The intertidal marine life here is also somewhat exotic and comparable to what one might find in the surf zone of an open ocean coast. The rapid currents discourage predators and permit the growth of huge brilliantly coloured anemones, urchins and giant barnacles. Special care must be exercised on the rocks overlooking the rapids as moss and lichens tend to become saturated, damp and slippery. The Parks Branch plans to construct a protective fence in the most dangerous areas. A common practice with young children is to tie them by a long rope to a tree so that if they fall in they can be yanked out before being carried away.

Yachtsmen without local knowledge who attempt to navigate through the Skookumchuck Rapids should only do so at slack water, preferably low water slack (when *entering* the inlet) so that one is going against the last of the ebb before entering the most difficult part between the Sechelt Islets and the Peninsula. If navigating the Skookumchuck at high water slack, which is recommended by the Canadian Hydrographic Service, one should be absolutely certain of the time of slack water. A miscalculation could result in one being drawn into the rapids before they have become safe enough to navigate or leave one too late to pass completely through before the ebb stream becomes too strong to stem. The maximum current at spring tides is 12 knots on the ebb and 10 knots on the flood.

At neap tides, when the tidal range is small, the B.C. *Small Craft Guide*, Volume 2, suggests that power boats could go through at times other than slack water on a course to the east of the Sechelt Islets light, in order to avoid the worst of the rips and eddies occurring off North Point on the ebb. On the flood, one can hold a central course past North and Roland Points, altering course southeast of Roland Point to avoid any overfalls. (see inset map).

The most dangerous part of the rapids are the whirlpools which generally occur along the edge of the Sechelt Islets (particularly on the ebb between the two islets east and north of North Point), and the overfalls which build up on the flood southeast of Roland Point. The whirlpools disappear and reappear at irregular intervals and are of tremendous power. I once saw a huge log, twice the size of a telephone pole, disappear completely in a whirlpool and suddenly, two or three hundred yards further on, come shooting out of the water with such force that it could easily have gone completely through any boat which happened to be over it. The flow of water through the Skookumchuck on a big tide is twice that of the Fraser River at New Westminster. (R. Harris).

Harry Roberts, in his book *The Trail of Chack Chack*, describes how he once tried to take a boat through the Skookumchuck against a strong ebb tide. They had anchored in a small cove to the north of North Point to build up steam. (This cove, incidentally is indicated as a ''boat moorage'' by the Parks Branch; — while not ideal as an anchorage it could serve as a moderately protected cove in which to secure or beach a small boat). After Roberts had built

Farm at Doriston in Sechelt Inlet.

up steam they attempted to power their way over the "hump" — a solid wall of water about 2 to 3 feet high opposite North Point. They tried twice and each time their boat was flung up out of the water onto the rocky islet opposite North Point, the second time, with such force that most of the boat was above the high tide line and they were unable to get it back into the water. They kept the boat in place by ropes from an overhanging tree and were lucky to salvage their boat at high water the next day. Roberts notes in his book: "It was not the people who went through occasionally who were in danger. The gravest danger was to those of us who became so used to going through that familiarity bred, if not contempt, at least a certain disregard and one cannot disregard the sea, particularly at the Skookum Chuck."

It is a sad fact that of at least 16 people known to have drowned here, the majority have been locals. It is not unusual to see small power boats blithely weaving their way through the rapids with no apparent concern, tempting fate.

In an emergency, temporary anchorage might be possible when there are back eddys behind the Sechelt Islets or behind Rapid Islet but I have never tried it and I suspect the holding ground would be poor as swift tidal currents tend to scour mud, sand and gravel from the sea bottom.

Sechelt Inlet

Winds on the B.C. coast tend to be strongly controlled by the nature of the topography, especially in narrow inlets where winds tend to blow along the length of the inlet rather than across it. In Sechelt Inlet this holds true some of the time, but, because of the configuration of the tributary Salmon and Narrows Inlets, not always. In the summer months winds often blow up Salmon and Narrows Inlets, starting around 10 or 11 each morning, becoming increasingly strong through the afternoon and dying out in the evening. Down-inlet winds generally occur at night or, in Salmon Inlet, when a strong southeaster is blowing out in the Gulf. The mouth of Salmon Inlet is notorious for rough water where any tidal currents meet contrary winds. When strong winds are blowing up Salmon and Narrows Inlets, winds may often blow across Sechelt Inlet from the southwest in "williwaw" fashion, being strongest, oddly enough, between Salmon and Narrows Inlets and not at the entrance to these inlets as one might expect.

Tides within Sechelt Inlet are very different from tides outside. There is a maximum range of only 10 feet (the maximum range at Egmont is 18 feet) with mean tidal ranges around 6 feet. The higher high water outside is sometimes the lower high water inside and the times of high or low water are 2 to 3 hours behind, so care should be taken in extrapolating heights and times from Point Atkinson tides.

There is a small community on the eastern shore opposite Rapid Islet with a private float serving logging operations in the surrounding hills. A logging

Tzoonie Narrows has a 200-acre marine park, the largest in Sechelt Inlet.

road provides access for a stimulating climb to the top of Mount Drew, known locally as "Red Top" and described in *Hiking Trails of the Sunshine Coast*.

Another mountain of considerable interest for hikers seeking an unobstructed view of the surrounding waterways is Mount Hallowell, the highest peak on the Sechelt Peninsula, located about four miles south of Egmont. This mountain is most accessible from the Pender Harbour side and is named after Admiral Sir Benjamin Hallowell, a Canadian who served in the Royal Navy. He was said to be a man of gigantic frame and vast personal strength who quelled any sign of mutiny with arm and fist. He was not without a sense of humour. Walbran notes that as a Captain he had:

> Commanded H.M.S. *Swiftsure*, 74 guns, at the battle of the Nile, and was another of the 'Band of Brothers' referred to by Nelson in his letter to Earl Howe. After the victory of the Nile gifts of all kinds were showered on Lord Nelson, but the most extraordinary of all was from Captain Hallowell, who, it is stated, on the authority of his brother, 'fearing the effect of all the praise and flattery lavished on his chief, determined to remind him that he was mortal,' and sent him, some months after the victory, a coffin, with a signed certificate pasted on the bottom that 'Every part of this coffin is made of the wood and iron of *L'Orient*, most of which was picked up by His Majesty's ship under my command, in the bay of Aboukir;' and with it a letter:-
>
> 'Swiftsure, 23 May, 1799.
> 'My Lord, — Herewith I send you a coffin made of part of *L'Orient's* mainmast, that when you are tired of this life you may be buried in one of your own trophies; but may that period be far distant is the sincere wish of your obedient and much obliged servant.'

Two years earlier, Captain Hallowell had been a passenger aboard H.M.S. *Victory* at the battle off Cape St. Vincent after his own ship has been wrecked a few weeks before near Gibraltar.

Narrows Inlet

Special care should be taken if rounding Highland Point at the entrance to Narrows Inlet to avoid the six foot drying rock which extends out some distance from the point and has proven to be more dangerous than it looks on the chart.

5   Tzoonie Narrows

The Tzoonie Narrows Marine Park site is the largest in the Sechelt Marine Park system with almost 200 acres of land protected. This park consists of a strip of land on both sides of the inlet surrounding the "bulge" in the inlet from Tzoonie Point to just beyond the Narrows themselves. The east side of the inlet was actively settled by a nunber of people who established a flourishing informal community here with gardens and fruit trees in the 1960s and '70s. The 1-foot islet which is a dot on the chart is actually a long narrow reef with large extensions under the surface, very deceptive at high tide. Temporary anchorage is possible inside this 1-foot islet or, with more protection from up-inlet winds, in a deep bight on the other side of the inlet where there is a nice beach.

Tidal streams through the Tzoonie Narrows run at maximum rates of 4 knots but there are no obstructions. Once inside the upper arm of Narrows Inlet, the surrounding mountains seem to come close and grow considerably higher giving one the impression of travelling down a remote mountain lake.

A mile east of the Narrows there is a 48-acre recreation reserve protecting a series of deltaic beaches and flat upland suitable for camping with fresh water nearby. There are also a number of small coves, particularly along the eastern shore, which could be used for temporary anchorage. The head of Narrows Inlet has been actively used as the site of a logging camp and for the dumping, booming and storage of logs. Fishermen make use of these log booms for temporary moorage while engaged in fishing up the Tzoonie River. It is also possible to find moderately protected anchorage behind the log booms at the edge of the Tzoonie estuary delta by passing around the booms in an open channel along the western shore of the inlet.

6   Storm Bay

Storm Bay, at the south entrance to Narrows Inlet, is probably the most protected anchorage in Sechelt Inlet. Strangely, M. Wylie Blanchet (*The Curve of Time*) felt this anchorage was unsafe and open to the influence of any night-time winds from Jervis Inlet. She had brought her children into the Inlet in search

of the places and animals they had remembered were visited by "Henry" in a story of a lost blackfish or killer whale, trapped inside the Inlet by the Skookumchuck. Mrs. Blanchet had felt like Saint Theresa when a goat had miraculously appeared on an islet in the bay, much to the delight of her children (and the goat as well).

Anchorage is possible in two locations, just inside the islets east of Cowley Point or behind a point projecting into the middle part of the bay. Care should be taken to avoid shoals east of the northern tip of the easternmost islet and just to the south of it. The remains of a brick factory which operated here from 1905 to 1907 can be found behind the drying flats at the head of the bay. There is a small community of hillside dwellers partially hidden in the forest above the eastern shore of the bay. The land surrounding Storm Bay is all private with the exception of the tiniest islet — a ¼-acre recreation reserve.

Just south of Storm Bay in Sechelt Inlet is a small nook with a sandy beach known as Friendly Cove which is being used at present for the booming of logs

Most protected anchorage in Sechelt Inlet is Storm Bay, at the entrance to Narrows Inlet.

Kunechin Point has a 111-acre marine park, at the entrance to Salmon Inlet.

cut from behind the hill directly above the cove. The immediate upland around the cove is designated as a 12-acre recreation reserve and when logging here finishes, this cove could provide temporary anchorage with fair protection from up- or down-inlet winds. There is a fresh water supply here and potential for camping ashore.

Salmon Inlet

7   Kunechin Point

The marine park site at Kunechin Point comprises 111 acres and includes the Kunechin Islets. This is a fascinating area to explore by small boat as there are several small "pocket" beaches and tiny coves where temporary anchorage can be found. Special care must be taken, however, to avoid a number of rocks which are not easy to delineate on the chart. The most protection is afforded in a small cove ½ mile north of Kunechin Point within Salmon Inlet. The western half of this cove is very shallow. There are drying rocks right in the middle of the cove and off the south entrance point. The best anchorage offering the most

protection from any light night-time down-inlet winds is along the northeastern shoreline of the cove where a log boom float and floathouse have been moored parallel to the shore. Strong down-inlet winds are not common in the summertime unless there is a strong southeaster blowing out in the Gulf. In such conditions, the tiny coves along the Sechelt Inlet side of the Kunechin Peninsula would offer more protection.

In the summer months the usual nightime conditions are generally so calm that one can hear the evening revellings and hymn-singing of campers at the Glad Tidings Youth Camp two miles across the mouth of Salmon Inlet. A short distance east of the Glad Tidings Camp there is a 17-acre recreational reserve.

Salmon Inlet is different from most other B.C. inlets in that the flood tide results in a current up the northwest side of the Inlet. This could be because the major inflow of fresh water into the Inlet is controlled by the power dam at the head. There is a high voltage power line from the head of the Inlet which passes over several small coves along the southern shore. At one time the lowest overhead clearance of the line was 12 feet but the minumum clearance is now 25 feet. No-one has yet been killed or had their boat explode by inadvertently striking the wires, but some unusual things have happened. One sailboat reportedly hit the wires with a brilliant display of sparks but no damage was noticed until the skipper attempted to anchor later that evening and found that all the links in his anchor chain were welded together. Other boats have had their radios, navigation lights and other electrical equipment blown to bits. As Chart 3589 warns: "Caution should be exercised when approaching the shore".

The "23-fathom" cove between Black Bear Bluff and Newcomb Point is very deep inside but small enough to take long bow and stern lines ashore. The power lines are over 50 feet above the water at this point.

8   Thornhill Creek

The Thornhill Creek Marine Park site, located less than a mile east of Chum Point, is 8 acres in size and covers the eastern shore of the creek delta. A small bight behind the delta was also used for booming logs and offers some protection from up-inlet winds. A flash flood caused by rapid erosion of the logged-over slopes took out the powerline and timber on both

Glad Tidings Youth Camp, across the inlet from Kunechin Point.

There is good temporary anchorage behind Lamb Islets. Note rock under surface of water.

Temporary anchorage north of Tuwanek Point.

sides of the creek east of Thornhill Creek in May of 1973, leaving a pile of rubble at the waterfront.

The Misery Creek falls north of Thornhill Point, while only 50 to 60 feet high, are a notable spectacle because of the bubbling intensity generated as they churn through a chasm less than ten feet wide at the waters edge. It is possible to sail right up to the base of the falls.

9   Misery Bay

Logging in the Misery Creek watershed is winding down and the bay is no longer actively used for log booming. The western end of Misery Bay now provides good protection from up-inlet winds. The sharp point at the east end of Misery Bay contains a group of rock paintings described by Lester Peterson in this manner:

> One painting . . . is quite interesting, and different from any other. It depicts, on a vertical rock face, accessible by means of a ledge, an open 'U', beside which stand a pair of deer, most accurately drawn. Strangely enough, it is the very symbol found years ago by James Churchward throughout the Pacific's islands and periphery, used, so he found, to depict the immersion of the legendary continent Mu. Near this painting, another shows the double-headed serpent encircling a tiny deer, and, near that again, a sort of herringbone pattern, which could well represent the primordial Tree of Life.

The extensive delta of Sechelt Creek stretches more than half way across Salmon Inlet from the eastern shore and is a hazard particularly near high water when the seaward extension of the delta is hidden. The east bank of the delta has served as a logging camp base with logs boomed in the protected bay behind the delta. Logging roads from here connect with roads from McNab Creek in Howe Sound, 14 miles away over a low, 2,000 foot high pass in the mountains. A 14-acre recreational reserve covers the south shore of the point a mile south of the head of the Inlet. Small coves here could be used as a temporary anchorage with no fears of overhead powerlines.

10   Clowhom Falls

Clowhom is one of the few geographical features in the local area to retain its aboriginal Sechelt name. "Clowhom" meaning "water running over rock" is no longer an accurate description, as the water runs through rock, pipes and turbines and only over rocks or spillways when B.C. Hydro wants it to.

The head of Salmon Inlet is occupied by log booms, log dump, a logging camp, floats, wharves, two power plants (one of which is much larger and newer than the other) each backed by surge water towers, two "dry" waterfall beds, and some resort style cabins known as the "Oregon Club" which somehow seem a bit out of place. Apparently, these cabins have long been used as a base for tourists, fishing and hunting in the upper Clowhom Lakes area. The water level in these lakes fluctuates between 135 and 175 feet above sea level, depending on the season. All the floats are private but permission for temporary moorage may be granted at the Weldwood floats north of the booming ground. It is possible to portage a light canoe or dinghy into Clowhom Lake by way of the logging road but be cautious — despite all the industrial activity, this area is notorious for black bears which do not always trundle off into the bush when you meet them unexpectedly lumbering down the road.

Outside Salmon Inlet, in the southern portion of Sechelt Inlet there are five additional marine park sites. None of these sites offers particularly good anchorage, but for small boats they offer some degree of shelter and an opportunity to camp ashore.

11   Halfway Islet

The first site is sixteen acres around a small delta with an attractive beach south of Halfway Islet. The second site is about half a mile south of Skaiakos Point and comprises a delta south of a small creek, one acre in size.

12   Nine Mile Point

The third site covers fifteen acres around a delta beach about three-quarters of a mile south of Nine Mile Point.

206

Lester Peterson notes that there is an interesting rock painting which is . . .

located on a concave cliff midway between Nine Mile Point and Gray Creek and depicts a face, full view. At this spot, so legend has it, a hunter was pulled overboard from his canoe by a porpoise he had speared, and was drowned. His spirit, seen sitting in a niche near the site of the painting, refused to come back to his people, but told them that he wished to return to the kingdom beneath the sea. There are overtones to the legend of the Greeks' boy on the green dolphin.

13 Tuwanek Point

The fourth site includes eighteen acres from a beach in the 20-fathom cove down to Tuwanek Point and 2 acres covering the islet south of Tuwanek Point. Between the point and the islet shoal draught boats can find very tightly enclosed shelter.

14 Piper Point

The last site incorporates thirteen acres to the south of Piper Point.

The extreme south end of Sechelt Inlet is described in Chapter 10.

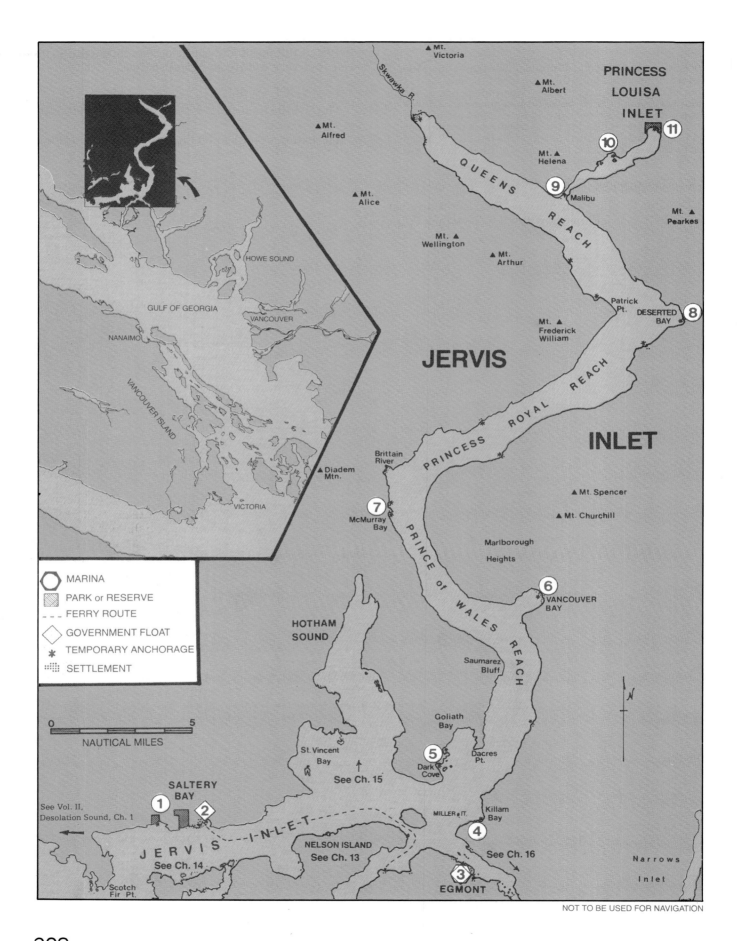

PRINCESS
LOUISA
INLET

⑪

⑩

Mt. ▲ Victoria

Skwawka R.

Mt. Albert ▲

▲ Mt. Alfred

Mt. ▲ Helena

Mt. ▲ Pearkes

⑨ Malibu

Q U E E N S   R E A C H

Mt. Alice ▲

Mt. ▲ Wellington

▲ Mt. Arthur

Patrick Pt.

DESERTED BAY ⑧

JERVIS

Mt. ▲ Frederick William

P R I N C E S S   R O Y A L   R E A C H

INLET

Brittany River

▲ Mt. Spencer

▲ Mt. Churchill

⑦ McMurray Bay

Marlborough Heights

⑥ VANCOUVER BAY

P R I N C E   o f   W A L E S   R E A C H

HOWE SOUND

GULF OF GEORGIA

VANCOUVER

NANAIMO

VANCOUVER ISLAND

▲ Diadem Mtn.

VICTORIA

Saumarez Bluff

HOTHAM SOUND

Goliath Bay

Dacres Pt.

| MARINA |
| PARK or RESERVE |
| FERRY ROUTE |
| GOVERNMENT FLOAT |
| TEMPORARY ANCHORAGE |
| SETTLEMENT |

St. Vincent Bay

See Ch. 15

⑤ Dark Cove

N

0   5
NAUTICAL MILES

SALTERY BAY

See Vol. II, Desolation Sound, Ch. 1

① ②

J E R V I S   -I-N-L-E-T

See Ch. 14

NELSON ISLAND
See Ch. 13

MILLER ● IT.

Killam Bay

④ See Ch. 16

Narrows

Inlet

Scotch Fir Pt.

③ EGMONT

CHAPTER SEVENTEEN

Jervis and Princess Louisa Inlets

Princess Louisa is one of two places in Georgia Strait (the other is Desolation Sound) which have top priority on the itineraries of cruising yachtsmen. With few anchorages or recreational opportunities ashore, the area relies solely on spectacular scenery for its popularity. The narrow inlet is walled in by towering mountains, snow-covered year-round, and cascading waterfalls roar down the sheer rock cliffs.

The 1864 *Pilot* gives this description of the approach to Princess Louisa Inlet:

Jervis Inlet is one of the most considerable of those numerous and remarkable arms of the sea which indent the continent; . . . it extends by winding reaches in a northerly direction for more than 40 miles, while its width rarely exceeds 1½ miles, and in most places is even less.

Neither in a commercial point of view, as a refuge for shipping, or as a means of communications with the interior of the country, does it appear likely ever to occupy any very prominent place, as it is hemmed in on all sides by mountains of the most rugged and stupendous character, rising from its almost perpendicular shores to five, six and sometimes eight thousand feet. The hardy pine, which flourishes where no other tree can find soil to sustain life; holds but a feeble and uncertain tenure here; and it is not uncommon to see whole mountain sides denuded by the blasts of winter, or the still more certain destruction of the avalanche which accompanies the thaw of summer. Strikingly grand and magnificent, there is a solemnity in the silence and utter desolation which prevail here during the months of winter, not a native, not a living creature to disturb the solitude and though in summer a few . . . Indians may occasionally be met with, and the reverberating echo of a hundred cataracts disturb the silence, yet the desolation remains, and seems inseparable from a scene which nature never intended as the abode of man. The depths below almost rival the height of the mountain summits; bottom is rarely reached under 200 fathoms, even close to the shore, and fre-

quently at much greater depths; there are a few spots where vessels may drop an anchor, but they are either open and exposed, (or) with an inconvenient depth of water . . .

Although the Inlet had long been used by the indigenous Sechelt Indians, the first white man to explore it was Captain George Vancouver, who named it Jervis's Channel. He also named the northern entrance point to the Inlet Scotch Fir Point because it produced the first Scotch firs they had yet seen. (See Chapter One of Vol. II, *Cruising Guide to Desolation Sound*). Vancouver had explored the Inlet in two small boats from H.M.S. *Discovery* which he had left anchored in Birch Bay with the *Chatham*. On his return, he met the Spanish vessels *Sutil* and *Mexicana*, anchored near Point Grey and four days after leaving it, all four vessels sailed together past the entrance to Jervis Inlet en route to Desolation Sound. Galiano and Valdes, the Spanish captains, named the Inlet Brazo de Mazaredo, after a naval officer (later Admiral) in the Spanish Navy. Almost all other place names in the Inlet were named around 1860 by coastal hydrographer Captain Richards.

Five years after Vancouver named the Inlet, Rear Admiral Sir John Jervis was created Earl St. Vincent in honour of his celebrated victory over the Spanish fleet in 1797.

Walbran had this to say about Jervis:

The Earl St. Vincent, which was Sir John's later title, and

CHARTS
3589 — JERVIS INLET and Approaches
    (1:76,385)

the name by which he is remembered by posterity, was a strict disciplinarian, and by many persons has been described as arbitrary and tyrannical. Such was not the case. When strict justice and sternness were necessary in upholding order in his fleet no person could be more unbending and inflexible than St. Vincent, but otherwise he was of an even and kindhearted disposition. Many anecdotes of St. Vincent's sternness, when necessary, and kind thoughtfulness at other times, might be given to exemplify his character. A striking one relates than when in command of the fleet off Cadiz, in 1799, a 74-gun ship named the *Marlborough,* having her crew in a state of mutiny, joined his fleet. A mutineer shortly after the arrival of the vessel was found guilty and sentenced to death; the crew refused to execute the prisoner, and the captain of the *Marlborough,* named Ellison, waited on the commander in chief and informed him of the decision of his crew. Lord St. Vincent received the captain on the quarterdeck, and after hearing his statement, replied: "Captain Ellison, do you mean to tell me you cannot command your ship. You are an old man and have been in command of His Majesty's ships for many years; if you were a younger man I should place an officer in command who can. You will return on board, sir, and hang that man to-morrow morning at eight o'clock." Captain Ellison returned to his ship. He was ordered to close his ports, which was done. Lord St. Vincent then gave orders and made such arrangements that at seven o'clock in the morning the boats of the fleet, heavily armed, surrounded the *Marlborough,* prepared to sink the line-of-battle ship where she lay, with all on board, should the execution be not carried out. It was an anxious moment. The bells of the fleet struck eight, the gun on the flagship fired, and the man was hanged at the foreyardarm of the *Marlborough.* The only remark Lord St. Vincent made as the sentence was carried out was, "discipline is preserved." (For a full account of this incident, *see* Tucker's "Life of Earl St. Vincent," I, IX, p. 305.)

On the other hand, when one of his seamen on the *Ville de Paris* had lost his savings, seventy pounds in bank notes, from jumping overboard with his clothes on, while bathing, Lord St. Vincent made him a present of the whole amount, and his gift of one thousand guineas to the seamen's orphanage, in remembrance of what he owed to the valour of British seamen, was never forgotten by the men of the British fleet during the weary months they were blockading Brest in 1800-1801, his lordship being in command on the *Ville de Paris.*

Moorage, Anchorage and Emergency Shelter

Jervis Inlet is not quite as desolate now as when Vancouver or the writer of the 1864 Pilot visited it. Although anchorages of any kind are scarce, there are a few projecting points and tiny bays or bights which offer some degree of shelter. In a few places there are small deltas projecting into the Inlet, usually at the mouths of rivers, creeks or waterfalls, although some of the waterfalls plunge off the mountainsides straight into the sea. The lee side of these deltas can often be used for the beaching of small boats. The flat upland above the beach can be used for camping ashore. Larger deltas at the mouths of the rivers coming into bends in the Inlet (usually at the end of a reach) are usually exposed to daytime winds, but

Most breathtakingly spectacular scenery on the coast is in Princess Louisa, when the weather is clear. Malibu Rapids, bottom, should be travelled at slack water.

Government floats are tucked in behind B.C. Ferry terminal at Saltery Bay.

could provide a night anchorage in stable weather. Moreover, there are several logging camps and a gravel quarry which might offer emergency moorage.

Winds

In the summer months, winds almost invariably blow up the Inlet to the end of Princess Royal Reach during the day, and are strongest in good weather. At night (in good weather), there is either very little wind, or if anything, a down-inlet wind. M. Wylie Blanchet, author of *The Curve of Time*, who cruised this coast for many years with her children, reports however, that in proceeding up this Inlet in July one year:

> The wind hit us as we came opposite Britain River, just as it usually does. It blows out of the deep valley of the Britain River, and then escapes out through Vancouver Bay. After we had slopped ahead out of that, we met the wind that blows out of Deserted Bay and down the full length of Princess Royal Reach. So for the next ten miles or so we battled wind. It is not a nice wind in among the mountains. It picks you up in its teeth and shakes you. It hits you first on one side and then on the other. There is nowhere to go, you just have to take it. But finally, everybody tired and hungry, we rounded Patrick Point into the gentle Queen's Reach — and there, there was no wind at all.

It is possible that this gusty, down-inlet wind occurs during very unsettled conditions when strong southeast winds are blowing out in the Strait of Georgia. Either that, or Mrs. Blanchet could possibly have been travelling after dusk or in the very early morning or even have confused her months, as the wind directions she describes (down the Inlet) are most unusual for summer daytimes. Otherwise, her description of wind conditions in general and in Queen's Reach in particular are fairly accurate.

In the winter months, the strongest winds blow down the Inlet. But because the valley at the head of the Inlet is not directly connected with the interior of the province as are most other mainland inlets, exceptionally strong winds like the "Bute" and the "Squamish" are uncommon here.

1   Saltery Bay Provincial Park

There are two separate sections of this park, as shown on the map, which together comprise almost 100 acres. There are 45 campsites in the eastern section which are intended primarily for visitors arriving by car. A conspicuous shorefront parking lot with a concrete launching ramp and picnicking facilities is located in the western portion of the park above a sandy beach. Temporary anchorage is possible here in calm conditions. The small bight just east of here has a number of drying boulders in it. The eastern park frontage is rocky with offshore rocks which dry 13 feet and 17 feet with no real opportunity for safe anchorage, although local residents use some of the small nooks as moorings.

2   Saltery Bay

Saltery Bay derives its name from an earlier use as the base for a fish packing plant and now serves as the western terminus of the Earls Cove ferry link to Powell River. Strong westerly winds result in swells curling into the bay. The ferry dock provides some protection for government floats that have up to 1,000 feet of berthage space. Just east of the floats is a log dump and booming ground. The government floats serve mainly as an access point for loggers commuting up Jervis Inlet. There are no facilities here, other than those at the ferry terminal, although a restaurant known as the Museum Inn was formerly in operation.

3   Egmont

Since Jervis has no marinas or permanent settlements where one can be sure of obtaining fuel or provisions in an emergency, it is wise to have sufficient supplies for a round trip. The community of Egmont has two marinas for final restocking. (See Chapter 16).

4   Killam Bay

Killam Bay is a temporary anchorage, sufficiently indented to be sheltered from most up- or down-inlet winds. One of the few sand beaches in Jervis Inlet can be found here.

Miller Islet, just west of Killam Bay, was formerly known as One Tree Islet and is most probably named after Ralph Willett Miller, an American Loyalist who joined the Royal Navy and commanded H.M.S. *Captain*, 74 guns, the flagship of Lord Nelson at the battle of Cape St. Vincent. There is a dangerous rock which dries 2 feet located about 200 yards to the southeast of Miller Islet.

5   Dark Cove

Like much of Jervis Inlet, this well named cove receives relatively few hours of sunlight each day due to the steepness of the surrounding mountains. A reasonably well protected anchorage is available off a beach at the head of the cove, north of Sydney Island behind a tiny islet (watch for a shallow patch just north of this islet), or in the extreme southwest end of Goliath Bay.

The northern portion of Goliath Bay is used as a massive log assembling and sorting area with huge machinery and cranes for breaking up booms and loading barges.

It is possible that Vancouver spent his last night in Jervis Inlet in one of these coves after a disappointing excursion to the head of the Inlet in the *Discovery's* yawl and a rough 17 hour row back down against a "southerly gale". Vancouver was searching for an elusive back entrance to the fabled "northwest passage" or a connection to the interior of the continent and was continually enticed and frustrated by each inlet up the British Columbia coast. Jervis Inlet had raised his expectations, and although he did not appear to appreciate what we now see as beautiful scenery, he may have changed his generally negative impressions of the B.C. coast if he had not missed Princess Louisa Inlet completely.

However, Vancouver's crew did not all share his view. Archibald Menzies, the expedition's botanist, relates how Vancouver's Lieutenant Peter Puget viewed Jervis Inlet:

In going up this Arm they here & there passed immense Cascades rushing from the Summits of high precipices & dashing headlong down Chasms against projecting Rocks & Cliffs with a furious wildness that beggard all description. Curiosity led them to approach one of the largest where it pourd its foaming pondrous stream over high rugged Cliffs & precipices into the fretted Sea with such stunning noise & rapidity of motion that they could not look up to its sourse without being affected with giddiness nor contemplate its romantic wildness without a mixture of awe & admiration.

Soda Water Falls in Princess Royal Reach.

213

Prevailing up-inlet winds in good weather give sailors an easy spinnaker run up Prince of Wales and Princess Royal Reaches.

Goliath Bay is named after H.M.S. *Goliath*, 74 guns, which was engaged in the battles of Cape St. Vincent and the Nile under Captain Thomas Foley. At the battle of the Nile, the *Goliath* led the line inside the anchored French fleet and the midshipman who first saw the enemy from the foreroyal yard was George Elliott, younger son of Sir Gilbert Elliott, afterwards Earl of Minto, ancestor of the Governor General of Canada, 1898-1904. The point which separates Goliath Bay from Jervis Inlet is named after Vice-Admiral James Richard Dacres, who, as Captain Dacres of H.M.S. *Barfleur*, 98 guns, was also engaged in the battle of St. Vincent.

Prince of Wales Reach

The view up the lower portion of Prince of Wales Reach is at first dominated by the pyramid shaped peak of Mount Churchill, 6,480 feet high. This peak seems to fade into the background upon closer approach as the somewhat lower, but bulky, Marlborough Heights (below 6,000 feet) rise up to

214

dominate the horizon. These mountains were all named around 1860, so it is possible that they are named after the ancestor of Sir Winston Churchill, John Churchill, the first Duke of Marlborough. It is also possible that Marlborough Heights could have been named after the 74 gun ship *Marlborough* which Admiral Jervis found necessary to discipline; or after Marlborough House, the residence of the Prince of Wales in London. Prince of Wales Reach is named after the first son of Queen Victoria and later King Edward VII.

Mount Spencer, 6,005 feet, which is hidden behind Mount Churchill and only visible from Princess Royal Reach may have been named after George John Spencer, first Lord of the Admiralty at the time of the battle of Cape St. Vincent. He was responsible for selecting Horatio Nelson to command the fleet which won the battle of the Nile.

6 Vancouver Bay

Vancouver Bay is not as inviting as it appears to be; strong up inlet winds often curl into it. There is not much space for safe anchorage at the edge of the wide delta which drops off rather abruptly to great depths. There is a small float at the southern end of this delta. A recently dredged channel crosses the delta just south of the Vancouver River outlet where the remains of an old logging camp are located. Trout fishing along the Vancouver River has been a popular pastime. It was while fishing here that M. Wylie Blanchet experienced a curious urge to crash back through the bush to where her children were playing on the beach. No one else was anywhere around except a tall man dressed in black at the far end of the beach who appeared to be a clergyman but, as he approached, turned out to be a bear. Black bears are common near the mouths of many rivers entering mainland inlets. At the heads of some major inlets, grizzlies are occasionally spotted.

Captain Vancouver stayed here the night of Sunday, 17 June, 1792. His journal relates:

The next morning, Monday the 18th, as usual, at four o'clock, we proceeded up the inlet about three miles in a N.N.W. direction, whence its width increases about half a league* in a direction nearly N.E. to a point which towards noon we reached, and ascertained its latitide to be 50° 1', longitude 236° 46'. The width of this channel still continuing, again flattered us with discovering a beach in the eastern range of snowy mountains, notwithstanding the disappointment we had met with in Howe's sound; and although since our arrival in the gulf of Georgia, it had proved an impenetrable barrier to that inland navigation, of which we had heard so much, and had sought with sanguine hopes and ardent exertions hitherto in vain, to discover.
* — 1½ miles.

7 McMurray Bay

Temporary anchorage is possible off a small delta in McMurray Bay. There is a tiny nook accessible by small boat at the east end of the bay. This bay is completely open to up-inlet winds. More shelter is obtainable in the second of two small bights just north of McMurray Bay. The first bight is completely rock encumbered but the second while shallow is relatively rock free, providing more protection from light to moderate up inlet-winds.

Moorsam Bluff across the inlet is an imposing sight. A band of volcanic rocks on the west wall of Marlborough Heights is cut by numerous quartz-feldspar prophyry dykes, some in excess of 100 feet wide. These dykes stand out as straight, sharply defined white lines against the darker outcrop of volcanic rocks.

Princess Royal Reach

Princess Royal Reach was named after Victoria, the first daughter of Queen Victoria. She later became the Empress of Germany when her husband, Frederick William of Prussia became Emperor. The majority of logging camps in the Inlet are located in this reach. Many have been abandoned but some are still active and could provide emergency moorage alongside booms or company floats. Camps which appeared to be active or showed some sign of habitation in 1979 were located at Seshal Creek, Glacial Creek and Stakawus (Bear River) Creek.

On nearing Patrick Point at the end of Princess Royal Reach, Vancouver noted in his journal:

> By the progress we had this morning made, which comprehended about six leagues, we seemed to have penetrated considerably into this formidable obstacle; and as the more lofty mountains were now behind us, and no very distant ones were seen beyond the vallies caused by the depressed parts of the snowy barrier in the northern quarters, we had great reason to believe we had passed the center of this impediment to our wishes, and I was induced to hope we should yet find this inlet winding beyond the mountains, by the channel through which we had thus advanced upwards of 11 leagues though for the most part it was not more than half a mile wide. Under these circumstances, our reduced stock of provisions was a matter of serious concern, fearing we might be obliged to abandon this pursuit without determining the source of this branch of the sea, having now been absent six days with subsistence for a week only, which would consequently very materially retard our survey, by rendering a second visit to this inlet indispensibly necessary. The surrounding country presented an equally dreary aspect with that in the vicinage of Howe's sound; and the serenity of the weather not adding at present to the natural gloominess of the prospect, was counterbalanced by the rugged surface of the mountains being infinitely less productive. A few detached dwarf pine trees, with some berry, and other small bushes, were the only signs of vegetation. The cataracts here rushed from the rugged snowy mountains in greater number, and with more impetuosity than in Howe's sound; yet the color of the water was not changed, though in some of the gullies there was the same chalky aspect. Hence it is probable, that the white appearance of the water in Howe's sound, may arise from a cause more remote, and which we had no oportunity of discovering.

This "chalky white" water has since been discovered to come from the remnants of the glaciers which originally carved out these inlets 10,000 years ago. Although the glaciers have retreated to the highest slopes on the inlet headwater mountains, they are still grinding the rock beneath them to a fine powder

Vancouver Bay, where Mrs. Blanchet met a "clergyman".

which each spring is washed down into the inlets as "glacial rock flour".

8 Deserted Bay

Deserted Bay was formerly a large settlement, known as Tsoh-nye and this is the name it is still known by for those involved with the Native Environmental Studies project which commenced in 1979. Native and non-Indian high school students from the Sechelt Peninsula spend up to four months here each year learning about the history, culture and environment of the local Sechelt Indians in conjunction with their regular school curriculum.

Deserted Bay was named by white men in the last century. On approaching the community two fishermen noticed that although many canoes were drawn up above the high tide mark, there was no smoke from the houses not a sign of any other activity. Going ashore they found the place deserted, the houses filled with dead . . . the victims of smallpox. Every house was silent except one where a baby girl still clung to her dead mother. This baby was rescued and . . . "grew up to be a beautiful lady . . . she married a good man and had many children" (Al Lloyd, *Coast News*).

Best temporary shelter from up-inlet winds is in second bight, right, north of McMurray Bay.

215

Mt. Alfred towers over the head of Jervis Inlet.

Deserted Bay does not provide particularly good afternoon anchorage as the up-inlet winds generate large seas after blowing up the 14 mile fetch of Princess Royal Reach. These seas are not dissipated in Deserted Bay as there is no delta to speak of, but reflect back to crash against the incoming swells. The seas tend to die away as the wind drops in the evening. However, as soon as the wind drops, hordes of voracious mosquitoes move out from shore thirsting for blood.

The most protected part of Deserted Bay is in the southeast corner where there are private floats which serve as the main access to Tsoh-Nye. Log booms to the west of here may also offer temporary moorage and slightly more protection from up-inlet swells. Oil Tank Point, two miles northwest of here, offers protection from down-inlet winds but is exposed to swells from Princess Royal Reach. Mount Pearkes,

End of a cruising day in Deserted Bay.

which rises 7,000 feet behind Oil Tank Point, is named after Major General George R. Pearkes, VC, CD, DSO, MC, Croix de Guerre, Lieutenant-Governor of British Columbia from 1960 to 1968. Directly across Queens Reach from Mount Pearkes is Mount Frederick William, named after the Princess Royal's husband. This mountain is also affectionately known as Mount Frankenstein due to its gruesome profile when viewed from the Malibu Rapids.

Patrick Point is named after Prince Arthur William Patrick Albert, third son of Queen Victoria, and namesake and godson of Arthur Wellesley, Duke of Wellington — the "Iron Duke" and the victor of Waterloo, after whom the two mountains opposite Princess Louisa Inlet are named.

Queens Reach

Queens Reach is particularly noted for its lack of wind. For some reason up-inlet winds do not usually enter this reach. Temporary anchorage at a number of nooks in this reach is generally fairly safe and comfortable. Boats waiting for slack water at Malibu Rapids can wait in a small nook behind Patrick Point or off Crabapple Creek.

Vancouver continued his search up Queens Reach:

Having dined, we pursued our examination. The inlet now took a N.W. by W. direction, without any contraction in its width, until about five o'clock in the evening, when all our hopes vanished, by finding it terminates, as others had done, in a swampy low land producing a few maples and pines, in latitude 50° 6', longitude 236° 33'. Through a small space of low land, which extended from the head of the inlet to the base of the mountains, that surrounded us, flowed three small streams of fresh water, apparently originating from one source in the N.W. or left hand corner of the bay, formed by the head of this inlet; in which point of view was seen an extensive valley, that took nearly a northerly uninterrupted direction as far as we could perceive, and was by far the deepest chasm we had beheld in the descending ridge of the snowy barrier, without the appearance of any elevated land rising behind. This valley much excited my curiosity to ascertain what was beyond it. But as the streams of fresh water were not navigable, though the tide had risen up to the habitations of six or seven Indians, any further examination of it in our boats was impracticable, and we had no leisure for excursions on shore.

Admiralty Chart 579(1864) has a dotted line leading north from the head of the Inlet and this notation: "Valley by which the Indians go to Clahoose in 2 days (Desolation Sound)." The Skwawka River valley connects Jervis Inlet with Little Toba River valley and thence to the Toba valley and the village of "Clahoose" at the head of Toba Inlet, 25 miles to the northwest; so it is likely that Vancouver would have been disappointed even if he had been able to proceed further.

Vancouver noted some peculiar hydrographic features at the head of the inlet:

In all these arms of the sea we had constantly observed, even in their utmost extremity, a visible and sometimes a

Running out of glaciers and icy lakes, Chatterbox Falls thunders through forests and down hundreds of feet of granite cliffs into the head of Princess Louisa, a mile below.

Ice floes dot lake below peak of Sunrise Mt, chief source of water for Chatterbox Falls.

material rise and fall of the tide, without experiencing any other current than a constant drain down to the seaward, excepting just in the neighbourhood of the gulf.

This outward current is caused by the continual discharge of fresh waters into the inlet and out to sea, over the denser seawater. Vancouver also noted:

> On our approach to the low land, we gained soundings at 70 fathoms, which soon decreased as we advanced, to 30, 14 and 3 fathoms, on a bank that stretches across the head of the inlet, similar to all the others we had before examined. So far as these soundings extended, which did not exceed half a league, the colour of the water was a little affected, probably by the discharge of the fresh water rivulets, that generally assumed a very light colour. Beyond these soundings the water again acquired its oceanic colour, and its depth was unfathomable.

The "whitish" colour of incoming fresh water is more rapidly diffused into the normal sea colour in Jervis Inlet as compared to Howe Sound (and other mainland inlets) because the drainage basin of the Inlet is relatively small with fewer tributary glaciers and no major rivers.

The head of Jervis Inlet is surrounded by very high mountains named after five of Queen Victoria's nine children, Alice, Alfred, Victoria, Albert, and Helena. Glacier capped Mount Albert rises to 8,350 feet above sea level directly north of the entrance to Princess Louisa Inlet behind Mount Helena, 5,100 feet high.

Princess Louisa Inlet

Princess Louisa Inlet is named after the mother of Queen Victoria, the Duchess of Kent, Victoria Maria Louisa. In earlier times it was known as Sway-We-Laht a reference to the fact that the entrance forms a change of direction. Some sources give the Inlet waters names as 'Suivoolot' meaning 'sunny and warm'. From outside nothing of the Inlet waters inside can be seen, hidden as they are behind a low peninsula.

Captain Vancouver passed by here without discovering the inlet inside:

> About two leagues from the head of the inlet we had observed, as we passed upwards on the northern shore, a small creek with some rocky islets before it, where I intended to take up our abode for the night. On our return, it was found to be full of salt water, just deep enough to admit our boats against a very rapid stream, where at low tide they would have grounded some feet above sea level of the water in the inlet. From the rapidity of the stream, and the quantity of water it discharged, it was reasonable to suppose, by its taking a winding direction up a valley to the N.E. that its source was at some distance. This not answering our purpose as a resting place, obliged us to continue our search along the shore for one less incommodius, which the perpendicular precipes precluded our finding until near eleven at night, when we disembarked on the only low projecting point the inlet afforded. (possibly Patrick Point).

9   Malibu Rapids

It is a surprise for many after travelling for over 30 miles down a nearly deserted inlet to find what appears to be a large, luxurious resort complex at the entrance to Princess Louisa Inlet. This is in fact what was built here by an American entrepreneur during the Second World War. The resort buildings now serve as a Christian youth camp run by the Young Life Association. Teenagers from the U.S.A. and Canada come here throughout the summer months to spend a week studying, exploring, and giving thanks for the fantastically beautiful surroundings. Facilities at Malibu include a heated outdoor pool and a 13-hole miniature golf course; and there are various other indoor and outdoor activities. In ensuing years they are invited back to serve newcomers and to take part in demanding programmes some of which include week-long hikes up and into the surrounding mountains. Visitors are welcome to tie up for half an hour or so at the floats just inside the Inlet where someone will greet you and show you around.

Because the Malibu Rapids run up to 9 knots at springs, entrance into Princess Louisa Inlet should be as close to slack water (about ½ hour after Point Atkinson tides) as possible. The passage to the west of Malibu Islet is straight forward and well charted with a 1:12,180 blow-up inset on Chart 3589. There is a tendency, when entering with a strong flood tide, to be carried against the eastern shoreline. As on Queens Reach, there are virtually no strong winds that penetrate into this inlet in the summer months. The strongest winds occur in winter and blow down the steep mountain sides as furious "williwaws".

During cold winters the Inlet often freezes over, especially near the head where the fresh water concentrations are highest. The waterfalls freeze and the only sound, beside the "whoosh" of williwaws, is the rumble and thump of avalanches crashing into the Inlet. In the summer months, the avalanche scars are plainly visible, and up to 60 separate waterfalls bring snow melt waters down over thousands of feet of sun warmed rock into the quiet stillness of the Inlet.

There have been many attempts to capture the

beauty of this Inlet in words. The B.C. Parks Branch and the Princess Louisa International Society have published a brochure entitled "The Legend of Princess Louisa Inlet" which quotes Earle Stanley Gardner:

> There is no use describing that Inlet. Perhaps an atheist could view it and remain an atheist, but I doubt it. There is a calm tranquility that stretches from the smooth surface of the reflecting water straight up into infinity. The deep calm of eternal silence is only disturbed by the muffled roar of throbbing waterfalls as they plunge down sheer cliffs. . . . One views the scenery with bared head and choking feeling of the throat. It is more than beautiful. It is sacred.

10 Macdonald Island

Relatively isolated anchorage is possible in either of two small nooks at the west end of a bight in the northern shoreline halfway down the Inlet. Anchorage is also possible behind Hamilton (now renamed as Macdonald) Island at the east end of this bight. This island and 40 acres of the adjacent mainland

Right: Falls 1800 feet above head of Princess Louisa creates lacy patterns as it tumbles to the sea.

Tide floods into Princess Louisa through Malibu Rapids.

Morning sun glints off converted tug at the head of Princess Louisa. Former editor of PY can be seen in dinghy to left.

Roar of Chatterbox provides background music for anchored crews.

shore is owned and cared for by the Princess Louisa International Society. This excellent organization was formed for the purpose of ensuring that the Inlet is never commercialized. It is made up of Canadian and American yachtsmen and provides an opportunity for concerned individuals to contribute to the protection and maintenance of such beautiful anchorages.

The eastern flank of Mount Albert (unseen from the Inlet) rises above Macdonald Island and was originally known as Tuh-Kohss'', roughly translated as "Old One-Eye". There are many creatures visible in the natural rock formations around the Inlet. Lester Peterson notes that near the head of the Inlet was Tah-Kay-Wah'-Lah-Klash-the horse. According to Sechelt myth, it came from the sea, as did most other creatures, in contrast to human beings, who were put on earth by Kwath-Am-Sahth'-AM, the Divine Spirit from the sky.

11 Princess Louisa Marine Park

The land surrounding Chatterbox Falls at the head of the Inlet was originally pre-empted by a James F. Macdonald in 1927. He had a log cabin built and took up residence. His presence here disturbed a few people at first who remembered the Inlet as totally secluded and uninhabited. Mrs. Blanchet refers to "The man from California . . . and his log cabin made the first thin wedge of civilization that had been driven into our favourite Inlet". James F. Macdonald (or "Mac" as he became known) did, however, recognize his intrusion and after generously welcoming yachtsmen for over 25 years he donated his land to the Princess Louisa International Society. He said "It should never have belonged to a private individual . . . I had a deep feeling that I was only the custodian of the property . . . I feel that (in returning the land) I am completing a trust". In 1964, the land was returned to Crown ownership and the administration of the provincial Parks Branch.

In addition to floats, there are five campsites and a communal rain shelter ashore. Visiting boats can moor at the floats or anchor over a shallow shelf at the base of Chatterbox Falls. The outflowing freshwater surface current is strong enough to keep the boat from swinging onto the shallows when the tide is low.

There is a trail from the floats to the base of Chatterbox Falls where a notice warns against proceeding further. The constant mist rising from the falls makes all rocks slippery and saturates the moss on bare rock surfaces. Where this moss rests on nearly flat rock and appears to be most stable, it is in fact most treacherous and the slightest footprint will start it moving. Eleven lives are reported to have been lost, by people failing to heed the warning and slipping over the falls. At night, the sound of the falls carries out over the water. M. Wylie Blanchet wrote: "That waterfall can laugh and talk, sing and lull you to sleep. But it can also moan and sob, fill you with awful apprehensions of you don't know what . . ."

There is also a hiking trail which starts out on an old skid road and snakes up the forested mountainside to a cabin near a waterfall, about 1,800 feet above sea level, with a view down the Inlet toward Malibu. More adventurous hikers can climb up above the tree line where there are alpine flowers, iceberg-filled lakes and perennial snowfields.

The head of Jervis Inlet circa 1860. H.M.S. Plumper anchors while surveyors take soundings from canoe, with hunting dog in bow, and sailing pinnace. Tapered cone is probably Mt. Victoria or "Anchor Mountain", also known as the mystic Kulse. Sechelt Indians who knew this area as Huhn'-ah-tchin, led Richard Charles Mayne, a Royal Navy officer, over an ancient trail from Deserted bay to Squamish, (see Chapter 8, page 125).

SELECTED BIBLIOGRAPHY

Several other references, listed previously in Volumes I and II are not included here. Most useful references are asterisked.

Alley, James. *Recreational Boating in Howe Sound*, Victoria: Islands Trust, 1976.

Anderson, Doris. *The Columbia is Coming!* Sidney: Gray's Publishing, 1982.

Bell, J.W. *British Columbia Memories*. Vancouver City Archives, 1946.

Blanchet, M. Wylie. *The Curve of Time*. Sidney: Gray's Publishing, 1968.

Brower, K. *The Starship and the Canoe*. New York: Holt, Rinehart and Winston, 1978.

*Canada, Hydrographic Service. *British Columbia Small Craft Guide, Vol. II. Boundary Bay to Cortes Island*. Ottawa: 1982.

Canada, Environment. *The Squamish River Estuary: Status of Environmental Knowledge to 1974*. 1975.

Carver, J.A. *The Vancouver Rowing Club. A History, 1886-1980*. Vancouver: A.F. Roberts, c1980.

Cates, Charles W. *Tidal Action in British Columbia Waters*, North Vancouver: B.C. Provincial Archives, 1952.

Creighton, H.E. *Coal Prospect on Coal Harbour*. Canadian Merchant Service Guild Yearbook. 1936.

*Davis, Chuck, ed. *The Vancouver Book*, Vancouver: J.J. Douglas Ltd. 1976.

*Dawson, Will. *Coastal Cruising*. Vancouver: Mitchell Press, 1973.

Drushka, Ken. *Against Wind and Weather: the History of Towboating in British Columbia*, Vancouver: Douglas and McIntyre, 1981.

Eisbacher, Gerhard H. *Vancouver Geology*, Geological Association of Canada, 1973.

Evans, Ginny and Beth. *The Vancouver Guide Book*. Victoria: Campbell's Pub. 1980.

Fox, Margaret, *Cha-Hai (Horseshoe Bay)*. Gleneagles Parent-Teacher Association, circa 1971.

Fraser River Estuary Study. *First Draft Report of the Area Designation Task Force to the Fraser River Estuary Planning Committee*. unpub. manuscript. Vancouver: 1981.

Fraser River Estuary Study. *"a living river by the door"*. Vancouver: Government of Canada and Province of British Columbia, 1981.

Hacking, Norman and W. Kaye Lamb. *The Princess Story*. Vancouver: Mitchell Press Ltd. 1974.

Hacking, Norman. *History of the Port of Vancouver*, NHB, 1900 Granville Square, No date.

Hattersley, Roy. *Nelson*, London: Weidenfeld and Nicolson, 1974.

Hoos, Lindsay M. and Glen A. Packman. *The Fraser River Estuary, Status of Knowledge to 1974*. Special Estuary Series No. 1., Vancouver: Environment Canada. 1974.

Howard, Irene. *Bowen Island 1872-1972*. Bowen Island Historians. 1973.

Hull, Raymond, Gordon Soules and Christine Soules. *Vancouver's Past*. Vancouver: Gordon Soules. 1974.

Humphreys, Pam. *The History of Wigwam Inn*. Vancouver: Western Pacific Resorts Inc., 1982.

Ince, John and Hedi Kottner. *Sea Kayaking Canada's West Coast*. Raxas Books, Vancouver: 1982.

Johnson, E. Pauline. *Legends of Vancouver*. Toronto: McClelland and Stewart, 1961.

Keeling, F. Temple. *Anvil Island*. Vancouver City Archives. 1961.

Lowry, Malcolm. *Hear Us O Lord From Heaven Thy Dwelling Place*. London: Cape, 1961.

Manson, Ainslie. *Mr. McUmphie of Caulfield Cove*. Winnipeg: Queenston House, 1981.

Mayne, R.C. *Four Years in British Columbia and Vancouver Island*. London: J. Murray, 1862.

Matthews, J.S. *Early Vancouver*, Volumes 1, 2. Vancouver City Archives, 1932.

Morley, Alan. *Vancouver, from Milltown to Metropolis*. Vancouver: Mitchell Press, 1974.

Nelson, Denys. *Place Names of the Delta of the Fraser*. Vancouver City Archives, 1923.

Nicol, Eric. *Vancouver*, Toronto: Doubleday, 1970.

Parsons, Marlene. *Fraser River Heritage Resource Inventory*. Victoria: Heritage Conservation Branch, Province of British Columbia. 1981.

Percheson, Rita, et al. *Hiking Trails of the Sunshine Coast*, Madeira Park: Harbour Publishing, 1979.

Peterson, Lester. *The Gibsons Landing Story*. Toronto: P. Martin Press, 1962.

Pethick, Derek. *Vancouver Recalled: Early Vancouver History to 1887*. Saanichton: Hancock House. 1974.

Pethick, Derek. *S.S. Beaver: The Ship that saved the West*. Vancouver: Mitchell Press. 1970.

Reeve, Phyllis. *Every Good Gift: a history of St. James*, Vancouver: 1981.

Roberts, L. Harry. *The Trail of Chack Chack*. New York: Carlton Press, 1968.

Roberts, L. Harry. *Natural Laws*, Gibsons: Coast News, 1969.

Robinson, J. Lewis. *How Vancouver has grown and changed*. Canadian Geographical Journal. October 1974.

Roper, E.L. *By Track and Trail through Canada*. London: W.H. Allen, 1891.

Rushton, Gerald A. *Whistle Up the Inlet*. Vancouver: Douglas and McIntyre. 1976.

Smith, Kathleen M. *Nature West Coast . . . Lighthouse Park*. Vancouver: Discovery Press, 1974.

Soules, Gordon, ed. *Vancouver at Your Feet*. Vancouver: Gordon Soules, 1970.

Stainsby, Donald and George Kuthon. *Vancouver: Sights and Insights*. Toronto: MacMillan. 1960.

*Thomson, Richard E. *Oceanography of the British Columbia Coast*. Canadian Special Publication of Fisheries and Aquatic Sciences 56. Victoria: Fisheries and Oceans Canada. 1981.

Vancouver Archives. *Portholes and Pilings: A retrospective look at the development of Vancouver Harbour up to 1933*. Occasional Paper No. 1. 1978.

Van der Ree, Frieda. *Exploring the Coast by Boat*. Vancouver: Gordon Soules, 1979.

Van Dyke, Henry. *The Story of the Other Wise Man*. New York: Peter Pauper Press.

Vardeman, Lynn and Freda Carr. *A guide to Stanley Park*. Vancouver: Seaside, 1973.

*Walbran, John, T. *British Columbia Coast Names*. Vancouver: The Library's Press, 1971.

*Ward, Peggy. *Explore the Fraser Estuary!* Vancouver: Environment Canada, Lands Directorate. 1980.

Warner, Oliver. *The Glorious First of June*. London: Batford, 1961.

White, Howard, ed. *Raincoast Chronicles*. Madeira Park: Harbour Publishing.

INDEX

ILLUSTRATION CREDITS

All photographs, except those listed below, were taken by George McNutt or the authors. Aerial photographs were taken from planes piloted by George McNutt.
Page 20, Chris Hatfield; page 39 top, Painting by John Horton, reproduced by kind permission of Harrison Galleries; bottom, P. Tough; page 40, Vancouver City Archives; page 41, Painting by L.A. Hamilton, Vancouver City Archives; page 51, Confederation Life; page 55, Painting by T.F.R. Thompson, photographed by N. Jill Newby, reproduced by kind permission of Richard Beard Gallery, West Vancouver; page 63, Barbara Cedroff, The Small Ship Society; bottom, B.C. Government; page 71, Federal Government; page 74 bottom; M. Dunn; page 77, B.R. Gates; page 86, Bill Ward; page 90, GVRD Parks; page 123, 132, Janet Stamper, The Jib Set; page 171, Painting by Harold Wylie, reproduced by kind permission of E. G. Cullwick, Captain (L) RCN (R), Ret'd, OBE; page 221, Engraving reproduced from Four Years in British Columbia and Vancouver Island by Commander R.C. Mayne, London, 1862, Provincial Archives, Victoria, B.C.
All maps except those listed below were draughted by Clementien Wolferstan or the authors.
End papers chart index, page 32, 33 tidal stream information: Canadian Hydrographic Service, Sidney, B.C.; page 4, Surveys and Mapping Branch, Victoria, B.C.

Copyright © 1982 by Bill Wolferstan
Whitecap Books
Vancouver/Toronto

Typeset by Vancouver Typesetting Co. Ltd., Vancouver
Printed and bound in Singapore by Khai Wah - Ferco Pte. Ltd.

First paperback edition 1992

Canadian Cataloguing in Publication Data

Wolferstan, Bill, 1942-
  Pacific Yachting's Cruising Guide to British Columbia.
  Includes bibliographies and indexes.
  Contents: v.1. Gulf Islands and Vancouver Island from Sooke to Courtenay—v.2. Desolation Sound and the Discovery Islands—v.3. Sunshine Coast, Fraser Estuary and Vancouver to Jervis Inlet.
  Vol. 1 also published separately as: Pacific Yachting's Cruising Guide to the Gulf Islands and Vancouver Island from Sooke to Courtenay.

  ISBN 0-921061-10-2 (v.1)—ISBN 0-921061-23-4 (v.2)—ISBN 1-55110-029-0 (v.3)
  1. British Columbia—Description and travel—1950— — Guide-books.* 2. Yachts and yachting—British Columbia. I. Pacific Yachting. II. Title. III. Title: Cruising Guide to British Columbia.
FC3817.4.W64   917.11'33   C80-091254-3
F1087.W64